Cancellation of Removal for Non-Permanent Residents

Getting the Green Card by being in the U.S. for 10 years

Attorney Brian D. Lerner

LAW OFFICES OF
BRIAN D. LERNER
A PROFESSIONAL CORPORATION

ATTORNEY DRAFTED IMMIGRATION PETITIONS

By

Brian D. Lerner

Attorney at Law

Disclaimer and Terms of Use:

Effort has been made to ensure that the information in this book is accurate and complete. However, the author and the publisher do not warrant that this particular petition will mirror or be exactly as your situation. There has not been any attorney-client agreement created by the purchase of this petition or application. No legal advice has occurred. The cases, regulations and/or statutes cited may change at any time without notice.

INTRODUCTION

There are a multitude of different immigration petitions and applications. They are complex and full of requirements. Obviously, it would be best to hire an immigration attorney to best prepare the petitions and applications. However, this can certainly cost thousands of dollars.

The next best option is to get a sample of the petition written by an experienced immigration attorney. The samples cost a fraction what would be charged by an immigration attorney. However, while the reader has to alter, amend and change the parts of the sample petition to reflect their actual situation, it is a fantastic roadmap for them to use. If the reader has purchased the entire petition or application, they will have real live samples of cover letters, forms, declarations, affidavits and the necessary exhibits to use. The samples come from real cases and the names of those clients have been redacted to protect the privacy of that person or corporation.

These are petitions and applications that have been drafted by an experienced immigration attorney with over 25 years of experience. Get the benefits of that experience without the costs.

CONTENTS

About the Law Offices of Brian D. Lerner

Brian D. Lerner has been a licensed attorney since 1992 and started the Law Offices of Brian D. Lerner, APC. The law practice consists of Immigration and Nationality Law and everything involved with and regarding immigration which includes citizenship, investment visas, family and employment visas, removal and deportation hearings, appeals, waivers, adjustment, consulate processing and all types of immigration and citizenship matters. Thousands of families have been reunited and/or permitted to stay in the U.S. and/or return to the U.S. because of the successful work of Immigration Attorney Brian D. Lerner.

This law offices handles all types of immigration cases including family based and employment based. Immigration issues range from immigration court proceedings to trying to fix what paralegals may have done that was neither correct nor proper. Foreign nationals must have experience lawyers admitted to practice law.

The Law Offices of Brian D. Lerner, APC, handles cases arising from business visas, work permits, Green Cards, non-immigrant visas, deportation, citizenship, appeals and all areas of immigration. The Law Offices of Brian D. Lerner, APC does EB-5 Investor Visas, H-1B Specialty Occupation, L-1 Intracompany Transferee, E-2 Treaty Investor, E-1 Treaty Trader, O-1 Extraordinary Ability among others. Regarding immigrant visas for the Green Card, the firm does PERM and advanced degree PERM, Family Petitions, and Extraordinary Alien Petitions. In addition to affirmative petitions, the Law Firm represents people in people in deportation and removal hearings, including political asylum, withholding of removal, and convention against torture cases.

Brian D. Lerner has been certified as an expert in Immigration & Nationality Law by the California State Bar, Board of Legal Specialization since 2000 and has been re-certified three times. He now passes on his decades of experience by allowing the Reader, Law Schools, Professors and other Immigration Attorneys to purchase sample petitions on every facet of Immigration Law.

Application for Cancellation of Removal and Adjustment of Status for Certain Non-Permanent Residents 42(B)

Application for Cancellation of Removal and Adjustment of Status for Certain Non-Permanent Residents 42(B). A Legal Permanent Resident can apply for cancellation of removal if they have maintained a continuous physical presence in the U.S. for 10 years, maintained a good moral character, and have not been convicted of an offense. The removal would result in exceptional and extremely unusual hardship to your U.S. or Legal Permanent Resident spouse, parent or child.

ATTORNEY COVER LETTER

Brian D. Lerner (#158536)
Christopher A. Reed (#235438)
Law Offices of Brian D. Lerner, APC
3233 E. Broadway
Long Beach, CA 90803
Telephone: (562) 495-0554
Facsimile: (562) 608-8672

UNITED STATES DEPARTMENT OF JUSTICE

EXECUTIVE OFFICE FOR IMMIGRATION REVIEW

IMMIGRATION COURT

LOS ANGELES, CALIFORNIA

In the Matter of:	)
	)
	)
▆▆▆▆▆▆▆▆▆▆	) File No.: A078-112-433
	)
	)
	)
Respondent,	)
	)
In Removal Proceedings.	)

Immigration Judge: Christine E. Stancill   Master Hearing: August 1, 2017 at 9:00 a.m.

APPLICATION FOR CANCELLATION OF REMOVAL AND ADJUSTMENT OF STATUS FOR CERTAIN NONPERMANENT RESIDENTS AND SUPPORTING DOCUMENTS

TABLE OF CONTENTS

Form:	Description:
EOIR-42B	Application for Cancellation of Removal and Adjustment of Status for Certain Nonpermanent Residents and Receipt Notice

FORMS

OMB#1125-0001

U.S. Department of Justice
Executive Office for Immigration Review

Application for Cancellation of Removal and Adjustment of Status for Certain Nonpermanent Residents

PLEASE READ ADVICE AND INSTRUCTIONS BEFORE FILLING IN FORM PLEASE TYPE OR PRINT	Fee Stamp (Official Use Only)

PART 1 - INFORMATION ABOUT YOURSELF

1) My present true name is: (Last, First, Middle)
████████████████████

2) Alien Registration (or "A") Number(s):
████████

3) My name given at birth was: (Last, First, Middle)
████████████████████

4) Birth Place: (City and Country)
████████

5) Date of Birth: (Month, Day, Year) 12/07/1985	6) Gender: ☒ Male ☐ Female	7) Height: 5'9"	8) Hair Color: Black	9) Eye Color: Brown

10) Current Nationality and Citizenship: Belize Belize	11) Social Security Number: ████████	12) Home Phone Number: ████████	13) Work Phone Number: N/A

14) I currently reside at:

Apt. number and/or in care of
Number and Street ████████ Fontana   CA   92336
City or Town   State   Zip Code

15) I have been known by these additional name(s):
N/A

16) I have resided in the following locations in the United States. (List PRESENT ADDRESS FIRST, and work back in time for at least 10 years.)

Street and Number - Apt. or Room # - City or Town - State - Zip Code				Resided From: (Month, Day, Year)	Resided To: (Month, Day, Year)
████████	Fontana	CA	92336	12/16/2016	PRESENT
	Norwalk	CA	90650	07/2016	11/16/2016
	Gladewater	TX	75647	02/2014	07/2016
	Norwalk	CA	90650	08/2007	02/2014
	Norwalk	CA	90650	04/2007	08/2007

PART 2 - INFORMATION ABOUT THIS APPLICATION

17) I, the undersigned, hereby request that my removal be cancelled under the provisions of section 240A(b) of the Immigration and Nationality Act (INA). I believe that I am eligible for cancellation of removal because: (Check all that apply.)

☒ My removal would result in exceptional and extremely unusual hardship to my:

	UNITED STATES CITIZEN	LAWFUL PERMANENT RESIDENT	TEMPORARY STATUS	NO STATUS
☐ spouse, who is a		X		
☒ father, who is a	X			
☒ mother, who is a	X			
☒ child/children, who is/are a	X			

With the exception of absences described in question #23, I have resided in the United States since: 07/03/1990
(Month, Day, Year)

☐ I, or my child, have been battered or subjected to extreme cruelty by a United States citizen or lawful permanent resident spouse or parent.

With the exception of absences described in question #23, I have resided in the United States since:

(Month, Day, Year)

Please continue answers on a separate sheet as needed.
(1)

Form EOIR-42B
Revised July 2016

PART 3 - INFORMATION ABOUT YOUR PRESENCE IN THE UNITED STATES

18) I first arrived in the United States under the name of: *(Last, First, Middle)*	19) I first arrived in the United States on: *(Month, Day, Year)*
▓▓▓▓▓▓▓▓▓▓▓▓	07/03/1990

20) Place or port of first arrival: *(Place or Port, City, and State)*

San Diego, CA

21) I: ☒ was inspected and admitted.

 ☐ I entered using my Lawful Permanent Resident card which is valid until _____ *(Month, Day, Year)*

 ☒ I entered using a **B-2** _____ visa which is valid until **01/02/1991** *(Month, Day, Year)*
 (Specify Type of Visa)

 ☐ was not inspected and admitted.

 ☐ I entered without documents. Explain: _____

 ☐ I entered without inspection. Explain: _____

 ☐ Other. Explain:

22) I applied on _____ *(Month, Day, Year)* for additional time to stay and it was ☐ granted on _____ *(Month, Day, Year)*

 and valid until _____ *(Month, Day, Year)*, or ☐ denied on _____ *(Month, Day, Year)*

23) Since the date of my first entry, I departed from and returned to the United States at the following places and on the following dates:
 (Please list all departures regardless of how briefly you were absent from the United States.)
 If you have never departed from the United States since your original date of entry, please mark an X in this box: ☒

	Port of Departure *(Place or Port, City and State)*	Departure Date *(Month, Day, Year)*	Purpose of Travel	Destination
1				
	Port of Return *(Place or Port, City and State)*	Return Date *(Month, Day, Year)*	Manner of Return	Inspected and Admitted? ☐ Yes ☐ No
2	Port of Departure *(Place or Port, City and State)*	Departure Date *(Month, Day, Year)*	Purpose of Travel	Destination
	Port of Return *(Place or Port, City and State)*	Return Date *(Month, Day, Year)*	Manner of Return	Inspected and Admitted? ☐ Yes ☐ No

24) Have you ever departed the United States: a) under an order of deportation, exclusion, or removal? .... ☐ Yes ☐ No

 b) pursuant to a grant of voluntary departure? .... ☐ Yes ☐ No

PART 4 - INFORMATION ABOUT YOUR MARITAL STATUS AND SPOUSE *(Continued on page 3)*

25) I am not married: ☒ I am married: ☐	26) If married, the name of my spouse is: *(Last, First, Middle)*	27) My spouse's name before marriage was:

28) The marriage took place in: *(City and Country)*	29) Date of marriage: *(Month, Day, Year)*

30) My spouse currently resides at:	31) Place and date of birth of my spouse: *(City & Country; Month, Day, Year)*
Apt. number and/or in care of	
No. and Street	32) My spouse is a citizen of: *(Country)*
City or Town *State/Country* *Zip Code*	

33) If your spouse is other than a native born United States citizen, answer the following:

 He/she arrived in the United States at: *(Place or Port, City and State)* _____

 He/she arrived in the United States on: *(Month, Day, Year)* _____

 His/her alien registration number(s) is: A# _____

 He/she was naturalized on: *(Month, Day, Year)* _____ at _____ *(City and State)*

34) My spouse ☐ is ☐ is not employed. If employed, please give salary and the name and address of the place(s) of employment.

Full Name and Address of Employer	Earnings Per Week *(Approximate)*
	$
	$
	$

Please continue answers on a separate sheet as needed.

(2)

Form EOIR-42B
Revised July 2016

PART 4 - INFORMATION ABOUT YOUR MARITAL STATUS AND SPOUSE (Continued)

35) I ☒ - have ☐ - have not been previously married: (If previously married, list the name of each prior spouse, the dates on which each marriage began and ended, the place where the marriage terminated, and describe how each marriage ended.)

Name of prior spouse: (Last, First, Middle)	Date marriage began: Date marriage ended:	Place marriage ended: (City and County)	Description or manner of how marriage was terminated or ended:
▓▓▓▓▓▓▓▓	7/11/02	Norwalk, CA	Divorce

36) My present spouse ☐ - has ☐ - has not been previously married: (If previously married, list the names of each prior spouse, the dates on which each marriage began and ended, the place where the marriage terminated, and describe how each marriage ended.)

Name of prior spouse: (Last, First, Middle)	Date marriage began: Date marriage ended:	Place marriage ended: (City and County)	Description or manner of how marriage was terminated or ended:

37) Have you been ordered by any court, or are otherwise under any legal obligation, to provide child support and/or spousal maintenance as a result of a separation and/or divorce? ☐ Yes ☐ No

PART 5 - INFORMATION ABOUT YOUR EMPLOYMENT AND FINANCIAL STATUS

38) Since my arrival into the United States, I have been employed by the following named persons or firms: (Please begin with present employment and work back in time. Any periods of unemployment or school attendance should be specified. Attach a separate sheet for additional entries if necessary.)

Full Name and Address of Employer	Earnings Per Week (Approximate)	Type of Work Performed	Employed From: (Month, Day, Year)	Employed To: (Month, Day, Year)
████████████████	$ 0	Unemployed	06/2016	PRESENT
	$ 200	Fence Builder	02/2014	06/2016
	$ 0		08/04/1999	06/18/2004

39) If self-employed, describe the nature of the business, the name of the business, its address, and net income derived therefrom:

40) My assets (and if married, my spouse's assets) in the United States and other countries, not including clothing and household necessities, are:

Self

Cash, Stocks, and Bonds	$ 0
Real Estate	$ 0
Auto (dollar value minus amount owed)	$ 0
Other (describe on line below)	$ 0
TOTAL	$

Jointly Owned With Spouse

Cash, Stocks, and Bonds	$
Real Estate	$
Auto (dollar value minus amount owed)	$
Other (describe on line below)	$
TOTAL	$

41) I ☐ - have ☒ - have not received public or private relief or assistance (e.g., Welfare, Unemployment Benefits, Medicaid, TANF, AFDC, etc.). If you have, please give full details including the type of relief or assistance received, date for which relief or assistance was received, place, and total amount received during this time:

42) Please list each of the years in which you have filed an income tax return with the Internal Revenue Service:

2007, 2011-2012, 2017

PART 6 - INFORMATION ABOUT YOUR FAMILY (Continued on page 5)

43) I have _____1_____ (Number of) children. Please list information for each child below, include assets and earnings information for children over the age of 16 who have separate incomes:

Name of Child: (Last, First, Middle) Child's Alien Registration Number:	Citizen of What Country: Birth Date: (Month, Day, Year)	Now Residing At: (City and Country) Birth Date: (City and Country)	Immigration Status of Child
F█████████ A#: N/A	USA 07/25/2009	Norwalk USA Whittier USA	USC
Estimated Total of Assets: $	Estimated Average Weekly Earnings $		
A#:			
Estimated Total of Assets: $	Estimated Average Weekly Earnings: $		
A#:			
Estimated Total of Assets: $	Estimated Average Weekly Earnings: $		

44) If your application is denied, would your spouse and all of your children accompany you to your:

Country of Birth - ☐ Yes ☒ No

Country of Nationality - ☐ Yes ☒ No

Country of Last Residence - ☐ Yes ☒ No

If you answered "No" to any of the responses, please explain _____

My parents and children have established their lives in the United States.

45) Members of my family, including my spouse and/or child(ren) ☐ - have ☒ - have not received public or private relief or assistance (e.g., Welfare, Unemployment Benefits, Medicaid, TANF, AFDC, etc.). If any member of your immediate family has received such relief or assistance, please give full details including identity of person(s) receiving relief or assistance, dates for which relief or assistance was received, place, and total amount received during this time: _____

46) Please give the requested information about your parents, brothers, sisters, aunts, uncles, and grandparents, living or deceased. As to residence, show street address, city, and state, if in the United States; otherwise show only country:

Name: (Last, First, Middle) Alien Registration Number:	Citizen of What Country: Birth Date: (Month, Day, Year)	Relationship to Me: Birth Date: (City and Country)	Immigration Status of Listed Relative
███████████ A#: █████████	Belize USA 03/18/1956	Father Belize City Belize	USC
Complete Address of Current Residence, if Living: 170 Country Road 2123 N, Longview, TX 75603			
███████████ A#: █████████	USA 12/16/1957	Mother Belize City Belize	USC
Complete Address of Current Residence, if Living: 16660 Raymond Avenue, Fontana, CA 92336			

PART 6 - INFORMATION ABOUT YOUR FAMILY *(Continued)*

IF THIS APPLICATION IS BASED ON HARDSHIP TO A PARENT OR PARENTS, QUESTIONS 47-50 MUST BE ANSWERED.

47) If your parent is not a citizen of the United States, give the date and place of arrival in the United States including full details as to the date, manner, and terms of admission into the United States _____

48) My father [X] - is [ ] - is not employed. If employed, please give salary and the name and address of the place(s) of employment.

Full Name and Address of Employer	Earnings Per Week *(Approximate)*
Headwaters Resources ▮▮▮▮ Tatum, TX 75691	$ 500

49) My mother [X] - is [ ] - is not employed. If employed, please give salary and the name and address of place(s) of employment.

Full Name and Address of Employer	Earnings Per Week *(Approximate)*
All Care Medical Management, Inc. 164 W. Hospitality Lane, Suite 14, San Bernardino, CA USA 92408	$ 600

50) My parent's assets in the United States and other countries not including clothing and household necessities are:

Assets of father consist of the following:		Assets of mother consist of the following:	
Cash, Stocks, and Bonds .... $	0	Cash, Stocks, and Bonds .... $	0
Real Estate .... $	0	Real Estate .... $	0
Auto (dollar value minus amount owed) ... $	0	Auto (dollar value minus amount owed) ... $	0
Other (describe on line below) .... $	0	Other (describe on line below) .... $	0
TOTAL $		TOTAL $	

PART 7 - MISCELLANEOUS INFORMATION *(Continued on page 6)*

51) I [ ] - have [X] - have not entered the United States as a crewman after June 30, 1964.

52) I [ ] - have [X] - have not been admitted as, or after arrival in the United States acquired the status of, an exchange alien.

53) I [ ] - have [X] - have not submitted address reports as required by section 265 of the Immigration and Nationality Act.

54) I [X] - have [ ] - have never (either in the United States or in any foreign country) been arrested, summoned into court as a defendant, convicted, fined, imprisoned, placed on probation, or forfeited collateral for an act involving a felony, misdemeanor, or breach of any public law or ordinance (including, but not limited to, traffic violations or driving incidents involving alcohol). *(If answer is in the affirmative, please give a brief description of each offense including the name and location of the offense, date of conviction, any penalty imposed, any sentence imposed, and the time actually served. You are required to submit documentation of any such occurances.)*

02/21/2012 - misdemeanor driving under influence in violation 23152(b) of the California Vehicle Code - 3 years probation

55) Have you ever served in the Armed Forces of the United States? [ ] Yes [X] No. If "Yes" please state branch *(Army, Navy, etc.)* and service number: _____

Place of entry on duty: *(City and State)* _____

Date of entry on duty: *(Month, Day, Year)* _____   Date of discharge: *(Month, Day, Year)* _____

Type of discharge: *(Honorable, Dishonorable, etc.)* _____

I served in active duty status from: *(Month, Day, Year)* _____ to *(Month, Day, Year)* _____

56) Have you ever left the United States or the jurisdiction of the district where you registered for the draft to avoid being drafted into the military or naval forces of the United States?   [ ] Yes [X] No

Please continue answers on a separate sheet as needed.

(5)

Form EOIR-42B
Revised July 2016

PART 7 - MISCELLANEOUS INFORMATION (Continued)

57) Have you ever deserted from the military or naval forces of the United States while the United States was at war? ☐ Yes ☒ No

58) If male, did you register under the Military Selective Service Act or any applicable previous Selective Service (Draft) Laws? ☐ Yes ☒ No
If "Yes," please give date, Selective Service number, local draft board number, and your last draft classification: _____

59) Were you ever exempted from service because of conscientious objection, alienage, or any other reason? ☐ Yes ☒ No

60) Please list your present or past membership in or affiliation with every political organization, association, fund, foundation, party, club, society, or similar group in the United States or any other place since your 16th birthday. Include any foreign military service in this part. If none, write "None." Include the name of the organization, location, nature of the organization, and the dates of membership.

Name of Organization	Location of Organization	Nature of Organization	Member From: (Month, Day, Year)	Member To: (Month, Day, Year)

61) Have you ever:

☐ Yes ☒ No been ordered deported, excluded, or removed?

☐ Yes ☒ No overstayed a grant of voluntary departure from an Immigration Judge or the Department of Homeland Security (DHS), formerly the Immigration and Naturalization Service (INS)?

☐ Yes ☒ No failed to appear for removal or deportation?

62) Have you ever been:

☐ Yes ☒ No a habitual drunkard?

☐ Yes ☒ No one whose income is derived principally from illegal gambling?

☐ Yes ☒ No one who has given false testimony for the purpose of obtaining immigration benefits?

☐ Yes ☒ No one who has engaged in prostitution or unlawful commercialized vice?

☐ Yes ☒ No involved in a serious criminal offense and asserted immunity from prosecution?

☐ Yes ☒ No a polygamist?

☐ Yes ☒ No one who brought in or attempted to bring in another to the United States illegally?

☐ Yes ☒ No a trafficker of a controlled substance, or a knowing assister, abettor, conspirator, or colluder with others in any such controlled substance offense (not including a single offense of simple possession of 30 grams or less of marijuana)?

☐ Yes ☒ No inadmissible or deportable on security-related grounds under sections 212(a)(3) or 237(a)(4) of the INA?

☐ Yes ☒ No one who has ordered, incited, assisted, or otherwise participated in the persecution of an individual on account of his or her race, religion, nationality, membership in a particular social group, or political opinion?

☐ Yes ☒ No a person previously granted relief under sections 212(c) or 244(a) of the INA or whose removal has previously been cancelled under section 240A of the INA?

If you answered "Yes" to any of the above questions, explain: _____

Please continue answers on a separate sheet as needed.
(6)
Form EOIR-42B
Revised July 2016

10 | Page

PART 7 - MISCELLANEOUS INFORMATION (Continued)

63) Are you the beneficiary of an approved visa petition? ☒ Yes ☐ No

If yes, can you arrange a trip outside the United States to obtain an immigrant visa? ☒ Yes ☐ No If no, please explain.

64) The following certificates or other supporting documents are attached hereto as a part of this application. *(Refer to the Instructions for documents which should be attached.)*

See Attached.

PART 8 - SIGNATURE OF PERSON PREPARING FORM, IF OTHER THAN APPLICANT

(Read the following information and sign below)

I declare that I have prepared this application at the request of the person named in Part 1, that the responses provided are based on all information of which I have knowledge, or which was provided to me by the applicant, and that the completed application was read to the applicant in a language the applicant speaks fluently for verification before he or she signed the application in my presence. I am aware that the knowing placement of false information on the Form EOIR-42B may subject me to civil penalties under 8 U.S.C. §1324c.

Signature of Preparer:	Print Name: Christopher A. Reed	Date: 12/15/2016
Daytime Telephone #: (562) 495-0554	Address of Preparer: *(Number and Street, City, State, Zip Code)* 3233 E. Broadway, Long Beach, CA 90803	

Please continue answers on a separate sheet as needed.

(7)

Form EOIR-42B
Revised July 2016

PART 9 - SIGNATURE

APPLICATION NOT TO BE SIGNED BELOW UNTIL APPLICANT APPEARS BEFORE AN IMMIGRATION JUDGE

I swear or affirm that I know the contents of this application that I am signing, including the attached documents and supplements, and that they are all true to the best of my knowledge, taking into account the correction(s) numbered _____ to _____, if any, that were made by me or at my request.

_____
(Signature of Applicant or Parent or Guardian)

Subscribed and sworn to before me by the above-named applicant at _____

_____
Immigration Judge

_____
Date (Month, Day, Year)

PART 10 - PROOF OF SERVICE

I hereby certify that a copy of the foregoing Form EOIR-42B was: ☐ - delivered in person   ☐ - mailed first class, postage prepaid

on _____ to the Assistant Chief Counsel for the DHS (U.S. Immigration and Customs Enforcement - ICE)
   (Month, Day, Year)

at _____
   (Number and Street, City, State, Zip Code)

_____
Signature of Applicant (or Attorney or Representative)

Addendum

████████████████████ , Form: EOIR-42B, A# 078-112-433 , 12/15/2016 (Page 1)

Part 1. 16) Additional Prior Address History:

████████████████████████

Part 4. 35) Additional Divorce History:

████████████████

Part 5. 38) Additional Employment History:

████████████████████████

Form I-797C, Notice of Action

THIS NOTICE DOES NOT GRANT ANY IMMIGRATION STATUS OR BENEFIT.

RECEIPT NUMBER SRC-17-062-50527		CASE TYPE I485 APPLICATION TO REGISTER PERMANENT RESIDENCE OR ADJUST STATUS
RECEIVED DATE December 27, 2016	PRIORITY DATE	APPLICANT
NOTICE DATE December 27, 2016	PAGE 1 of 1	

CHRISTOPHER ALLAN REED LAW OFFICES OF BRIAN D LERNER 3233 E BROADWAY LONG BEACH CA 90803	**Notice Type:** Receipt Notice Fee Previously Collected

Receipt Notice - This notice confirms that USCIS received your application or petition ("this case") as shown above. If any of the above information is incorrect, please immediately call 800-375-5283 to let us know. This will help avoid future problems.

This notice does not grant any immigration status or benefit, nor is it evidence that this case is still pending. It only shows that the application or petition was filed on the date shown.

Processing time - Processing times vary by case type. You can check our website at www.uscis.gov for our current "processing times" for this case type at the particular office to which this case is or becomes assigned. On our website's "case status online" page, you can also view status or sign up to receive free e-mail updates as we complete key processing steps on this case. During most of the time this case is pending, however, our systems will show only that the case has been received, and the processing status will not have changed, because we will be working on other cases that were filed earlier than this one. We will notify you by mail, and show in our systems, when we make a decision on this case or if we need something from you. If you do not receive an initial decision or update from us within our current processing time, check our website or call 800-375-5283. Please save this notice, and any other notice we send you about this case, and please make and keep a copy of any papers you send us by any means, along with any proof of delivery to us. Please have all these papers with you if you contact us about this case.

If this case is an I-130 Petition - Filing and approval of a form I-130, Petition for Alien Relative, is only the first step in helping a relative immigrate to the United States. The beneficiaries of a petition must wait until a visa number is available before they can take the next step to apply for an immigrant visa or adjustment of status to lawful permanent residence. To best allocate resources, USCIS may wait to process I-130 forms until closer to the time when a visa number will become available, which may be years after the petition was filed. Nevertheless, USCIS processes I-130 forms in time not to delay relatives' ability to take the next step toward permanent residence once a visa number does become available. If, before final action on the petition, you decide to withdraw your petition, your family relationship with the beneficiary ends, or you become a U.S. citizen, call 800-375-5283.

Applications requiring biometrics- In some types of cases USCIS requires biometrics. In such cases, USCIS will send you a separate appointment notice with a specific date, time and place for you to go to a USCIS Application Support Center (ASC) for biometrics processing. You must WAIT for that separate appointment notice and take it (NOT this receipt notice) to your ASC appointment along with your photo identification. Acceptable kinds of photo identification are: a passport or national photo identification issued by your country, a drivers license, a military photo identification, or a state-issued photo identification card. If you receive more than one ASC appointment notice, even for different cases, take them both to the first appointment.

If your address changes- If your mailing address changes while your case is pending, call 800-375-5283 or use the "Online Change of Address" function on our website. Otherwise, you might not receive notice of our action on this case.

NOTICE: Pursuant to the terms of the United States Immigration & Nationality Act (INA), the information provided on and in support of applications and petitions is submitted under penalty of perjury. USCIS and the U.S. Department of Homeland Security reserve the right to verify this information before and/or after adjudication to ensure conformity with applicable laws, rules, regulations, and other authorities. Methods used for verifying information may include, but are not limited to, the review of public information and records, contact by correspondence, the Internet, or telephone, and site inspections of businesses and residences. Information obtained during the course of verification will be used to determine eligibility for the benefit sought. Applicants, petitioners, and representatives of record will be provided an opportunity to address derogatory information before any formal decision is made and/or proceeding is initiated.

Please see the additional information on the back. You will be notified separately about any other cases you filed.
TEXAS SERVICE CENTER
US CITIZENSHIP & IMMIGRATION SVCS
P.O. BOX 851488-DEPT A
MESQUITE   TX   75185-1488
Customer Service Telephone: (800) 375-5283

If this is an interview or biometrics appointment notice, please see the back of this notice for important information.   Form I-797C 07/11/14 Y

EXHIBITS

TAB 'A'

Respondent's Birth Certificate

Antonio REGISTRAR GENERAL DEPARTMENT

VITAL STATISTICS UNIT
BIRTH CERTIFICATE

I. CHILD'S INFORMATION

1. Entry No: 6   2. Date of Registration: 02 January 1986

3. Name of Child: ▮▮▮▮▮▮▮

4. Date of Birth: 07 December 1985   5. Sex: Male

6. Place of Birth: Santiago Castillo Hospital, Belize City, BELIZE DISTRICT

II. FATHER'S INFORMATION

7. Name: ▮▮▮▮▮▮▮

8. Country of Birth: BELIZE   9. Age: 29

10. Occupation: Technician

11. Address: ▮▮▮▮▮▮▮

III. MOTHER'S INFORMATION

12. Name: ▮▮▮▮▮▮▮

13. Country of Birth: BELIZE   14. Age: 28

15. Occupation: Housewife   16. Marital Status: Married

17. Address: ▮▮▮▮▮▮▮

IV. INFORMANT'S INFORMATION

18. Name: ▮▮▮▮▮▮▮

19. Relation to Child: Father

20. Address: ▮▮▮▮▮▮▮

V. N ▮▮▮▮▮▮▮

1. This is a certificate of the record officially registered in the VITAL STATISTICS UNIT, Registrar General Department

2. This certificate is not valid unless displaying the Embossed Seal and Signature of the Appropriate Registrar

Given at Belize City, this 23 day of February, 2007.

Lovinia A. Daniels (Miss)
Registrar
Births, Deaths, Marriages

064374

Respondent's Father Permanent Resident Card

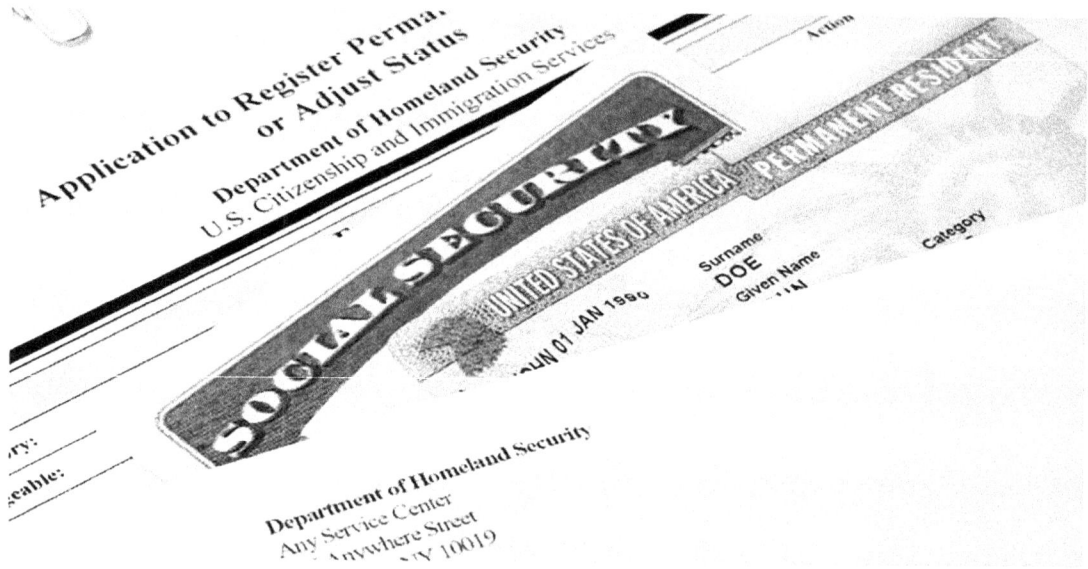

PERMANENT RESIDENT CARD
[redacted]
C1USA0795245526SRC0615751379<<
5603185M1605125BLZ<<<<<<<<<<<4
[redacted]

TAB 'C'

Respondent's Mother Naturalization Certificate

THE UNITED STATES OF AMERICA

No. 32405554

CERTIFICATE OF NATURALIZATION

Personal description of holder as of date of naturalization:

Date of birth DECEMBER 16, 1957

Sex: FEMALE

Height: 5 feet 2 inches

Marital status: MARRIED

Country of former nationality: BELIZE

CIS Registration No:

I certify that the description given is true, and that the photograph affixed hereto is a likeness of me.

Be it known that, pursuant to an application filed with the Secretary of Homeland Security

at: LOS ANGELES, CALIFORNIA

The Secretary having found that such

then residing in the United States, intends to reside in the United States when so required by the Naturalization Laws of the United States, and had in all other respects complied with the applicable provisions of such naturalization laws and was entitled to be admitted to, and had taken the oath of allegiance in a ceremony conducted by the

US DISTRICT COURT CENTRAL DISTRICT

at LOS ANGELES, CALIFORNIA on JULY 24, 2009

that such person is admitted as a citizen of the United States of America.

Director, U.S. Citizenship and Immigration Services

FORM N-550 REV 6/04

CERTIFICATE OF SERVICE

Re: ██████████████████████

I, Christopher A. Reed, hereby certify that I am a resident of or employed in the County of Los Angeles, State of California over 18 years of age, not a party to the within action and that I am employed at and my business address is:

Law Offices of Brian D. Lerner, APC
3233 E. Broadway
Long Beach, CA 90803
Telephone: (562) 495-0554
Facsimile: (562) 608-8672

On January 5, 2017, I served a copy of the attached *APPLICATION FOR CANCELLATION OF REMOVAL AND ADJUSTMENT OF STATUS FOR CERTAIN NONPERMANENT RESIDENTS AND SUPPORTING DOCUMENTS* on the following person(s) by the following method(s):

Office of the Assistant Chief Counsel
Department of Homeland Security
606 S. Olive Street, 8th Floor
Los Angeles, CA 90014
(Personal Service)

I declare under penalty of perjury that the foregoing is true and correct. Executed in Long Beach, California.

DATED: January 5, 2017

By: _____
Christopher A. Reed
Attorney at Law

Brian D. Lerner (#158536)
Christopher A. Reed (#235438)
Law Offices of Brian D. Lerner, APC
3233 E. Broadway
Long Beach, CA 90803
Telephone: (562) 495-0554
Facsimile: (562) 608-8672

UNITED STATES DEPARTMENT OF JUSTICE

EXECUTIVE OFFICE FOR IMMIGRATION REVIEW

IMMIGRATION COURT

LOS ANGELES, CALIFORNIA

In the Matter of:	)	
	)	
	)	
████████████████	)	File No.: ████████
	)	
	)	
	)	
Respondent,	)	
	)	
In Removal Proceedings.	)	

Immigration Judge: Christine E. Stancill   Master Hearing: March 20, 2018 at 9:00 a.m.

SUPPLEMENTAL DOCUMENTS FOR APPLICATION FOR CANCELLATION OF REMOVAL AND ADJUSTMENT OF STATUS FOR CERTAIN NONPERMANENT RESIDENTS #1

TABLE OF CONTENTS

TAB 'D'

Respondent's DACA Denial Notice

September 26, 2017

U.S. Department of Homeland Security
U.S. Citizenship and Immigration Services
California Service Center
Laguna Niguel, CA 92607-0590

U.S. Citizenship and Immigration Services

CHRISTOPHER ALLAN REED
LAW OFFICES OF BRYAN D LERNER
3233 E BROADWAY
LONG BEACH, CA 90803
USA

IOE0901450274

RE: ▓▓▓▓▓▓▓▓▓▓▓▓▓▓
I-821D, Deferred Action for Childhood Arrivals

A078-112-433

DECISION

USCIS has evaluated your Form I-821D, Consideration of Deferred Action for Childhood Arrivals. Based on a review of your case, it appears that the following occurred:

You have not established that you have continuously resided in the United States since June 15, 2007, until the date of filing your request.

Accordingly, USCIS has determined, in its unreviewable discretion, that you have not demonstrated that you warrant a favorable exercise of prosecutorial discretion and it will not defer action in your matter. Accordingly, your Form I-765, Application for Employment Authorization, has also been denied. Deferred action is a discretionary determination to defer removal action of an individual as an act of prosecutorial discretion. You may not file an appeal or motion to reopen/reconsider this decision.

Sincerely,

Kathy A. Baran

Kathy A. Baran
Director
Officer: SG8555

Respondent's DNA Test Report

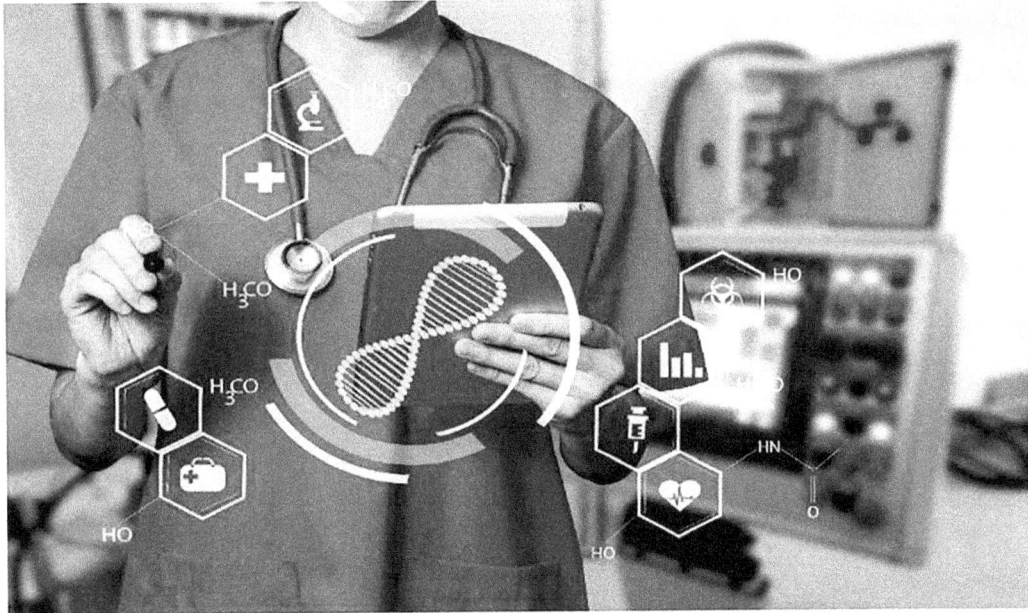

DDC
DNA Diagnostics Center

DNA Test Report

BY937199

Los Angeles CSSD-Division V

DDC is accredited/certified by AABB, CAP, ACLASS-International, ISO/IEC 17025, CLIA, NYSDOH & ASCLD/LAB-International.

Case 1063754	MOTHER		CHILD		Alleged FATHER	
Name	▉▉▉		▉▉▉		▉▉▉	
Race	Hispanic				Other	
Date Collected	3/17/2010		3/17/2010		3/10/2010	
Test No.	1063754-10		1063754-20		1063754-30	
Locus **PI**	Allele Sizes		Allele Sizes		Allele Sizes	
D3S1358 2.07	15	17	15	17	15	
TH01 1.94	6	8	8	9.3	6	9.3
D21S11 35.57	28	32.2	28	32	31	32
D18S51 2.01	12	13	12	13	12	16
D5S818 2.81	11	12	11		11	
D13S317 1.70	11	13	12	13	12	13
D7S820 3.23	8	12	8	12	12	
D16S539 6.11	12		12	13	13	
CSF1PO 1.72	10	12	11	12	11	12
Penta D 7.24	13		11	13	11	
vWA 1.01	16	17	16	17	16	18
TPOX 11.32	10	11	10	12	11	12
Amelogenin	X		X	Y	X	Y

Interpretation:

RN: 257013

Combined Paternity Index: **3,820,970**   Probability of Paternity **99.99997%**

The alleged father is not excluded as the biological father of the tested child. Based on testing results obtained from analyses of the DNA loci listed, the probability of paternity is 99.99997%. This probability of paternity is calculated by comparing to an untested, unrelated, random individual of the general population (assumes prior probability equals 0.50).

Subscribed and sworn to before me on March 26, 2010

Glenda R. Sturtevant
Notary Public/State of Ohio
My Commission Expires October 4, 2013

I, the undersigned Laboratory Director, verify that the interpretation of the results is correct as reported on 3/26/2010.

Michael L. Baird, Ph.D.   Thomas M. Reid, Ph.D.
Keen A. Wilson, Ph.D.   L. Farris Hanna, Ph.D.
Pierig Lepont, Ph.D.   Marco Scarpetta, Ph.D.

TAB 'F'

Respondent's License and Certificate of Marriage and Spouse's
Certificate of Death

COUNTY OF LOS ANGELES • REGISTRAR-RECORDER/COUNTY CLERK

4 2013 19 005721

LICENSE AND CERTIFICATE OF MARRIAGE
MUST BE LEGIBLE - MAKE NO ERASURES, WHITEOUTS, OR OTHER ALTERATIONS
USE BLACK INK ONLY

04/02/1987	CALIFORNIA	0

13030 ROSETON AVE — NORWALK — CALIFORNIA 90650

DANNY JOSE MUNOZ — NICARAGUA

MEXICO

JEREMY — EDWARD

12/07/1985	BELIZE	0

NORWALK — CALIFORNIA 90650

BELIZE

BELIZE

/S/ JENNIFER MUNOZ — /S/ JEREMY EDWARD BURROWES

02/05/2013	05/06/2013	DEAN C. LOGAN	

P2160400	LOS ANGELES	12400 Imperial Highway, Norwalk, CA 90650

MATILDE CABRERA

/S/PEDRO REAL

37724 45TH ST EAST, PALMDALE CA 93552

02/17/2013	NORWALK	LOS ANGELES

NON-DENOM

ROBERTO CABRERA — REVEREND

12629 FAIRFORD AVE, NORWALK, CA 90650

JENNIFER	MUNOZ	BURROWES

DEAN C. LOGAN — APR 18 2013

STATE OF CALIFORNIA, DEPARTMENT OF PUBLIC HEALTH, OFFICE OF VITAL RECORDS

This is to certify that this document is a true copy of the official record filed with the Registrar-Recorder/County Clerk.

SEP 23 2013

DEAN C. LOGAN
Registrar-Recorder/County Clerk

1000000719865

This copy not valid unless prepared on engraved border displaying the Seal and Signature of the Registrar-Recorder/County Clerk.

ANY ALTERATION OR ERASURE VOIDS THIS CERTIFICATE

STATE OF CALIFORNIA
CERTIFICATION OF VITAL RECORD

COUNTY OF ORANGE
CLERK-RECORDER

CERTIFICATE OF DEATH

CA	616-16-0763	DIVORCED — 08/02/2015 — 1763 — F
HS GRADUATE [X] MEXICAN AMERICAN	HISPANIC	
CARE TAKER	MEDICAL FIELD	2

7931 DEVON COURT
RIVERSIDE — RIVERSIDE — 92508 — 26 — CA
7931 DEVON COURT, RIVERSIDE, CA 92508

	JOSE	MUNOZ	NICARAGUA
	REFUGIO		MEXICO

RESURRECTION CEMET

09/14/2015			EMB202
BU	ROBERT CERDA		
FD245	ERIC O. HANDLER M.D.		08/14/2015

UNIVERSITY OF CALIFORNIA IRVINE MED CTR E/D APH — [X] — ORANGE
ORANGE — 101 THE CITY DR S

DEVASTATING TRAUMATIC BRAIN INJURY WITH SUBDURAL — DAYS — 15-01115-EK
HEMATOMA — DAYS
MOTOR VEHICLE ACCIDENT

NONE

NO

	COLETTE SAORI INABA M.D.	A133742 — 08/14/2015
	COLETTE SAORI INABA M.D.	
	101 THE CITY DR S, BLDG 53 #204, ORANGE, CA 92801	
07/31/2015 — 08/02/2015	[X] NO — 07/00/2015 — 2150	

STREET

PEDESTRIAN VS. AUTO

BEACH BLVD SOUTH OF LA HABRA BLVD, LA HABRA, CA 90631
DANIEL P. AKIN — 08/14/2015 — DANIEL P. AKIN, DEPUTY CORONER

103279

00348647C

CERTIFIED COPY OF VITAL RECORDS

STATE OF CALIFORNIA } SS
COUNTY OF ORANGE } DATE ISSUED SEP 28 2015

HUGH NGUYEN
CLERK-RECORDER
ORANGE COUNTY, CALIFORNIA

TAB 'G'

Respondent's High School Diploma

Norwalk High School

Norwalk, California

This Certifies that

███████████████████

has completed the Course of Study prescribed by the Board of Trustees of the Norwalk-La Mirada Unified School District for graduation from this School and is therefore awarded this

Diploma

Given this fifteenth day of June, One thousand nine

Charles Zapadla
Principal

Leonard Krupet
President of the Board of Trustees

Douglas Lelland
Superintendent

TAB 'H'

Respondent's Father Naturalization Certificate and Mother's U.S. Passport

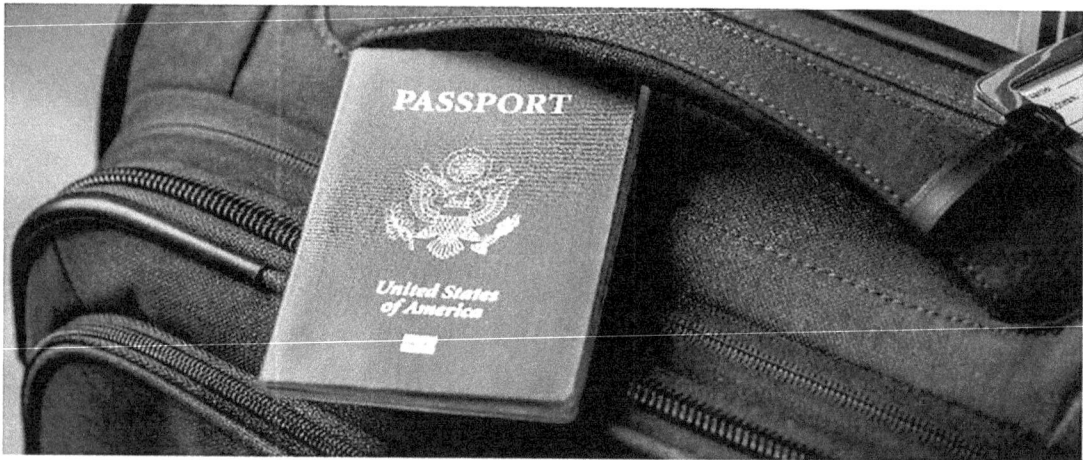

We the People

Of the United States,

Darin Albino Burrowes
SIGNATURE OF BEARER / SIGNATURE DU TITULAIRE / FIRMA DEL TITULAR

PASSPORT
PASSEPORT
PASAPORTE

USA

UNITED STATES OF AMERICA

Type / Type / Tipo   Code / Code / Código   Passport No / No du Passeport / No de Pasaporte
P   USA   493970765

Surname / Nom / Apellidos

Given Names / Prénoms / Nombres

UNITED STATES OF AMERICA

Date of birth / Date de naissance / Fecha de nacimiento
16 Dec 1957

Place of birth / Lieu de naissance / Lugar de nacimiento
BELIZE

Date of issue / Date de délivrance / Fecha de expedición
15 Jun 2012

Date of expiration / Date d'expiration / Fecha de caducidad
14 Jun 2022

Endorsements / Mentions Spéciales / Notaciones
SEE PAGE 27

Sex / Sexe / Sexo
F

Authority / Autorité / Autoridad
United States
Department of State

USA

4939707654USA5712160F2206149324957951<685062

TAB 'I'

Evidence of Respondent's U.S. Citizen Siblings

CALIFORNIA

COUNTY OF LOS ANGELES • REGISTRAR-RECORDER/COUNTY CLERK
CERTIFIED ABSTRACT OF BIRTH

NAME: ▮▮▮▮▮

DATE OF BIRTH: FEBRUARY 03, 1992   SEX: MALE

COUNTY OF BIRTH: LOS ANGELES

BIRTH NAME OF MOTHER: ▮▮▮▮▮

NAME OF FATHER: ▮▮▮▮▮

DATE FILED: FEBRUARY 28, 1992

DATE ISSUED: JUNE 24, 1992

LOCAL REGISTRATION NUMBER: 0012252

This certified document is a true
abstract of the official record
filed with the Registrar-Recorder.

CHARLES WEISSBURD
REGISTRAR-RECORDER/COUNTY CLERK

19- 0631705

THE UNITED STATES OF AMERICA

DEPARTMENT OF HOMELAND SECURITY

CERTIFICATE OF NATURALIZATION

No. 32751458

Personal description of holder
as of date of naturalization:

Date of birth: JULY 04, 1979

Sex: MALE

Height: 6 feet 0 inches

Marital status: MARRIED

Country of former nationality:
BELIZE

INS Registration No.

I certify that the description given is true, and that the photograph affixed
hereto is a likeness of me:

(Complete and true signature of holder)

Be it known that, pursuant to an application filed with the Secretary of
Homeland Security

at SANTA ANA, CALIFORNIA

The Secretary having found that:

that residing in the United States, intends to reside in the United States when so
required by the Naturalization Laws of the United States, and had in all other
respects complied with the applicable provisions of such naturalization laws and
was entitled to be admitted to citizenship, such person having taken the oath of
allegiance at a ceremony conducted by the

US DISTRICT COURT CENTRAL DISTRICT

at LOS ANGELES, CALIFORNIA on OCTOBER 27, 2010

that such person is admitted as a citizen of the United States of America.

Alejandro N Mayorkas

Director, U.S. Citizenship and Immigration Services

We the People

Of the United States,
in Order to form a more perfect Union,
establish Justice, insure Domestic Tranquility,
provide for the common defence,
promote the general Welfare, and secure
the Blessings of Liberty to ourselves and
our posterity, do ordain and establish this
Constitution for the United States of America.

Noelle Burrowes
SIGNATURE OF BEARER / SIGNATURE DU TITULAIRE / FIRMA DEL TITULAR

PASSPORT
PASSEPORT
PASAPORTE

USA

UNITED STATES OF AMERICA

Type / Type / Tipo   Code / Code / Código   Passport No. / No. du Passeport / No. de Pasaporte
P   USA

Surname / Nom / Apellidos

Given names / Prénoms / Nombres

Nationality / Nationalité / Nacionalidad
UNITED STATES OF AMERICA

Date of birth / Date de naissance / Fecha de nacimiento
22 May 1981

Place of birth / Lieu de naissance / Lugar de nacimiento
BELIZE

Date of issue / Date de délivrance / Fecha de expedición
21 Apr 2016

Date of expiration / Date d'expiration / Fecha de caducidad
20 Apr 2026

Endorsements / Mentions Spéciales / Anotaciones
SEE PAGE 27

Sex / Sexe / Sexo
F

Authority / Autorité / Autoridad
United States
Department of State

USA

5450504360USA8105222F2604206613070327<116098<<<<<<<<<<<<<<<

TAB 'J'

Evidence of Respondent's U.S. Citizen Nephews/Nieces

UNITED STATES OF AMERICA

P   USA   490467910

UNITED STATES OF AMERICA

02 Feb 2010

CALIFORNIA U S A

02 Nov 2012

01 Nov 2017

SEE PAGE 27

United State
Department of State

USA

P<USABURROWES<<MYLAH<ADRIELLE<<<<<<<<<<<<<
4964679100USA1002023F1711017253331293<874220

Passport 1

We the People
Of the United States,

UNITED STATES OF AMERICA

PASSPORT / PASSEPORT / PASAPORTE

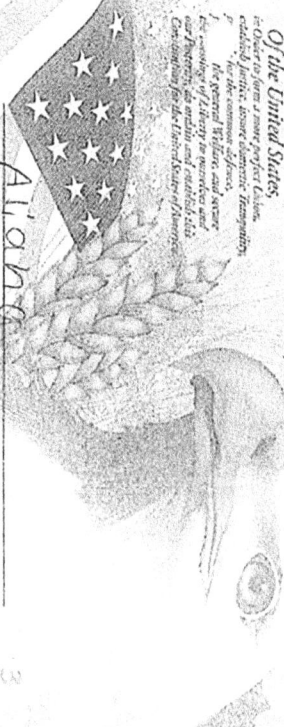

SIGNATURE OF BEARER / SIGNATURE DU TITULAIRE / FIRMA DEL TITULAR
Aliana

Type / Type / Tipo: P
Code / Code / Código: USA
Passport No. / No. du Passeport / No. de Pasaporte: 532824961

Surname / Nom / Apellidos
Given Names / Prénoms / Nombres

Nationality / Nationalité / Nacionalidad: UNITED STATES OF AMERICA
Date of birth / Date de naissance / Fecha de nacimiento: 29 Jan 2009
Place of birth / Lieu de naissance / Lugar de nacimiento: CALIFORNIA, U.S.A.
Date of issue / Date de délivrance / Fecha de expedición: 30 Jun 2015
Date of expiration / Date d'expiration / Fecha de caducidad: 29 Jun 2020
Sex / Sexe / Sexo: F
Authority / Autorité / Autoridad: United States Department of State
Endorsements / Mentions Spéciales / Anotaciones: SEE PAGE 27

```
5328249614USA0901299F2006291331102510<081456
```

Passport 2

We the People
Of the United States,

UNITED STATES OF AMERICA

PASSPORT / PASSEPORT / PASAPORTE

SIGNATURE OF BEARER / SIGNATURE DU TITULAIRE / FIRMA DEL TITULAR
Alyssa

Type / Type / Tipo: P
Code / Code / Código: USA
Passport No. / No. du Passeport / No. de Pasaporte: 532824960

Surname / Nom / Apellidos
Given Names / Prénoms / Nombres

Nationality / Nationalité / Nacionalidad: UNITED STATES OF AMERICA
Date of birth / Date de naissance / Fecha de nacimiento: 29 Jan 2009
Place of birth / Lieu de naissance / Lugar de nacimiento: CALIFORNIA, U.S.A.
Date of issue / Date de délivrance / Fecha de expedición: 30 Jun 2015
Date of expiration / Date d'expiration / Fecha de caducidad: 29 Jun 2020
Sex / Sexe / Sexo: F
Authority / Autorité / Autoridad: United States Department of State
Endorsements / Mentions Spéciales / Anotaciones: SEE PAGE 27

```
5328249603USA0901299F2006291331102499<081384
```

TAB 'K'

Proof of Respondent's Child Support Payments

MoneyGram.

2

R 2074363585 70

207436358857
131   NN

08/18/2017
$100.00
00

MONEYGRAM PAYMENT SYSTEMS, INC. DRAWER
P.O. BOX 9476
MINNEAPOLIS, MN 55480

▶ DETACH HERE ◀

698 (12/12) 500/5000
M 77060-X
EMPLOYEE

KEEP A COPY OF THIS STUB
FOR YOUR RECORDS/
MANTENGA UNA COPIA DE
ESTE RECIBO PARA SUS ARCHIVOS

MoneyGram.

1

R 2071074310 91

20710743109
993   NN

01/15/2017
$100.00
00

MONEYGRAM PAYMENT SYSTEMS, INC. DRAWER
P.O. BOX 9476
MINNEAPOLIS, MN 55480

▶ DETACH HERE ◀

698 (12/12) 500/5000
M 77065-X
EMPLOYEE

KEEP A COPY OF THIS STUB
FOR YOUR RECORDS/
MANTENGA UNA COPIA DE
ESTE RECIBO PARA SUS ARCHIVOS

MoneyGram.

1

R 2067771649 35

20
161   NN

$80.00
00

MONEYGRAM PAYMENT SYSTEMS, INC. DRAWER
P.O. BOX 9476
MINNEAPOLIS, MN 55480

▶ DETACH HERE ◀

698 (12/12) 500/5000
M 77781-W
EMPLOYEE

KEEP A COPY OF THIS STUB
FOR YOUR RECORDS/
MANTENGA UNA COPIA DE
ESTE RECIBO PARA SUS ARCHIVOS

17106749787

17106749904

17270969316

17163279651

FGT 806987 LOC 000079 DT 050115 $70.00 70DOLLARS AND NO CENT

MoneyGram.

R 206126675645

MoneyGram.

04/26/2015
$100.00

06/10/2015
$120.00

$120.00

$110.00

PURCHASER'S RECEIPT
PLEASE COMPLETE AND SIGN THIS
MONEY ORDER PROMPTLY

PURCHASER'S RECEIPT
PLEASE COMPLETE AND SIGN THIS
MONEY ORDER PROMPTLY

PURCHASER'S RECEIPT
PLEASE COMPLETE AND SIGN THIS
MONEY ORDER PROMPTLY

PURCHASER'S RECEIPT
PLEASE COMPLETE AND SIGN THIS
MONEY ORDER PROMPTLY

PURCHASER'S RECEIPT
PLEASE COMPLETE AND SIGN THIS
MONEY ORDER PROMPTLY

355004459 355004664 355004142 361084118 361084281

PAID TO

07/03/2015
$110.00

07/10/2015
$120.00

08/03/2015
$140.00

$150.00

08/28/2015
$120.00

PURCHASER'S RECEIPT
PLEASE COMPLETE AND SIGN THIS
MONEY ORDER PROMPTLY

PURCHASER'S RECEIPT
PLEASE COMPLETE AND SIGN THIS
MONEY ORDER PROMPTLY

PURCHASER'S RECEIPT
PLEASE COMPLETE AND SIGN THIS
MONEY ORDER PROMPTLY

PURCHASER'S RECEIPT
PLEASE COMPLETE AND SIGN THIS
MONEY ORDER PROMPTLY

361084850 361085203 361315563 361316446

10/02/2015
$120.00

10/27/2015
$110.00

11/16/2015
$110.00

$100.00

N, THIS SIDE UP →

← LOAD THIS DIREC

* 1 7 1 0 6 7 4 9 6 1 1 *

ECTION, THIS SIDE UP →

← LOAD THIS DIRECTION

* 1 7 1 0 6 7 4 9 6 3 4 *

MONEYGRAM PAYMENT SYSTEMS, INC. DRAWER
P.O. BOX 9476
MINNEAPOLIS, MN 55403
PLEASE READ REVERSE SIDE   www.moneygram.com/moneyorders   DATE/AMOUNT

COPY OF THIS STUB
FOR YOUR RECORDS
NGA UNA COPIA DE
D PARA SUS ARCHIVOS

R2060 86072929 698 (12/12) 500/5000 M 73395-V
▼ ▼DETACH HERE▼ ▼

MONEYGRAM PAYMENT SYSTEMS, INC. DRAWER
P.O. BOX 9476
MINNEAPOLIS, MN 55403
PLEASE READ REVERSE SIDE   www.moneygram.com/moneyorders   DATE/AMOUNT

2048707811   12/09/2014
145                $140.00
5852009960399   08

KEEP A COPY OF THIS STUB
FOR YOUR RECORDS
MANTENGA UNA COPIA DE
ESTE RECIBO PARA SUS ARCHIVOS

R2048 87878118 698 (12/12) 500/5000 M 70403-U
EMPLOYEE
▼ ▼DETACH HERE▼ ▼

MONEYGRAM PAYMENT SYSTEMS, INC. DRAWER
P.O. BOX 9476
MINNEAPOLIS, MN 55403
PLEASE READ REVERSE SIDE   www.moneygram.com/moneyorders   DATE/AMOUNT

COPY OF THIS STUB
FOR YOUR RECORDS
NGA UNA COPIA DE
O PARA SUS ARCHIVOS

R2058 26291605 698 (12/12) 500/5000 M 72870-V
EMPLOYEE
▼ ▼DETACH HERE▼ ▼

MONEYGRAM PAYMENT SYSTEMS, INC. DRAWER
P.O. BOX 9476
MINNEAPOLIS, MN 55403
PLEASE READ REVERSE SIDE   www.moneygram.com/moneyorders   DATE/AMOUNT

2058471364   11/26/2014
375                $50.00
5528057210572   08

KEEP A COPY OF THIS STUB
FOR YOUR RECORDS
MANTENGA UNA COPIA DE
ESTE RECIBO PARA SUS ARCHIVOS

R2058 64713648 698 (12/12) 500/5000 M 72871-V
EMPLOYEE
▼ ▼DETACH HERE▼ ▼

MONEY ORDER PROMPTLY

361316097

361520672

361520170

PLEASE COMPLETE AND SIGN THIS
MONEY ORDER PROMPTLY

361520485

PLEASE COMPLETE AND SIGN THIS
MONEY ORDER PROMPTLY

361519991

$100.00

**$100.00*

$100.00

**$100.00*

03/24/2016

$100.00

FIDELITY EXPRESS
P.O. Box 758 • Sulphur Springs, TX 75483-0758
For Money Order Inquiries call 800-621-8030

FIDELITY EXPRESS

FIDELITY EXPRESS

FIDELITY EXPRESS

FIDELITY EXPRESS

PURCHASER'S RECEIPT
PLEASE COMPLETE AND SIGN THIS
MONEY ORDER PROMPTLY

361704379

PURCHASER'S RECEIPT
PLEASE COMPLETE AND SIGN THIS
MONEY ORDER PROMPTLY

361703985

PURCHASER'S RECEIPT
PLEASE COMPLETE AND SIGN THIS
MONEY ORDER PROMPTLY

361703388

PURCHASER'S RECEIPT
PLEASE COMPLETE AND SIGN THIS
MONEY ORDER PROMPTLY

361077436

04/16/2016
**$100.00*

05/26/2016
$100.00

05/26/2016
$120.00

06/17/2016
$120.00

FIDELITY EXPRESS
P.O. Box 758 • Sulphur Springs, TX 75483-0758
For Money Order Inquiries call 800-621-8030

FIDELITY EXPRESS

FIDELITY EXPRESS

FIDELITY EXPRESS

2
MoneyGram.

R 207 569 715 683

1
MoneyGram.

R 207 436 354 004

3
MoneyGram.

R 207 678 251 495

KEEP A COPY OF THIS STUB
FOR YOUR RECORDS!
MANTENGA UNA COPIA DE
ESTE RECIBO PARA SUS ARCHIVOS

0099

NOV 11th 2017

█████████████████

Pay to the
Order of _____ $ 100 00

one hundred _____ Dollars

WELLS FARGO Wells Fargo Bank, N.A.
California
wellsfargo.com

For _Logan_

1598.66

NOV. 25th 2017   **0100**

█████████████████

Pay to the
Order of _____ $ 100 00

one hundred _____ Dollars

WELLS FARGO Wells Fargo Bank, N.A.
California
wellsfargo.com

For _Logan_

JEREMY E BURROWES
16660 RAYMOND AVE
FONTANA, CA 92336-2346   **101**

DEC 7th 2017

█████████████████

PAY TO THE
ORDER OF _____ $ 100 00

ONE HUNDRED _____ DOLLARS

WELLS FARGO Wells Fargo Bank, N.A.
California
wellsfargo.com

FOR _Logan_

JEREMY E BURROWES
16660 RAYMOND AVE
FONTANA, CA 92336-2346   **102**

DEC 28th 2017

█████████████████

PAY TO THE
ORDER OF _____ $ 100 00

one hundred _____ DOLLARS

WELLS FARGO Wells Fargo Bank, N.A.
California
wellsfargo.com

FOR _Logan_

TAB 'L'

Docket Sheet – 2JB011494 (Driving under the Influence)

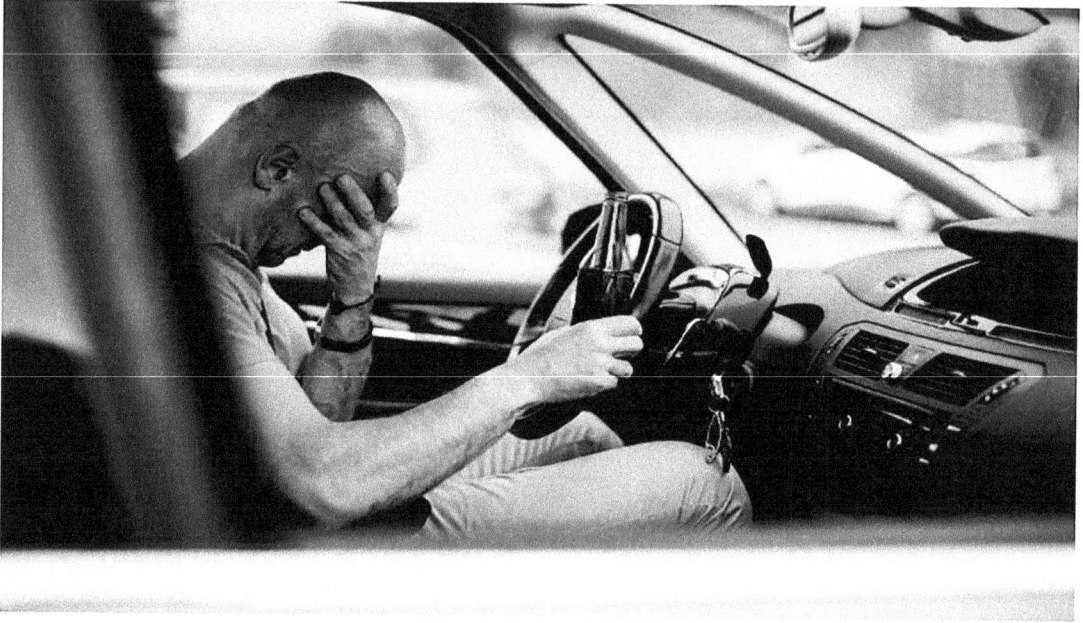

NO. 2JB01194   PAGE NO. 1
THE PEOPLE OF THE STATE OF CALIFORNIA   VS.   CURRENT DATE 08/15/16
DEFENDANT 01: ████████████
LAW ENFORCEMENT AGENCY EFFECTING ARREST: IRWINDALE POLICE DEPARTMENT

BAIL: APPEARANCE   AMOUNT   DATE   RECEIPT OR SURETY COMPANY   REGISTER
       DATE   OF BAIL   POSTED   BOND NO.   NUMBER

CASE FILED ON 02/09/12.
   COMPLAINT FILED, DECLARED OR SWORN TO CHARGING DEFENDANT WITH HAVING
   COMMITTED, ON OR ABOUT 12/27/11 IN THE COUNTY OF LOS ANGELES, THE FOLLOWING
OFFENSE(S) OF:
   COUNT 01: 23152(A) VC MISD
   COUNT 02: 23152(B) VC MISD
   COUNT 03: 12500(A) VC MISD
NEXT SCHEDULED EVENT:
   02/21/12   830 AM ARRAIGNMENT   DIST WEST COVINA COURTHOUSE DEPT 009

ON 02/21/12 AT 830 AM IN WEST COVINA COURTHOUSE DEPT 009

CASE CALLED FOR ARRAIGNMENT ████████████ ██████ ██████ (CLERK)
PARTIES ██████████████████████████████████ RICHMAN (DA)

DEFENDANT DEMANDS COUNSEL.
COURT REFERS DEFENDANT TO THE PUBLIC DEFENDER.
PUBLIC DEFENDER APPOINTED. JAMES DUFFY - P.D.
DEFENDANT IS PRESENT IN COURT, AND REPRESENTED BY JAMES DUFFY DEPUTY PUBLIC
   DEFENDER
DEFENDANT STATES HIS/HER TRUE NAME AS CHARGED.
A COPY OF THE COMPLAINT AND THE ARREST REPORT GIVEN TO DEFENDANTS COUNSEL.
DEFENDANT'S FINANCIAL STATEMENT FILED.
DEFENDANT ADVISED OF AND PERSONALLY AND EXPLICITLY WAIVES THE FOLLOWING RIGHTS:
   WRITTEN ADVISEMENT OF RIGHTS AND WAIVERS FILED, INCORPORATED BY REFERENCE
HEREIN
TRIAL BY COURT AND TRIAL BY JURY
   CONFRONTATION AND CROSS-EXAMINATION OF WITNESSES;
   SUBPOENA OF WITNESSES INTO COURT TO TESTIFY IN YOUR DEFENSE;
   AGAINST SELF-INCRIMINATION;

DEFENDANT ADVISED OF THE FOLLOWING:
   THE NATURE OF THE CHARGES AGAINST HIM, THE ELEMENTS OF THE OFFENSE IN THE
   COMPLAINT, AND POSSIBLE DEFENSES TO SUCH CHARGES;
   THE POSSIBLE CONSEQUENCES OF A PLEA OF GUILTY OR NOLO CONTENDERE, INCLUDING
   THE MAXIMUM PENALTY AND ADMINISTRATIVE SANCTIONS AND THE POSSIBLE LEGAL
   EFFECTS AND MAXIMUM PENALTIES INCIDENT TO SUBSEQUENT CONVICTIONS FOR THE
   SAME OR SIMILAR OFFENSES;
   THE EFFECTS OF PROBATION;
   IF YOU ARE NOT A CITIZEN, YOU ARE HEREBY ADVISED THAT A CONVICTION OF THE
   OFFENSE FOR WHICH YOU HAVE BEEN CHARGED WILL HAVE THE CONSEQUENCES OF
   DEPORTATION, EXCLUSION FROM ADMISSION TO THE UNITED STATES, OR DENIAL OF
   NATURALIZATION PURSUANT TO THE LAWS OF THE UNITED STATES.
COUNSEL FOR THE DEFENDANT JOINS IN THE WAIVERS AND CONCURS IN THE PLEA.
COURT FINDS THAT EACH SUCH WAIVER IS KNOWINGLY, UNDERSTANDINGLY, AND EXPLICITLY
   MADE;

THE DEFENDANT WITH THE COURTS APPROVAL, PLEADS NOLO CONTENDERE TO COUNT 02 A
VIOLATION OF SECTION 23152(B) VC. THE COURT FINDS THE DEFENDANT GUILTY.
COUNT (02) : DISPOSITION: CONVICTED
COURT FINDS THAT THERE IS A FACTUAL BASIS FOR DEFENDANT'S PLEA, AND COURT
ACCEPTS PLEA.
THE DEFENDANT IS ADVISED THAT THIS IS A PRIORABLE OFFENSE.

WRITTEN WAIVER SIGNED AND FILED.

COUNSEL STIPULATES TO A FACTUAL BASIS FOR THE
PLEA AND A BLOOD ALCOHOL OF .16 PERCENT, PURSUANT TO THE
POLICE REPORT.

THE DEFENDANT ADMITS THE ALLEGATION OF DRIVING WITH A BLOOD
ALCOHOL LEVEL OF 15% OR HIGHER PURSUANT TO VEHICLE CODE SECTION
23578 AND THE COURT FINDS IT TO BE TRUE.

WAIVES TIME FOR SENTENCE.

NEXT SCHEDULED EVENT:
SENTENCING
DEFENDANT WAIVES ARRAIGNMENT FOR JUDGMENT AND STATES THERE IS NO LEGAL CAUSE
WHY SENTENCE SHOULD NOT BE PRONOUNCED. THE COURT ORDERED THE FOLLOWING
JUDGMENT:
AS TO COUNT (02):
IMPOSITION OF SENTENCE SUSPENDED
DEFENDANT PLACED ON SUMMARY PROBATION
FOR A PERIOD OF 003 YEARS UNDER THE FOLLOWING TERMS AND CONDITIONS:
PAY A FINE OF $360.00
PLUS A STATE PENALTY FUND ASSESSMENT OF $1,008.00
PLUS $1.00 NIGHT COURT.
PLUS $72.00 CRIMINAL FINE SURCHARGE (PURSUANT TO 1465.7 P.C.)
$30.00 CRIMINAL CONVICTION ASSESSMENT (PURSUANT TO 70373 G.C.)
$40.00 COURT SECURITY ASSESSMENT (PURSUANT TO 1465.8(A)(1) P.C.)
$33.00 LABORATORY SERVICE FUND(PURSUANT TO 1463.14(B) P.C.)
$75.00 ALCOHOL AND DRUG PROBLEM ASSESSMENT (23649 V.C.)
$50.00 ALCOHOL ABUSE/PREVENTION ASSESSMENT (23645 V.C.)
DEFENDANT TO PAY FINE TO THE COURT CLERK
IN LIEU OF FINE, DEFENDANT MAY:
PERFORM 183 HOURS OF COMMUNITY SERVICE, AND FILE PROOF OF COMPLETION WITH THE

CLERK'S OFFICE BY 02/21/13;
DEFENDANT TO PAY COURT COST OF $170 .
THE DEFENDANT SHALL ENROLL AND PARTICIPATE IN, AND SUCCESSFULLY COMPLETE, A
6-MONTH LICENSED FIRST-OFFENDER ALCOHOL AND OTHER DRUG EDUCATION AND COUNSELING
PROGRAM
DEFENDANT SHALL PAY A RESTITUTION FINE IN THE AMOUNT OF $120.00 TO THE COURT
TOTAL DUE: $1,959.00
IN ADDITION:
-DEFENDANT SHALL REPORT TO THE PUBLIC HEALTH INVESTIGATOR IN
ROOM 128 TODAY, TO ENROLL IN THE ALCOHOL PROGRAM.
-DO NOT DRIVE A MOTOR VEHICLE WITHOUT A VALID DRIVER'S LICENSE IN
YOUR POSSESSION OR WITHOUT LIABILITY INSURANCE IN AT LEAST THE
MINIMUM AMOUNTS REQUIRED BY LAW.
-DO NOT DRIVE ANY VEHICLE WITH ANY MEASURABLE AMOUNT OF ALCOHOL
OR DRUGS IN YOUR BLOOD OR REFUSE TO TAKE AND COMPLETE ANY BLOOD

ALCOHOL OR DRUG CHEMICAL TEST, ANY FIELD SOBRIETY TEST, AND ANY
PRELIMINARY ALCOHOL SCREENING TEST, WHEN REQUESTED BY ANY PEACE
OFFICER.
-DEFENDANT IS ORDERED TO PAY A PROBATION REVOCATION RESTITUTION
FINE PURSUANT TO PENAL CODE SECTION 1202.44, IN THE AMOUNT OF
$ 120.00. THIS FINE SHALL BECOME EFFECTIVE UPON THE REVOCATION
OF PROBATION.
-OBEY ALL LAWS AND ORDERS OF THE COURT.
-DEFENDANT ACKNOWLEDGES TO THE COURT THAT THE DEFENDANT
UNDERSTANDS AND ACCEPTS ALL THE PROBATION CONDITIONS, AND
DEFENDANT AGREES TO ABIDE BY SAME.
COURT ORDERS AND FINDINGS:
-THE DEFENDANT WAS ADVISED AND UNDERSTOOD THAT BEING UNDER THE
INFLUENCE OF ALCOHOL OR DRUGS, OR BOTH, IMPAIRS HIS/HER ABILITY
TO SAFELY OPERATE A MOTOR VEHICLE, AND IT IS EXTREMELY DANGEROUS
TO HUMAN LIFE TO DRIVE WHILE UNDER THE INFLUENCE OF ALCOHOL OR
DRUGS, OR BOTH. DEFENDANT WAS FURTHER ADVISED THAT IF HE/SHE
CONTINUES TO DRIVE WHILE UNDER THE INFLUENCE OF ALCOHOL OR

DRUGS, OR BOTH, AND AS A RESULT OF HIS/HER DRIVING, SOMEONE IS
KILLED, THE DEFENDANT CAN BE CHARGED WITH MURDER.
OBEY ALL LAWS AND FURTHER ORDERS OF THE COURT.
THE DEFENDANT IS GIVEN CUSTODY CREDIT FOR 1 DAY ($30) TOWARD
THE FINE, FOR A NEW BASE FINE OF $360.00.

COURT COSTS OF $170 INCLUDE, $10 CITATION PROCESSING, $30
INSTALLMENT, $4 EMERGENCY TRANSPORTATION AND $126 IN ATTORNEY
FEES.

THE DEFENDANT IS ADVISED THAT THE DEPARTMENT OF MOTOR VEHICLES
WILL REQUIRE INSTALLATION OF AN IGNITION INTERLOCK DEVICE FOR
A PERIOD OF 5 MONTHS.

PAYMENT OF THE FINE OF $1959 OR PROOF OF COMPLETION OF 183
HOURS OF COMMUNITY SERVICE PLUS PAYMENT OF $489 IS DUE TO
CLERK ON 2-21-13.

COUNT (02): DISPOSITION: CONVICTED
REMAINING COUNTS DISMISSED:
COUNT (01): DISMISSED DUE TO PLEA NEGOTIATION

COUNT (03): DISMISSED DUE TO PLEA NEGOTIATION
ABSTRACT ISSUED ON 02/21/12 FOR COUNT 02
DMV JUDGMENT CODE QCG
NEXT SCHEDULED EVENT:
02/21/13 900 AM PROOF OF COMPLETION/FINE   DIST WEST COVINA COURTHOUSE
DEPT CLK

03/02/12 ARREST DISPOSITION REPORT SENT VIA FILE TRANSFER TO DEPARTMENT OF
JUSTICE

ON 02/21/13 AT 1000 AM :

UPON DEFENDANT'S REQUEST, CASE IS CONTINUED TO 03/21/13
AT 8:30 AM IN DEPARTMENT 009 FOR AN EXTENSION ON THE FINE.

DEFENDANT IS INFORMED TO APPEAR ON SAID DATE.

FILED: PROOF OF COMPLETION OF 183 HOURS OF COMMUNITY SERVICE.

CASE NO. 2J801194   PAGE NO.   4
DEF NO. 01   DATE PRINTED 08/15/16

NEXT SCHEDULED EVENT:
     03/21/13   830 AM FURTHER PROCEEDINGS   DIST WEST COVINA COURTHOUSE DEPT 009

ON 03/21/13 AT 830 AM IN WEST COVINA COURTHOUSE DEPT 009

CASE CALLED FOR FURTHER PROCEEDINGS
PARTIES: VICTOR D. MARTINEZ (JUDGE) DEBORAH SUSTAYTA (CLERK)
         ANTOINETTE DAVIS   (REP) SYLVIA M. MOORE (DA)
DEFENDANT IS NOT PRESENT IN COURT, AND NOT REPRESENTED BY COUNSEL
MATTER IS BEFORE THE COURT PURSUANT TO THE DEFENDANT'S
"SPECIAL PETITION FOR WALK-INS".

   THE DEFENDANT IS NOT PRESENT IN COURT BUT THE COURT NOTES FOR
   RECORD THAT PROOF OF COMPLETION FOR COMMUNITY SERVICE HAS
   BEEN FILED.

   THE COURT ORDERS THE BALANCE OF $489.00 REFERRED FOR
   ABSTRACT OF JUDGMNET.
NEXT SCHEDULED EVENT:
PROBATION IN EFFECT

CUSTODY STATUS: ON PROBATION

ON 03/25/13 AT 900 AM :

   PAID IN FULL.
   PAYMENT IN THE AMOUNT OF $489.00 PAID ON 03/25/13 RECEIPT # CIT514853011

ON 07/18/16 AT 900 AM :

   PETITION FOR DISMISSAL PURSUANT 1203.4 P.C. FILED. REQUEST TO
   WAIVE COURT FEES FORWARDED TO DEPT. 9 FOR JUDICIAL REVIEW. MG

ON 07/25/16 AT 930 AM :

   CHAMBERS:
   ORDER ON COURT FEE WAIVER SIGNED BY THE COURT AND FILED.
PROCEEDINGS TERMINATED

ON 07/27/16 AT 900 AM :

   MAILED COPY OF ORDER ON COURT FEE WAIVER TO DEFENDANT. RL

   PETITION FOR DISMISSAL IS SET FOR HEARING ON 08/10/16 AT 8:30 AM
   IN DEPARTMENT 9
NEXT SCHEDULED EVENT:
     08/10/16   830 AM MOTN/DISM PURSNT PC SEC 1203.4   DIST WEST COVINA
          COURTHOUSE DEPT 009

ON 08/10/16 AT 830 AM IN WEST COVINA COURTHOUSE DEPT 009

CASE CALLED FOR MOTN/DISM PURSNT PC SEC 1203.4
PARTIES: DAVID C. BROUGHAM (JUDGE) ELIZABETH RIVERA   (CLERK)
         REBECA HORAN (REP)   ANET BADALI (DA)
DEFENDANT IS PRESENT IN COURT, AND NOT REPRESENTED BY COUNSEL
   DEFENDANT APPEARS IN PRO PER
AS TO COUNT (02):
MOTION PURSUANT TO SECTION 1203.4/1203.4A OF THE CALIFORNIA PENAL CODE IS
HEREBY GRANTED. IT IS HEREBY ORDERED THAT THE PLEA, VERDICT, OR FINDING OF
GUILT BE SET ASIDE AND VACATED AND A PLEA OF NOT GUILTY BE ENTERED; AND THAT
THE COMPLAINT BE, AND IS HEREBY DISMISSED
COUNT (02): IS DISMISSED: DISMISSED PER 1203.4 P.C.
   NOTICE REGARDING ABILITY TO REIMBURSE COST OF SERVICES
RENDERED FILED.

   THE COURT FINDS THE DEFENDANT DOES NOT HAVE THE ABILITY TO
REIMBURSE THE COURT FOR THE ACTUAL COSTS OF SERVICES

   RENDERED.

   ORDER FOR DISMISSAL SIGNED BY THE COURT AND FILED.
COUNT (02): DISPOSITION: DISMISSED PER 1203.4 P.C.
DMV ABSTRACT NOT REQUIRED
NEXT SCHEDULED EVENT:
   DISMISSD PURSUANT TO 1203.4 PC

ON 08/11/16 AT 900 AM :

   SUBSEQUENT ADR FORWARDED TO THE DEPARTMENT OF JUSTICE. RL
PROCEEDINGS TERMINATED

Brian D. Lerner (#158536)
Christopher A. Reed (#235438)
Law Offices of Brian D. Lerner, APC
3233 E. Broadway
Long Beach, CA 90803
Telephone: (562) 495-0554
Facsimile: (562) 608-8672

UNITED STATES DEPARTMENT OF JUSTICE

EXECUTIVE OFFICE FOR IMMIGRATION REVIEW

IMMIGRATION COURT

LOS ANGELES, CALIFORNIA

In the Matter of:	)
	)
	)
▇▇▇▇▇▇▇▇▇▇▇	) File No.: ▇▇▇▇▇
	)
	)
	)
Respondent,	)
	)
In Removal Proceedings.	)

Immigration Judge: Christine E. Stancill   Individual Hearing: July 24, 2018 at 1:00 p.m.

SUPPLEMENTAL DOCUMENTS FOR APPLICATION FOR CANCELLATION OF REMOVAL AND ADJUSTMENT OF STATUS FOR CERTAIN NONPERMANENT RESIDENTS #2

Brian D. Lerner (#158536)
Christopher A. Reed (#235438)
Law Offices of Brian D. Lerner, APC
3233 E. Broadway
Long Beach, CA 90803
Telephone: (562) 495-0554
Facsimile: (562) 608-8672

UNITED STATES DEPARTMENT OF JUSTICE

EXECUTIVE OFFICE FOR IMMIGRATION REVIEW

IMMIGRATION COURT

LOS ANGELES, CALIFORNIA

In the Matter of:	)	
	)	
███████████████	)	File No.: A ███████
	)	
Respondent,	)	
In Removal Proceedings.	)	

Immigration Judge: Christine E. Stancill

Individual Hearing: July 24, 2018 at 1:00 p.m.

SUPPLEMENTAL DOCUMENTS FOR APPLICATION FOR CANCELLATION OF REMOVAL AND ADJUSTMENT OF STATUS FOR CERTAIN NONPERMANENT RESIDENTS #2

TABLE OF CONTENTS

TAB 'M'

Witness List

WITNESS LIST

If necessary, the following individual(s) will provide testimony in support of Respondent's applications for relief from removal:

1. Name: Daria Albina BURROWES – Respondent's Mother
   Summary of Testimony: Respondent's mother will testify about her relationship with Respondent, Respondent's physical presence in this country, Respondent's good moral character and the hardship she and her family will suffer if Respondent is removed from the United States.
   Alien Number: A███████████
   Length of Testimony: 20 Minutes
   Language: English

2. Name: ███████████ – Respondent's Sister
   Summary of Testimony: Respondent's sister will testify about her relationship with Respondent, Respondent's physical presence in this country, Respondent's good moral character and the hardship her family will suffer if Respondent is removed from the United States.
   Alien Number: ███████████
   Length of Testimony: 10 Minutes
   Language: English

3. Name: ███████████ – Respondent's Brother
   Summary of Testimony: Respondent's brother will testify about his relationship with Respondent, Respondent's physical presence in this country, Respondent's good moral character and the hardship his family will suffer if Respondent is removed from the United States.
   Alien Number: N/A
   Length of Testimony: 10 Minutes
   Language: English

4. Name: ███████████ – Respondent's Son's Mother
   Summary of Testimony: Respondent's son's mother will testify about her relationship with Respondent, Respondent's good moral character, Respondent's physical presence in this country, Respondent's relationship with his son and the hardship her son will suffer if Respondent is removed from the United States.
   Alien Number: N/A
   Length of Testimony: 15 Minutes
   Language: English

5.   Name: ██████████ -- Respondent's Friend
Summary of Testimony: Respondent's friend will testify about her relationship with Respondent, Respondent's physical presence in this country and Respondent's good moral character.
Alien Number: N/A
Length of Testimony: 10 Minutes
Language: English

6.   Name: ██████████ -- Respondent's Friend
Summary of Testimony: Respondent's friend will testify about his relationship with Respondent, Respondent's physical presence in this country and Respondent's good moral character.
Alien Number: N/A
Length of Testimony: 10 Minutes
Language: English

7.   Name: ██████████ - Respondent's Family Friend
Summary of Testimony: Respondent's friend will testify about his relationship with Respondent, Respondent's physical presence in this country and Respondent's good moral character.
Alien Number: N/A
Length of Testimony: 10 Minutes
Language: English

TAB 'N'

Respondent's Sister Certificate of Naturalization

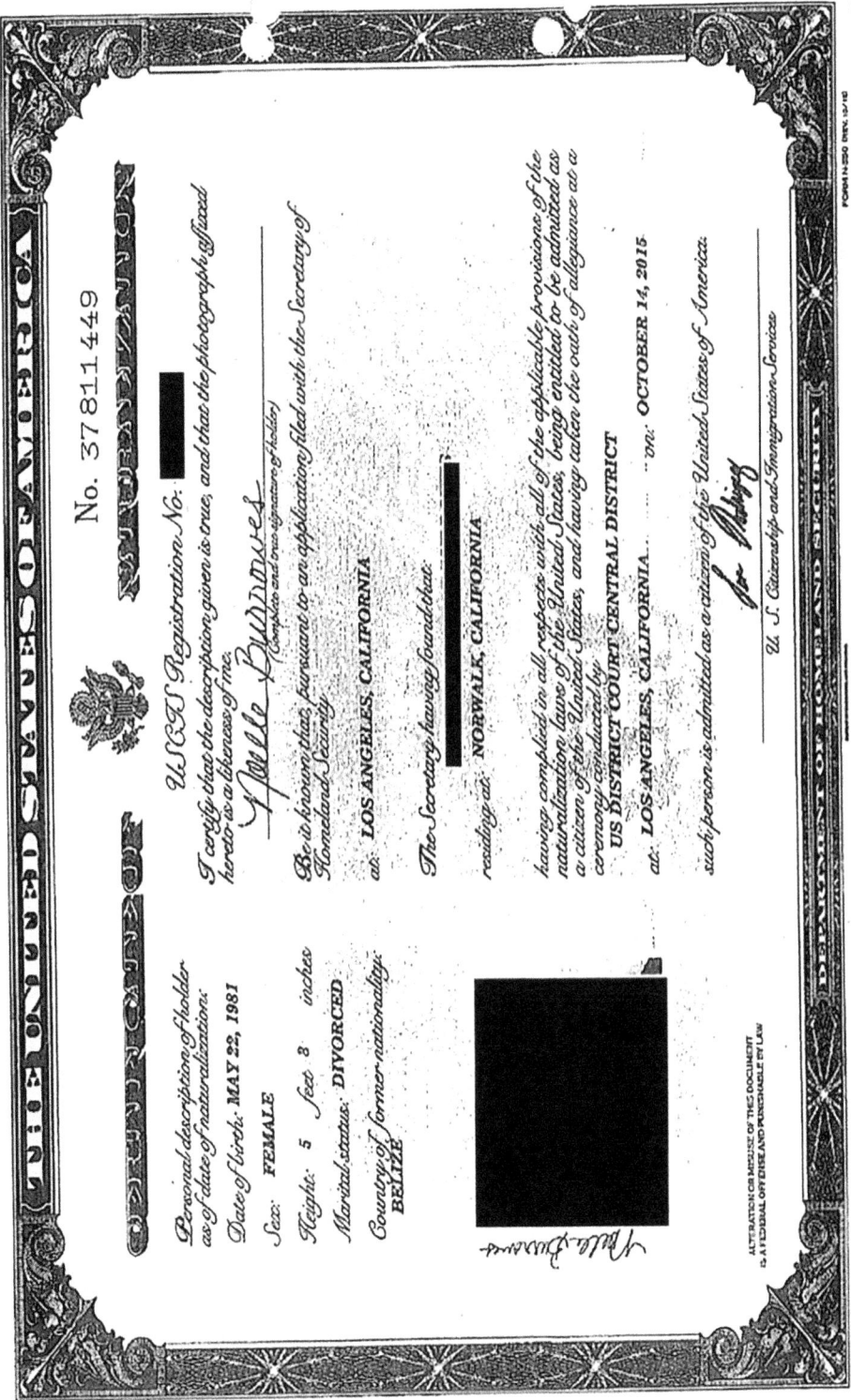

THE UNITED STATES OF AMERICA

No. 37811449

DEPARTMENT OF HOMELAND SECURITY

Personal description of holder as of date of naturalization:

Date of birth: MAY 22, 1981

Sex: FEMALE

Height: 5 feet 3 inches

Marital status: DIVORCED

Country of former nationality: BELIZE

USCIS Registration No.:

I certify that the description given is true, and that the photograph affixed hereto is a likeness of me,

(Complete and true signature of holder)

Be it known that, pursuant to an application filed with the Secretary of Homeland Security

at: LOS ANGELES, CALIFORNIA

The Secretary having found that:

residing at: NORWALK, CALIFORNIA

having complied in all respects with all of the applicable provisions of the naturalization laws of the United States, being entitled to be admitted as a citizen of the United States, and having taken the oath of allegiance at a ceremony conducted by

US DISTRICT COURT CENTRAL DISTRICT

at: LOS ANGELES, CALIFORNIA .... on: OCTOBER 14, 2015

such person is admitted as a citizen of the United States of America.

U.S. Citizenship and Immigration Services

FORM N-550 (REV. 13/10)

TAB 'O'

Respondent's Approved I-130

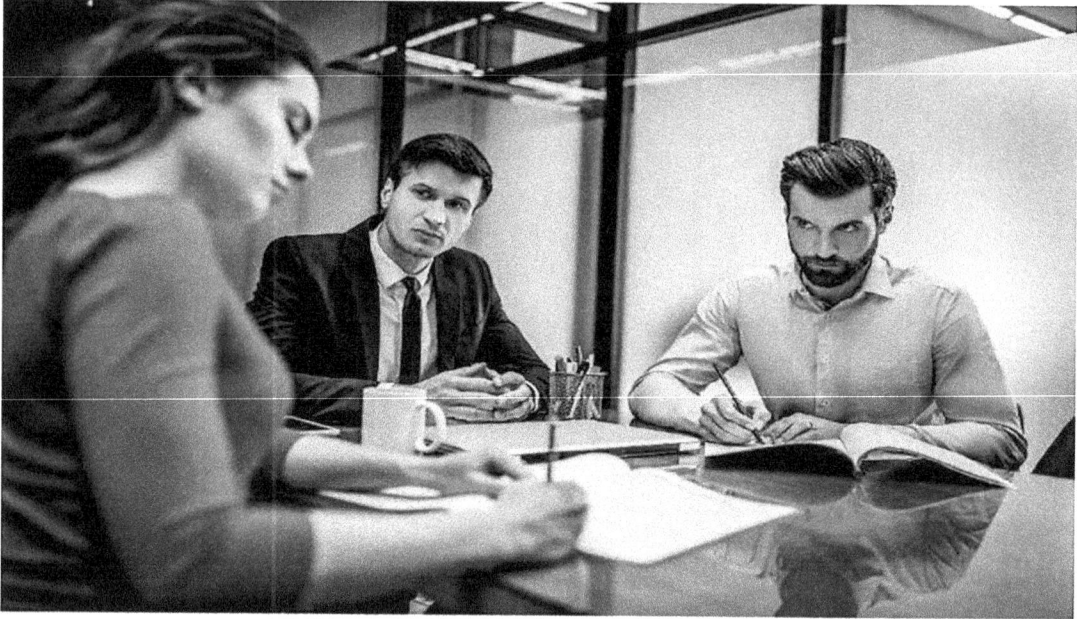

Department of Homeland Security
U.S. Citizenship and Immigration Service

I-797C, Notice of Action

THE UNITED STATES OF AMERICA

Receipt Number: WAC-09-331-11455		Case Type: I-130 - Petition for Alien Relative
Received Date: August 26, 2009	Priority Date:	Petitioner: ▮▮▮▮▮
Notice Date: August 31, 2009	Page 1 OF 1	Beneficiary: ▮▮▮▮▮

Notice Type:	Receipt Notice
Amount Received	$355.00
Section: Unmarried child (age 21 or older) of U.S. Citizen, 201(a)(1) INA	

Receipt Notice - This notice confirms that USCIS received your application or petition ("this case") as shown above. If any of the above information is incorrect, please immediately call 800-375-5283 to let us know. This will help avoid future problems.

This notice does not grant any immigration status or benefit. It is not even evidence that this case is still pending. It only shows that the application or petition was filed on the date shown.

Processing Time - Processing times vary by kind of case. You can check our website at www.uscis.gov for our current processing times for this kind of case at the particular office to which this case is or becomes assigned. At our website's "case status online" page, you can also view status or sign up to receive free e-mail updates as we complete key processing steps in this case. During most of the time this case is pending, however, our systems will show only that the case has been received, and the processing status will not have changed, because we were working on other cases that were filed earlier than this one. We will notify you by mail, and show in our systems, when we make a decision on this case or if we need something from you. If you do not receive an initial decision or update from us within our current processing time, check our website or call 800-375-5283. Please save this notice and any other notice we send you about this case, and please make and keep a copy of any papers you send us by any means, along with any proof of delivery to us. Please have all these papers with you if you contact us about this case.

If this case is an I-130 Petition - Filing and approval of a Form I-130, Petition for Alien Relative, is only the first step in helping a relative immigrate to the United States. The beneficiaries of a petition must wait until a visa number is available before they can take the next step to apply for an immigrant visa or adjustment of status to lawful permanent residence. To best allocate resources, USCIS may wait to process forms I-130 until closer to the time when a visa number will become available, which may be years after the petition was filed. Nevertheless, USCIS processes forms I-130 in time not to delay relatives ability to take the next step toward permanent residence once a visa number does become available. If, before final action on the petition, you decide to withdraw your petition, your family relationship with the beneficiary ends, or you become a U.S. citizen, call 800-375-5283.

Applications requiring biometrics - In some types of cases USCIS requires biometrics. In such cases, USCIS will send you a SEPARATE appointment notice with a specific date, time and place for you to go to a USCIS Application Support Center (ASC) for biometrics processing. You must WAIT for that separate appointment notice and take it (NOT this receipt notice) to your ASC appointment along with your photo identification. Acceptable kinds of photo identification are: a passport or national photo identification issued by your country, a drivers license, a military photo identification, or a state issued photo identification card. If you receive more than one ASC application notice, even for different cases, take them both to the first appointment.

If your address changes - If your mailing address changes while your case is pending, call 800-375-5283 or use the "Online Change of Address" function on our website. Otherwise, you might not receive notice of our action on this case.

Please see the additional information on the back. You will be notified separately about any other cases you filed
U. S. Citizenship and Immigration Services
USCIS California Service Center
P.O. Box 30111
Laguna Niguel, CA 92607-0111

Form I-797C (Rev. 01/31/05) N

**U.S. Citizens
and Immigration
Services**

FORMS   NEWS   RESOURCES   LAWS   OUTREACH   ABOUT US

- Check My Case Status
- Sign in to My Account
- Sign up for Case Updates
- Check Processing Times
- Change Of Address Online
- e-Request
- Office Locator

My Case Status

Para tener acceso a este sitio en Español, presione aquí

Your Current Case Status for Form I130, IMMIGRANT PETITION FOR RELATIVE, FIANCE(E), OR ORPHAN

Enter your Receipt Number
wac0303311455
[Check Status]

○ Acceptance   ○ Initial Review   ○ Decision   ● Post Decision Activity

Your Case Status:
Post Decision Activity

Post Decision Activity

On August 11, 2011, we mailed you a notice that we have approved this I130 IMMIGRANT PETITION FOR RELATIVE, FIANCE(E), OR ORPHAN. Please follow any instructions on the notice. If you move before you receive the notice, call customer service at 1-800-375-5283.

For approved applications/petitions, post-decision activity may include USCIS sending notification of the approved application/petition to the National Visa Center or the Department of State. For denied applications/petitions, post decision activity may include the processing of an appeal and/or motions to reopen or reconsider and revocations.

You can register for automatic case status updates by email and text message by creating an account.
To submit a service request for an inquiry for an application please click e-Request.

Processing Times

1). Select a form type
[Select one...   ] ▼

[NEXT] [RESET]

View national volumes and trends for all applications

USCIS Privacy Act Statement

Case Status Online

Authority: The information requested by My Case Status is collected pursuant to the Immigration and Nationality Act of 1952, Public Law 82-414, as amended.

Purpose: The primary purpose for collecting your case receipt number is to provide you with a status update and estimated processing times for a pending immigration benefit application or petition.

Routine Uses: The information may be used by and disclosed to DHS personnel and contractors or other agents who need the information to assist in activities related to providing status information on a pending immigration benefit application or petition. Additionally, DHS may share this information with law enforcement or other government agencies as necessary to respond to potential or actual threats to national security pursuant to the agency's published Privacy Policy and the routine uses outlined in the Benefits Information System system of records notice, DHS-USCIS-007, September 29, 2008 73 FR 56596.

Disclosure: The information you provide is voluntary. However, failure to provide the requested information may prevent USCIS from providing a status update on your pending case.

OMB control no. 1615-0080

Expiration date 6-30-2012

TAB 'P'

Respondent's Judgement of Dissolution of Marriage

HUSBAND:		CASE NUMBER:
WIFE		VD 065868.

NOTICE OF ENTRY OF JUDGMENT

6. You are notified that a judgment of dissolution of marriage was entered on *(date)*: JUL 0 1 2008

Date: JUL 0 1 2008

JOHN A CLARKE

Clerk, by _____ S. Thompson _____) Deputy

CLERK'S CERTIFICATE OF MAILING

I certify that I am not a party to this cause and that a true copy of the *Notice of Entry of Judgment* was mailed first class, postage fully prepaid, in a sealed envelope addressed as shown below, and that the notice was mailed at *(place):* NORWALK , California,

on *(date):* JUL 14 2008

Date: JUL 14 2008

JOHN A CLARKE

Clerk, by _____ S. Thompson _____ , Deputy

HUSBAND'S ADDRESS

WIFE'S ADDRESS

FL-820 [Rev. January 1, 2003]

REQUEST FOR JUDGMENT, JUDGMENT OF DISSOLUTION
OF MARRIAGE, AND NOTICE OF ENTRY OF JUDGMENT
(Family Law—Summary Dissolution)

Page 2 of 2

70 | P a g e

FL-820

ATTORNEY OR PARTY WITHOUT ATTORNEY *(Name and address):*
PETITIONER IN PRO PER

████████████████████

Norwalk, CA 90650
TELEPHONE NO.: 562-864-7747
FAX NO. *(Optional)*:
ATTORNEY FOR *(Name)*: Teresa A. Torres

SUPERIOR COURT OF CALIFORNIA, COUNTY OF LOS ANGELES
STREET ADDRESS: 12720 NORWALK BOULEVARD
MAILING ADDRESS: SAME
CITY AND ZIP CODE: NORWALK, CA 90650
BRANCH NAME: SOUTHEAST DISTRICT

MARRIAGE OF PETITIONERS
HUSBAND: ████████████████
WIFE: ████████████

FOR COURT USE ONLY

FILED
LOS ANGELES SUPERIOR COURT

JUL 01 2008

JOHN A. CLARKE, CLERK

BY S. THOMPSON, DEPUTY

Received Norwalk Superior Court JUL 01 2008

REQUEST FOR JUDGMENT, JUDGMENT OF DISSOLUTION OF MARRIAGE, AND NOTICE OF ENTRY OF JUDGMENT	CASE NUMBER: VD 065868

1. The *Joint Petition for Summary Dissolution of Marriage* (form FL-800) was filed on *(date)*: 12-27-07
2. No notice of revocation has been filed and the parties have not become reconciled.
3. I request that judgment of dissolution of marriage be
   a. X entered to be effective now.
   b.   entered to be effective (nunc pro tunc) as of *(date)*:
          for the following reason:

I declare under penalty of perjury under the laws of the State of California that the foregoing is true and correct.

Date: 6-30-08

TERESA A. TORRES
_____
(TYPE OR PRINT NAME)

_____
(SIGNATURE OF HUSBAND OR WIFE)

4. ☐ Husband, ☐ Wife, who did not request his or her own former name be restored when he or she signed the joint petition, now requests that it be restored. The applicant's former name is:

Date: ████████

_____
(TYPE OR PRINT NAME)

_____
(SIGNATURE OF PARTY WISHING TO HAVE HIS OR HER NAME RESTORED)

(For Court Use Only)
JUDGMENT OF DISSOLUTION OF MARRIAGE

5. THE COURT ORDERS
   a. A judgment of dissolution of marriage will be entered, and the parties are restored to the status of unmarried persons.
   b. The judgment of dissolution of marriage will be entered nunc pro tunc as of *(date)*:
   c. Wife's former name is restored *(specify)*:
   d. Husband's former name is restored *(specify)*:
   e. Husband and wife must comply with any agreement attached to the petition.

Date: JUL 01 2008

_____
JUDGE OF THE SUPERIOR COURT

NOTICE: Dissolution may automatically cancel the rights of a spouse under the other spouse's will, trust, retirement benefit plan, power of attorney, pay on death bank account, transfer on death vehicle registration, survivorship rights to any property owned in joint tenancy, and any other similar thing. It does not automatically cancel the rights of a spouse as beneficiary of the other spouse's life insurance policy. You should review these matters, as well as any credit cards, other credit accounts, insurance policies, retirement benefit plans, and credit reports to determine whether they should be changed or whether you should take any other actions.

Page 1 of 2

Form Adopted for Mandatory Use
Judicial Council of California
FL-820 [Rev. January 1, 2003]

REQUEST FOR JUDGMENT, JUDGMENT OF DISSOLUTION
OF MARRIAGE, AND NOTICE OF ENTRY OF JUDGMENT
(Family Law—Summary Dissolution)

Family Code, § 2403

TAB 'Q'

Respondent's Termination of Child Support

LOS ANGELES COUNTY CSSD - ANTELOPE VALLEY
5500 S EASTERN AVE
COMMERCE CA 90040-2947

11/24/2017

CSE Case Number:
200000000596659
Custodial Party:
LISA M RAMIREZ
Noncustodial Parent:
JEREMY BURROWES
Court Case Number:
BZ216402

Dear JEREMY BURROWES:

This letter is to let you know that on 11/24/2017 the local child support agency terminated child support services and closed the support case for the child(ren) listed below:

Case closure only means that the local child support agency will stop providing collection services. Child support orders will remain in effect. If you are currently ordered to pay child support, you must continue to pay until the order is changed. If you believe the court order should be changed you must contact the Family Law Facilitator at or Customer Connect at (866) 901-3212. If you would like us to continue handling your child support case, please contact Customer Connect.

☒ Your case may remain open with the State of California for payment processing only.

If you have any questions, please visit CustomerConnect on the web, http://www.childsup-connect.ca.gov for assistance on-line or call CustomerConnect at (866) 901-3212. Persons with hearing or speech impairments, please call the TTY number (866) 399-4096.

Sincerely,

TRAYSENA WOODS
Child Support Representative

NOTICE OF TERMINATION OF IV-D SERVICES
DCSS 0080 (06/20/12)

STATE OF CALIFORNIA - HEALTH AND HUMAN SERVICES AGENCY
DEPARTMENT OF CHILD SUPPORT SERVICES
TEAM 3

GOVERNMENTAL AGENCY (Under Family Code, §§ 17400,17406):
ALEXANDRA BAUER , CHIEF ATTORNEY
LOS ANGELES COUNTY CSSD - COMMERCE
5000 S EASTERN AVE
COMMERCE CA 90040-2917

200000000596659

TELEPHONE NO. : (866) 901-3212   FAX NO.: (323) 869-0590
E-MAIL ADDRESS :
ATTORNEY FOR (name): Under Family Code §§ 17400 & 17406

SUPERIOR COURT OF CALIFORNIA, COUNTY OF LOS ANGELES
STREET ADDRESS: 600 S COMMONWEALTH AVE
MAILING ADDRESS: 600 S COMMONWEALTH AVE
CITY AND ZIP CODE: LOS ANGELES 90005-4001
BRANCH NAME: CENTRAL CIVIL WEST

PETITIONER/PLAINTIFF: COUNTY OF LOS ANGELES
RESPONDENT/DEFENDANT: ██████████
OTHER PARENT/PARTY: ██████████

STIPULATION FOR   [X] JUDGMENT   [ ] SUPPLEMENTAL JUDGMENT
REGARDING PARENTAL OBLIGATIONS AND JUDGMENT

CASE NUMBER:
BZ216402

1. This matter proceeded as follows:
   a. [X] By written stipulation without court appearance.
   b. [ ] By court hearing, appearances as follows:
      (1) Date: Dept.:   Judicial Officer:
      (2) [ ] Petitioner/plaintiff present   [ ] Attorney present (name):
      (3) [ ] Respondent/defendant present   [ ] Attorney present (name):
      (4) [ ] Other parent/party present   [ ] Attorney present (name):
      (5) Local child support agency (Family Code, §§ 17400, 17406) by (name):
      (6) [ ] Other (specify):

   c. The parent ordered to pay support is the   [ ] petitioner/plaintiff [X] respondent/defendant [ ] other parent/party.

2. [ ] This order is based on the attached documents (specify):

3. The parties agree that:
   a. The parent ordered to pay support has read and understands the *Advisement and Waiver of Rights for Stipulation* on page 5 of this form. The parent ordered to pay support gives up these rights and freely agrees that a judgment may be entered in accordance with this stipulation.
   b. The amount of support payable by the party ordered to pay support as calculated under the guideline is: $128.00   per month.
      [X] We agree to guideline support.
      [ ] The guideline amount should be rebutted because of the following:
      (1) [ ] We have been fully informed of the guideline amount of support; we agree voluntarily to child support in the amount of $ per month; the agreement is in the best interest of the children; the needs of the children will be met adequately by the agreed amount; the children are not receiving public assistance; no application for public assistance is pending; and application of the guideline would be unjust and inappropriate in this case. We understand that if the order is below guideline, no change of circumstances need be shown for the court to raise this order to the guideline amount. If the order is above the guideline, a change of circumstances will be required to modify this order.
      (2) [ ] Other rebutting factors (specify):

   c. [X] The computer printout attached shows the parents' incomes and percentage of time each parent spends with the children. The printout, which shows the calculation of child support payable, will become the court's findings.

NOTICE: Any party required to pay child support must pay interest on overdue amounts at the legal rate, which is currently 10 percent per year.

Form Adopted for Alternative Mandatory
Use Instead of Form FL-692
Judicial Council of California
FL-615 [Rev. January 1, 2017]

STIPULATION FOR JUDGMENT OR SUPPLEMENTAL JUDGMENT
REGARDING PARENTAL OBLIGATIONS AND JUDGMENT
(Governmental)

Page 1 of 5
Family Code, §§ 17400,
17402, 17406
www.courts.ca.gov

74 | Page

PETITIONER/PLAINTIFF: COUNTY OF LOS ANGELES	CASE NUMBER:
RESPONDENT/DEFENDANT: JEREMY BURROWES	BZ216402
OTHER PARENT/PARTY: LISA M RAMIREZ	

3. d. ☐ Petitioner/plaintiff ☒ Respondent/defendant ☒ Other parent/party are the parents of the children named in item 3e below.

e. The parent ordered to pay support must pay current child support as follows:

Name of child	Date of birth	Monthly support amount
▓▓▓▓▓▓▓	07/25/2009	$128.00

(1) ☒ Mandatory additional child support.

  (a) The parent ordered to pay support must pay additional monthly support for reasonable child-care costs, as follows:

    ☐ one-half or ☐   % or ☐ (specify amount): $ per month of the costs.

    Payments must be made to the ☐ other parent ☐ State Disbursement Unit ☐ child-care provider.

  (b) The parent ordered to pay support must pay reasonable uninsured health-care costs for the children, as follows:

    ☒ one-half or ☐   % or ☐ (specify amount): $ per month of the costs.

    Payments must be made to the ☒ other parent ☐ State Disbursement Unit ☐ health-care provider.

(2) ☐ Other (specify):

(3) ☒ For a total of: $128.00   payable on the: 1st   day of each month

    beginning (date): 11/1/17

(4) ☒ The low-income adjustment applies.

    ☐ The low-income adjustment does not apply because (specify reasons):

(5) Any support ordered will continue until further order of court, unless terminated by operation of law.

(6) When a person who has been ordered to pay child support is in jail or prison or is involuntarily institutionalized for any period of more than 90 days in a row, the child support order is temporarily stopped. However, the child support order will not be stopped if the person who owes support has the financial ability to pay that support while in jail, prison, or an institution. It will also not be stopped if the reason the person is in jail, prison, or an institution is because the person didn't pay court ordered child support or committed domestic violence against the supported person or child. The child support order starts again on the first day of the month after the person is released from jail, prison, or an institution.

f. ☒ The parent ordered to pay support ☒ The parent receiving support   must (1) provide and maintain health insurance coverage for the children if available at no or reasonable cost, and keep the local child support agency informed of the availability of the coverage (the cost is presumed to be reasonable if it does not exceed 5 percent of gross income to add a child); (2) if health insurance is not available, provide coverage when it becomes available; (3) within 20 days of the local child support agency's request, complete and return a health insurance form; (4) provide to the local child support agency all information and forms necessary to obtain health-care services for the children; (5) present any claim to secure payment or reimbursement to the other parent or caretaker who incurs costs for health-care services for the children; and (6) assign any rights to reimbursement to the other parent or caretaker who incurs costs for health-care services for the children. The parent ordered to provide health insurance must seek continuation of coverage for the child after the child attains the age when the child is no longer considered eligible for coverage as a dependent under the insurance contract, if the child is incapable of self-sustaining employment because of a physically or mentally disabling injury, illness, or condition and is chiefly dependent upon the parent providing health insurance for support and maintenance.

STIPULATION FOR JUDGMENT OR SUPPLEMENTAL JUDGMENT REGARDING PARENTAL OBLIGATIONS AND JUDGMENT

PETITIONER/PLAINTIFF: COUNTY OF LOS ANGELES	CASE NUMBER:
RESPONDENT/DEFENDANT: JEREMY BURROWES	BZ216402
OTHER PARENT/PARTY: LISA M RAMIREZ	

3. g. ☐ The parent ordered to pay support must pay child support for the past periods and in the amounts set forth below.

Name of child	Date of birth	Period of support	Amount

    (1) ☐ Other *(specify):*

    (2) ☐ For a total of: $. payable: $ on the: day of each month
           beginning *(date):*

    (3) ☐ Interest accrues on the entire principal balance owing and not on each installment as it becomes due.

h. If this is a judgment on a *Supplemental Complaint*, it does not modify or supersede any prior judgment or order for support or arrearages, unless specifically provided.

i. No provision of this judgment may operate to limit any right to collect the principal (total amount of unpaid support) or to charge and collect interest and penalties as allowed by law. All payments ordered are subject to modification.

j. All payments, unless specified in item 3e(1) above, must be made to the State Disbursement Unit at the address listed below *(specify address):* CALIFORNIA STATE DISBURSEMENT UNIT
                      PO BOX 989067
                      WEST SACRAMENTO CA 95798-9067

k. **An earnings assignment order is issued.**

l. In the event that there is a contract between a party receiving support and a private child support collector, the party ordered to pay support must pay the fee charged by the private child support collector. This fee must not exceed 33 1/3 percent of the total amount of past due support nor may it exceed 50 percent of any fee charged by the private child support collector. The money judgment created by this provision is in favor of the private child support collector and the party receiving support, jointly.

m. If "The parent ordered to pay support" box is checked in item 3f, a health insurance coverage assignment must issue.

n. The parents must notify the local child support agency in writing within 10 days of any change in residence or employment.

o. The *Notice of Rights and Responsibilities (Health-Care Costs and Reimbursement Procedures)* and *Information Sheet on Changing a Child Support Order* (form FL-192) is attached.

p. ☒ The following person (the "other parent") is added as a party to this action *(name):*
    ████████████

q. ☒ Other *(specify):*
    Child support is extended pursuant to Family Code Section 3901. Both parents are equally responsible for all uncovered health expenses and can collect reimbursement through Family Code Section 4063.

FL-615 [Rev. January 1, 2017]   **STIPULATION FOR JUDGMENT OR SUPPLEMENTAL JUDGMENT**   Page 3 of 5
                               REGARDING PARENTAL OBLIGATIONS AND JUDGMENT
                                    (Governmental)

PETITIONER/PLAINTIFF: COUNTY OF ANGELES	CASE NUMBER
RESPONDENT/DEFENDANT: ████	BZ216402
OTHER PARENT/PARTY: ████	

Date: 11/9/17

████████████

▷ _____
(SIGNATURE OF ATTORNEY FOR LOCAL CHILD SUPPORT AGENCY)

Date:

_____
(TYPE OR PRINT NAME)

▷ _____
(SIGNATURE OF PETITIONER)

Date:

_____
(TYPE OR PRINT NAME)

▷ _____
(SIGNATURE OF ATTORNEY FOR PETITIONER)

Date: 11/9/17

JEREMY BURROWES
_____
(TYPE OR PRINT NAME)

▷ _____
(SIGNATURE OF RESPONDENT)

Date:

_____
(TYPE OR PRINT NAME)

▷ _____
(SIGNATURE OF ATTORNEY FOR RESPONDENT)

Date: 11/9/17

████████
_____
(TYPE OR PRINT NAME)

▷ _____
(SIGNATURE OF OTHER PARENT)

Date:

_____
(TYPE OR PRINT NAME)

▷ _____
(SIGNATURE OF ATTORNEY FOR OTHER PARENT)

JUDGMENT

4. THE COURT SO ORDERS.

Date: NOV 0 9 2017

ANGELA VILLEGAS
_____
JUDICIAL OFFICER

Number of pages attached: _____

☐ SIGNATURE FOLLOWS LAST ATTACHMENT

FL-615 [Rev. January 1, 2017]

STIPULATION FOR JUDGMENT OR SUPPLEMENTAL JUDGMENT REGARDING PARENTAL OBLIGATIONS AND JUDGMENT (Governmental)

Page 4 of 5

PETITIONER/PLAINTIFF: COUNTY OF LOS ANGELES	CASE NUMBER:
RESPONDENT/DEFENDANT: ▊▊▊▊▊▊▊	BZ216402
OTHER PARTY/PARENT: ▊▊▊▊▊	

ADVISEMENT AND WAIVER OF RIGHTS FOR STIPULATION

1. **RIGHT TO BE REPRESENTED BY A LAWYER.** I understand that I have the right to be represented by a lawyer of my choice at my expense. If I cannot afford a lawyer to represent me, I can ask the court to appoint one to represent me free of charge only if I dispute that I am the parent of the children named in this action and only on the issue of parentage. I understand that the attorney for the local child support agency does not represent me.

2. **RIGHT TO A TRIAL.** I understand that I have a right to have a judicial officer (1) determine if I am the parent of the children named in the stipulation, (2) decide how much child support I must pay, and (3) decide how much I owe for arrearages (unpaid support).

3. **RIGHT TO CONFRONT AND CROSS-EXAMINE WITNESSES.** I understand that in a trial any allegations made against me must be proved. At the trial I may be present with a lawyer when witnesses testify, and I may ask them questions. I may also present evidence and witnesses.

4. **RIGHT TO HAVE PARENTAGE TESTS WHERE THE LAW PERMITS.** I understand that, where the law permits, I have the right to have the court order parentage tests. The court will decide on the tests. The court could order that I pay none, some, or all of the costs of the tests.

5. **ADMISSION AND WAIVER OF RIGHTS.** I understand that by agreeing to the terms of this stipulation, I am admitting that I am the parent of the children named in the stipulation and I am giving up the rights stated above.

6. **WHERE THE STIPULATION INCLUDES CHILD SUPPORT.**

   a. I understand that I will have the duty to obey the support order for the children named in the stipulation until the order is changed by the court or ended by law.

   b. I also understand that the court will order any support payments to be paid directly from my wages or other earnings and sent to the local child support agency if one is assigned to collect the support.

   c. I have been advised of the amount of guideline child support and how the proposed child support amount was determined.

7. **WHERE THE STIPULATION INCLUDES A PROVISION FOR HEALTH INSURANCE.** I understand that I must keep health insurance coverage for the minor children if insurance is available or becomes available to me at no or reasonable cost. A health insurance coverage assignment/*National Medical Support Notice* may be ordered to get health insurance for my children.

8. I agree to the terms of this stipulation freely and voluntarily.

9. I understand that the local child support agency is required by state law to enforce the duty of support.

10. **I UNDERSTAND THAT IF I WILLFULLY FAIL TO SUPPORT MY CHILDREN, CRIMINAL PROCEEDINGS MAY BE INITIATED AGAINST ME.**

11. **COLLECTION OF SUPPORT.** I understand that any support I owe may be collected from any of my property. This collection may be made by intercepting money owed to me by the state or federal government (such as tax refunds, unemployment and disability benefits, and lottery winnings), by taking property I own, by placing a lien on my property, or by any other lawful means.

12. **IF I AM REPRESENTED BY AN ATTORNEY, MY ATTORNEY HAS READ AND EXPLAINED TO ME THE TERMS OF THE STIPULATION AND THIS ADVISEMENT AND WAIVER OF RIGHTS, AND I UNDERSTAND THESE TERMS.**

☑ I have read and understand the *Advisement and Waiver of Rights for Stipulation;* or

☐ Attached is a translation of this *Advisement and Waiver of Rights for Stipulation* in *(specify language):*

☐ I understand the translation.   ☐ I understand the translation.

Date: 11/9/17   Date:

JEREMY BURROWES
_____   _____
(TYPE OR PRINT NAME)   (TYPE OR PRINT NAME)

▷ _____   ▷ _____
(PARTY'S SIGNATURE)   (PARTY'S SIGNATURE)

DECLARATION OF PERSON PROVIDING INTERPRETATION/TRANSLATION: The party/parties indicated below is/are unable to read or understand this *Stipulation for Judgment or Supplemental Judgment Regarding Parental Obligations and Judgment* because

☐ (Insert name): _____ 's primary   ☐ (Insert name): _____ 's primary
language is *(specify):*   language is *(specify):*

and he or she ☐ has ☐ has not read the form   and he or she ☐ has ☐ has not read the form
stipulation translated into this language.   stipulation translated into this language.

I certify under penalty of perjury under the laws of the State of California that I am competent to interpret or translate in the primary language indicated above and that I have, to the best of my ability, read to, interpreted for, or translated for the above-named party the *Stipulation for Judgment or Supplemental Judgment Regarding Parental Obligations and Judgment* in the party's primary language. The above-named party said he or she understood the terms of this *Stipulation for Judgment or Supplemental Judgment Regarding Parental Obligations and Judgment* before signing it.

Date: Date:

_____   _____
(TYPE OR PRINT NAME)   (TYPE OR PRINT NAME)

▷ _____   ▷ _____
(SIGNATURE)   (SIGNATURE)

FL-615 [Rev. January 1, 2017]   **STIPULATION FOR JUDGMENT OR SUPPLEMENTAL JUDGMENT**   Page 5 of 5
                                        REGARDING PARENTAL OBLIGATIONS AND JUDGMENT

TAB 'R'

Vendor Agreement for Transportation Services

VENDOR AGREEMENT FOR TRANSPORTATION SERVICES (2017)

THIS VENDOR AGREEMENT IS FOR TRANSPORTATION SERVICES ("AGREEMENT") entered into as of the 5 day of November , 2017 ("Effective Date"), by and between Jeremy Burrowes with its principal office located at 16660 Raymond ave., Fontana, CA 92336 (the "Vendor") and 1A Distribution, Inc, a corporation organized under the laws of the State of California, with its principal office located at P.O. Box 2847, Fullerton, CA 92837 ("1A Distribution"). Vendor and 1A Distribution are sometimes hereinafter individually referred to as a "Party" or collectively as the "Parties".

WITNESSETH:

WHEREAS, 1A Distribution is a duly licensed motor carrier operating pursuant to authorities issued by the United States Department of Transportation ("DOT"); and

WHEREAS, 1A Distribution is engaged in the business of referring transportation services for its customers ("Customer(s)") with respect to general merchandise (hereinafter referred to as "Packages" and/or "Package"), throughout the State of California; and

WHEREAS, in connection with the operation of such business, 1A Distribution has the need, from time to time, for the services of delivery vendors to pick up, transport and deliver Packages for 1A Distribution's Customers; and

WHEREAS, Vendor owns and operates a business that provides transportation services and owns, leases, rents, and/or otherwise has access to a motor vehicle and other equipment and accessories as are necessary to conduct such business; and

WHEREAS, Vendor is engaged in providing transportation and delivery services to the general public and desires to receive offers to provide transportation services for 1A Distribution's Customers, as its own business, which offers Vendor shall be free to accept or decline.

NOW, THEREFORE, it is mutually agreed between the Parties as follows:

1.   Vendor Relationship. The Parties agree and acknowledge that the relationship of Vendor with 1A Distribution hereunder is that of a distinct operating business and any and all services provided by Vendor hereunder shall be provided in such capacity. Vendor shall in no way and for no purpose hereunder be considered an agent, servant, employee, partner or joint venture of 1A Distribution or be deemed to hold any relationship with 1A Distribution other than that of an independently established business. Neither Vendor nor Vendor's officers, directors, agents, subcontractors, substitute drivers, employees, helpers or servants ("Vendor Support Personnel") are to be considered employees of 1A Distribution at any time, under any circumstances or for any purpose. Vendor and 1A Distribution acknowledge and agree that 1A Distribution shall have no right to direct or control the manner, means, details or methods by which Vendor provides its services hereunder.

Vendor shall be solely responsible for the direction and control of its Vendor Support Personnel, including selecting, hiring, firing, supervising, directing, servicing accepted pickups and deliveries, sorting, staging, and loading trucks with packages, making payments for services rendered, withholding and paying applicable state and federal payroll taxes, providing workers' compensation insurance, paying workers' compensation and unemployment insurance premiums, setting wages, hours of work, and performance standards, regulatory compliance, assigning routes of travel, providing all necessary tools or assistance to safely accomplish the work, working conditions and handling any grievances with Vendor Support Personnel.

2.   Term of Agreement. This Agreement shall commence as of the Effective Date, and shall continue in effect for a period of twelve (12) months thereafter ("Initial Term"). The Initial Term of this Agreement shall automatically extend for additional twelve (12) month periods ("Renewal Term") unless earlier terminated by either Party providing written notice to the other at least sixty (60) days prior to the end of the Initial Term or the Renewal Term. Notwithstanding anything to the contrary set forth above, this Agreement may be terminated earlier by either Party in accordance with Section 15 of this Agreement. The Initial Term and any Renewal Term are hereinafter collectively referred to as the "Term".

3.   Vendor's Control of Services. During the Term of this Agreement, 1A Distribution may, from time to time, in its sole discretion, based on Customer requests, provide Vendor with offers of transportation services by notifying Vendor of the place and time frame of pick-up and delivery, together with any customer completion schedules. Vendor shall have the right to decline or accept any such offer. Vendor, upon acceptance of an offer, agrees to provide the transportation services and, in connection

therewith, Vendor shall be solely responsible for selecting the route(s) to be taken. Vendor shall be solely responsible to determine and control the manner and means to be utilized in providing the transportation services under this Agreement. All matters relating to the pick-up, transport and/or delivery of Packages, including, but not limited to, the priority which may be given to the pick-up and/or delivery of any particular item in relation to any other item which may be picked up and/or delivered, shall be in the control of and at the discretion of Vendor; provided, however, that Vendor shall conform with any time constraints and special conditions required by Customers of which it is specifically advised at the time Vendor accepts the offer. It is assumed that Vendor shall have the skills necessary to fulfill the terms of this Agreement thus not be provided with any training by 1A Distribution during the Term of this Agreement. However, Vendor may receive general orientation information relating to the applicable Customer expectations. Vendor shall use its best efforts to resolve any and all disputes, claims, or complaints made by Customers during the Term of this Agreement.

4.   Availability of Vendor. Vendor shall determine, in its sole discretion whether and when to provide services to 1A Distribution. Vendor is not on-call for 1A Distribution and is not be eligible for any on-call payments from 1A Distribution. When declining an offer to provide transportation services, Vendor shall not be required to provide any justification for Vendor's refusal. Vendor shall not be penalized for declining an offer from 1A Distribution. Vendor acknowledges that 1A Distribution may offer its services equally to other companies and to the public generally, in a manner consistent with the other provisions of this Agreement. With the exception of exclusive use arrangements that may be agreed to by Vendor in its discretion, Vendor may perform concurrent delivery services for companies other than 1A Distribution and commingle cargo to the extent allowed by law. Notwithstanding the foregoing, Vendor agrees that the DOT operating authority that may apply when providing transportation services referred by 1A Distribution to Customers will not apply in any manner to any other operations or services provided by Vendor.

5.   Vendor's Compensation and Payment.
      (a) Rate of Settlement. 1A Distribution agrees to pay, and Vendor agrees to accept, as full and complete compensation for each delivery made by Vendor pursuant to this Agreement a mutually agreed upon sum of money which has been negotiated and shall be computed as provided for in the bid submitted by Vendor as set forth in Schedule A attached hereto and incorporated herein (such compensation shall hereinafter be referred to as "Settlement").   The provisions of Schedule A may only be modified by written agreement signed by Vendor and 1A Distribution. 1A Distribution will not be liable to Vendor for any settlement or loss associated with suspension of services due to acts of God or other events beyond the control of 1A Distribution, including, but not limited to, war, civil disturbance, acts of terrorism, acts or demands of any government or governmental agency, labor disturbances, fires, floods or other casualty, severe weather, or Vendor suspension or termination of service. The determination of when and how often 1A Distribution may provide Vendor with offers of transportation services hereunder shall be at the sole discretion of 1A Distribution and nothing contained herein shall constitute a guarantee to Vendor that 1A Distribution will make any such offers. Vendor understands and agrees that from time to time circumstances such as traffic or shipment delays, adverse weather, and other potentially cost increasing circumstances will occur and Vendor will not be guaranteed any additional payment from 1A Distribution for such occurrences. Vendor shall be free to request additional compensation due to extenuating circumstances, and Vendor and 1A Distribution may negotiate for additional compensation subject to mutual agreement. Vendor hereby acknowledges that financial gain or loss may be recognized by Vendor while providing transportation services under this Agreement. Notwithstanding anything to the contrary in this Agreement, 1A Distribution makes no promises or representations whatsoever as to the amount of business Vendor will be offered at any time under this Agreement.
      (b) Payment. Vendor shall provide 1A Distribution with completed manifests, proofs of delivery, bills of lading, and/or invoices detailing the applicable sums Vendor that are due under this Agreement. Vendor shall receive payment for services within fifteen (15) days from the most recent prior two (2) week incremental period.   Vendor's payments shall be reconciled by 1A Distribution on a bi weekly basis and paid within two (2) weeks following the completion of Vendor's services ("Settlement Payment"). Vendor shall be issued a statement which shall contain a computation of the Settlement Payment Vendor is entitled to receive net of any deductions agreed to by Vendor. Vendor hereby authorizes 1A Distribution and agrees as directed by Vendor, to deduct from its bi weekly settlement any monies owed by Vendor to third Parties with regard to its rental, leasing, or purchasing of vehicles or equipment necessary to perform the transportation services performed by Vendor under this Agreement.
      (c) Documentation. It is the responsibility of Vendor to provide completed proofs of delivery, manifests, or bills of lading or invoices detailing items such as addresses and legible signatures as proof that pick-up and/or deliveries have been completed in order that Vendor can be paid for its services. Vendor shall also be responsible for the expense of generating proofs of delivery, manifests or bills of lading and Vendor may purchase same from any source. 1A Distribution reserves the right to refuse payment for services if Vendor does not submit completed manifest documentation, bills of lading, invoices and/or proofs of delivery.

(d) Settlement Disputes. 1A Distribution and Vendor agree that each Settlement Payment by 1A Distribution to Vendor under this Agreement shall be considered to be proper and accurate unless written notice disputing the amount of such Settlement Payment is provided by Vendor to 1A Distribution within fourteen (14) days of Vendor's receipt of such Settlement Payment. In the absence of such timely notice by Vendor, the Settlement Payment shall be conclusively presumed to be correct.

(e) Final Settlement. Vendor agrees that 1A Distribution shall have the right to withhold its final Settlement Payment under this Agreement for a maximum period of thirty (30) days in order to allow 1A Distribution sufficient time to account for, calculate and provide a complete reconciliation of the amount of Vendor's final settlement after making any and all deductions or offsets allowed under the terms of this Agreement.

6. No Fringe Benefits.

(a) Vendor agrees and acknowledges that neither it nor its Vendor Support Personnel shall (i) have the status of an employee of 1A Distribution or (ii) participate in 1A Distribution's employee benefit plans or group insurance plans or programs including, but not limited to, salary, bonus or incentive plans, stock options or purchase plans, medical or dental plans, or plans pertaining to retirement, vacation, personal time off, deferred savings, disability, (hereinafter collectively referred to as "Fringe Benefits").

(b) Vendor hereby agrees to indemnify, hold harmless and defend 1A Distribution, its parent, subsidiaries, affiliates, assignees, and their employees. Officers, directors, equity holders, members, managers, and Board of Managers against any claim, cost, penalty, loss or expense (including attorneys' fees) arising out of or relating to any claim, demand, or suit for Fringe Benefits by Vendor and/or Vendor Support Personnel.

7. Independently Owned Business.

(a) Business Licenses and Operating Authorities. Vendor warrants and represents that it is an independently owned business and as such is responsible for complying with any applicable corporate and local laws of its state of residence and the Internal Revenue Service ("IRS") either as a corporation, partnership, limited liability company, unincorporated business association, d/b/a, or sole proprietorship and that it has obtained and completed a W9 (Report for Taxpayer Identification Number and Certification) in accordance with IRS regulations. Vendor further warrants and represents that it has obtained and shall maintain at all times during the Term of this Agreement for itself and its Vendor Support Personnel any applicable and all motor carrier operating authorities, permits, or licenses of any nature required by the United States DOT and/or required under the laws of any jurisdiction in which Vendor operates.

(b) Taxes. (a) The relationship of Vendor and/or Vendor Support Personnel with 1A Distribution is that of an independently established business.. It is fully understood by 1A Distribution and Vendor that neither federal, state, nor local income taxes nor payroll taxes of any kind, including, but not limited, to F.I.C.A. or F.U.T.A., will be withheld or paid by 1A Distribution on behalf of Vendor and Vendor Support Personnel. Therefore Vendor understands that payments, including, but not limited to, sales taxes, payroll taxes of any kind, income taxes, social security taxes, unemployment insurance, state disability insurance and estimates thereof, and all workers' compensation insurance payments as may be required under the laws, rules or regulations of any governmental agency having jurisdiction over Vendor and/or Vendor Support Personnel. Vendor hereby agrees to indemnify and to hold harmless 1A Distribution, its parent, subsidiaries, affiliates, assignees, and their employees. officers, directors, equity holders, members, managers, and Board of Managers against any claim, cost, penalty, loss or expense (including attorneys' fees) arising out of or related to such taxes, costs or payments.

(c) Cost of Vendor's Business. Vendor agrees that it is solely responsible for all the costs and expenses of its business arising out of or relating to the transportation services provided by Vendor under this Agreement including, but not limited to, costs for Vendor Support Personnel, vehicle costs, fuel costs, scanners, load moving and securing devices, costs of generating proofs of delivery, licenses, insurance coverage, vehicle maintenance and repair, uniforms (if required), signage for its vehicles, worker's compensation insurance or occupational accident insurance, cargo insurance, background checks and drug tests, as well as any other costs or expenses described in this Agreement. and any fines, and assessments by any and all regulatory agencies, boards or municipalities. Vendor hereby indemnifies and agrees to hold harmless 1A Distribution and its officers, directors, equity holders, members, managers, and Board of Managers against any claim, cost, penalty, loss or expense (including attorneys' fees) arising out of or related to Vendor's nonpayment or underpayment of any such costs, expenses, taxes, fines, assessments or payments as well as penalties and interest thereon for Vendor or Vendor Support Personnel.

(d) Unemployment Compensation. Vendor agrees that, as a sole proprietor or business, the services Vendor shall provide pursuant to the Agreement are not covered by the unemployment compensation laws of any state. Therefore Vendor is NOT ENTITLED to be paid any UNEMPLOYMENT INSURANCE BENEFITS during or after its engagement with 1A Distribution.

8. Vendor's Vehicle(s).

(a) Vehicle - Vendor warrants that it shall provide and use for the performance of its services hereunder a lawfully registered and safe vehicle capable of meeting any safety standards acceptable to Customers. Vendor shall, at Vendor's sole cost and expense, keep and maintain such vehicle(s) in good operating condition and working order and shall perform all preventive and corrective maintenance and repairs required to insure safe and efficient operation and the good appearance of the vehicle(s). Vendor shall be responsible for procuring and paying the cost of all expenses incurred in or incidental to the operation of such vehicle(s) including, but not limited to, gas, oil, tires, repairs, insurance, purchase of equipment, inspections, fees, permits, and storage, and will do all that is required in order for the vehicle(s) to meet the requirements of all applicable state, federal and local laws, rules and regulations. Vendor shall direct, in all respects, the operation and maintenance of the equipment used in performance of this Agreement, which direction includes, but is not limited to, selection of substitute drivers, helpers, places of repair, stopping, parking, replacement, maintenance, purchases of fuel, equipment, insurance, parts and accessories. Notwithstanding the terms of this provision, the undersigned Parties agree that both Parties shall benefit by adhering to certain recognized industry standards. Vendor agrees to meet any applicable Customer contractual requirements regarding drivers' qualifications. The Parties mutually agree that observance of Customer expectations shall protect both Parties from excessive insurance rates, cancellation of insurance coverage, and contractual breach.

(b)   Department of Transportation. Vendor agrees to create, maintain and make available to 1A Distribution or any governmental agency having jurisdiction over Vendor, documents required for DOT compliance, including, but not limited to, driver qualification files, vehicle inspection reports, vehicle maintenance and repair reports, daily drivers logs, hours of service, and vehicle condition reports.

(c)   Signage. Many Customers have concerns regarding safety and allowing access to their workplace. To the extent required by those Customers Vendor chooses to service under this Agreement, Vendor shall obtain and pay the costs of all appropriate and Customer required signage for its vehicle(s). Vendor agrees that it has the sole responsibility and shall bear the cost and expense of painting, obtaining, affixing, and removing such signage. Upon termination of this Agreement, Vendor shall immediately remove and return any Customer required signage to either Customer or 1A Distribution. Should Vendor obtain and install signage, 1A Distribution agrees to pay Vendor an advertising/marketing fee as set forth in Schedule A.

9.   Uniforms and Identification Badges. Vendor agrees that while providing services pursuant to the Agreement, Vendor will maintain a professional appearance. Vendor may refer transportation services to Customers who require that Vendor be easily identified for security purposes. Should Vendor accept an offer to provide such referral, Vendor agrees to purchase, wear, and maintain, at Vendor's own cost and expense, uniforms which clearly identify Vendor as a contracted provider of services for 1A Distribution. Vendor may not use 1A Distribution's logos or any uniforms purchased through 1A Distribution other than for the purposes of providing referred services under this Agreement.

10.   Tools and Equipment. Vendor agrees that it will provide all tools and equipment necessary for providing services under this Agreement. Vendor shall furnish and maintain, at its own cost and expense, shipment handling equipment, radios, cellular telephones, beepers, scanners, and any other type of equipment utilized by Vendor. Vendor shall provide a commercial scanner or other communication device compatible with any existing technology to allow Vendor to handle and track shipments according to the Customer's package tracking requirements. Vendor may purchase its own scanner from any third party of its choosing or may elect to lease such equipment from 1A Distribution under the terms and conditions.

11.   Insurance.

(a) Public Liability Insurance Vendor, at its expense, shall carry and keep in full force and effect for the duration of this Agreement, Commercial Auto Liability Insurance covering Bodily Injury and Property Damage, with a limit of liability not less than (i) $500,000 Combined Single Limit for vehicles weighing under 10,001 pounds, and (ii) $1,000,000.00 combined single limit for vehicles with a gross vehicle weight rating of 10,001 or more pounds. Each such policy of insurance shall name 1A Distribution, parent, subsidiaries, affiliates, and their assignees, officers, directors, equity holders, members, and Board of Managers as Additional Insureds on such policy. If the scope of this Agreement involves more than one vehicle, coverage must apply to all other owned or hired and non-owned vehicles. Vendor agrees to provide 1A Distribution with a customary Certificate of Insurance as evidence of such insurance. Each such insurance policy obtained by Vendor shall require the insurer to provide 1A Distribution with thirty (30) days written notice of any changes in coverage, expiration, termination or cancellation of such insurance. Vendor agrees to immediately notify 1A Distribution of any changes in coverage, expiration, termination or cancellation of such insurance. All such insurance maintained by Vendor shall provide that insurance, as it applies to 1A Distribution, shall be primary and 1A Distribution's insurance shall be noncontributing notwithstanding any insurance 1A Distribution maintains.

(b)   Workers' Compensation Insurance/Occupational Accident Insurance. Vendor, at its expense, shall obtain and keep in full force during the term of this Agreement accident insurance that compensates Vendor for injuries incurred while performing referred services under this agreement, including medical expenses, loss of income, and death/ dismemberment/ paralysis benefits. This requirement can be met through either a statutory Workers Compensation policy that explicitly extends coverage to Vendor as well as any employees or uninsured subcontractors of Vendor, or Occupational Accident insurance covering Vendor or any subcontractors.

12.   Vendor's Liability for Packages. It is Vendor' responsibility to obtain cargo insurance at its own expense. Should Vendor not obtain such insurance Vendor will be responsible for a minimal charge of $300.00 for any lost or damaged item per occurrence. Should Vendor obtain its own insurance Vendor shall provide 1A Distribution with a customary Certificate of Insurance as evidence of such insurance and related deductible. Each such insurance policy obtained by Vendor shall require the insurer to provide 1A Distribution with thirty (30) days written notice of any changes in coverage, expiration, termination or cancellation of such insurance. Vendor shall be liable to 1A Distribution for loss or damage to Packages shipped under this Agreement whether or not the loss is covered by the insurance. Packages picked up by Vendor shall be deemed to be in the care, custody, possession, and control of Vendor until the same shall have been delivered to, and accepted by, the designated consignee, recipient, or its authorized agent. In the event of damage, shortage, spillage, contamination or other loss to any Packages that occurs while in Vendor's care, custody, possession or control, Vendor shall notify the shipper and/or 1A Distribution of the damage or loss as soon as practicable after damage or loss occurs. It is Vendor's responsibility to complete accepted transportation services and make any corrections with respect to the Customer expectations. If it should become necessary for 1A Distribution to intervene due to Vendor's inability or refusal to complete services accepted by Vendor, 1A Distribution reserves the right, upon notice, to setoff unavoidable costs against any Settlement Payment due Vendor. Vendor agrees to cooperate with 1A Distribution and/or the shipper to resolve cargo claims/damages as quickly as possible and agrees that in the event 1A Distribution is held liable for any loss or damage to any Packages caused by Vendor's intentional or negligent acts or omissions, 1A Distribution shall have the right to recover such amount from Vendor. Vendor reserves the right to dispute liability for damage or loss, and to pursue the claim through arbitration after paying the total disputed amount.

13.   Indemnification. Vendor agrees to indemnify, defend and hold harmless 1A Distribution and its parent, subsidiaries, affiliates, assignees, and their employees, officers, directors, equity holders, managers, members, and Board of Managers from and against any and all claims or suits for injury to or death of Vendor, its agents, representatives, Vendor Support Personnel, assistants, employees and/or subcontractors or loss of or damage to their property and from and against any and all other claims or suits for injury or death to person or loss of or damage to property of 1A Distribution or referred Customers, agents, members, employees or any third Party, resulting from Vendor's breach of this Agreement or Vendor's intentional or negligent acts or omissions, and/or those of its agents, representatives, assistants, employees, Vendor Support Personnel, and/or subcontractors. 1A Distribution shall have the right to set off and deduct from any and all amounts owing from 1A Distribution to Vendor the full value of any damage, loss or liability incurred by 1A Distribution or any third Party arising out of any negligent or intentional act or omission by Vendor or its agents, representatives, assistants, employees or subcontractors.

14.   Substance Abuse and Drivers Qualifications Policies. In order to comply with applicable DOT rules, regulations, guidelines, and Customers, Vendor agrees that it and its Vendor Support Personnel, including, but not limited to, any substitute drivers and any person having access to Customer shipments or facilities, will comply with applicable state laws, rules, and regulations regarding driver qualifications, safety, and substance abuse.

15.   Termination of Agreement.
     (a)   Notwithstanding anything to the contrary set forth in Section 2, this Agreement may be terminated at any time and for any reason by either Party upon fifteen (15) days prior written notice.
     (b)   Notwithstanding anything to the contrary in Section 2 or Section 15(a) above, in the event either Party commits a Material Breach of the terms of this Agreement, the other Party shall have the right to terminate this Agreement immediately.

The term "Material Breach" includes but is not limited to any of the following events:

(i)   Vendor fails to carry and keep in full force and effect at all times during the Term hereof the policies of insurance required in this Agreement;

(ii)   Vendor willfully fails or refuses to provide referral services required hereunder in accordance with the terms set forth by the Customer and terms of this Agreement;

(iii)   the Vendor fails to perform to a Customer's satisfaction;

(iv)   Proven use of drugs or alcohol by Vendor or Vendor Support Personnel while in providing services under this Agreement;

(v)   Violation of applicable laws by Vendor or Vendor Support Personnel during the Term of this Agreement;

(vi)   Taking any action that the non-breaching Party reasonably determines to be adverse to the non-breaching Party's business, its reputation and/or its relationship with Customers;

(vii)   Operation of a vehicle while performing the services hereunder by Vendor or Vendor Support Personnel without a valid and current commercial or other drivers license as required by law;

(viii)   The filing by or against either Party of a claim or cause of action under any bankruptcy related law or statute;

(ix)   Failure by Vendor to maintain any necessary state or federal motor carrier authority required by applicable law to deliver Packages under this Agreement;

(x)   The providing of false or fraudulent documentation by either Party to the other Party;

(xi)   Failure of either Party to perform as required pursuant to the terms of this Agreement (other than failures identified above in this Section 15(b)), if such breach is not cured within three (3) days of receipt of written notice of the breach.

(c) This Agreement may be terminated immediately by either Party without further obligation in the event there is a decline in service referrals hereunder or 1A Distribution ceases to do business with a Customer whose services are being referred to Vendor.

(d) Upon the termination of this Agreement through the expiration of its Term, non-renewal or as otherwise provided for in this Section 15, 1A Distribution's only liability and sole responsibility to Vendor shall be to make payment to Vendor of unpaid sums, for services completed prior to termination, which have been incurred pursuant to Section 5 hereof.

16.   Waiver. The waiver of a breach of any of the terms or conditions hereof shall be limited to the act or acts constituting such breach and shall not be construed as a waiver of future acts or happenings.

17.   Headings. The headings set forth herein have been inserted for convenience only and are not to be considered when construing the provisions of this Agreement.

18.   Governing Law – Waiver of Trial by Jury.
(a) Except as otherwise set forth in this Agreement, the laws of the state of residence of the Vendor shall govern this Agreement.
(b) The Parties voluntarily agree to waive any right to a trial by jury in any suit filed hereunder and agree to adjudicate any dispute pursuant to Paragraph 19 below.

19.   Arbitration and Waiver To Join A Class.
(a) Agreement to Arbitrate. The Parties agree that any dispute, difference, question, or claim arising out of or in any way relating to this Agreement, the transportation services provided hereunder, the relationship of the Parties or between the Vendor and the Customers, and/or the termination of any such relationship shall be submitted for resolution to binding arbitration in accordance with the Arbitration Agreement attached hereto and incorporated herein as Schedule B.
(b) Voluntary Waiver to Join a Class. Vendor hereby voluntarily and expressly waives any right it may have to join any suit, action, arbitration, or other legal proceeding arising out of or in any way relating to this Agreement or the services provided hereunder, the relationship of the Parties or between the Vendor and the Customers, and/or the termination of any such relationship on a class-wide, multiple plaintiff, collective or similar basis as such waiver is more particularly described in Schedule B attached hereto and incorporated herein.

20.   Entire Agreement. This Agreement and the Schedules hereto constitute the entire agreement of the Parties relating to the subject matter hereof and supersedes any and all oral or written agreements or negotiations relating to any such

subject matter. Each Party to this Agreement acknowledges that no representations, inducements, promises or agreements, oral or otherwise, have been made by either Party or anyone acting on behalf of any Party hereto which are not embodied herein. This Agreement supersedes any prior agreement between 1A Distribution, its predecessors, successors or affiliates, and Vendor relating to the subject matter hereof. Any modification of or amendment to this Agreement or any Schedule hereto will be effective only if it is in writing signed by the Party to be charged.

21.   Gender, Etc. Whenever used herein, the singular number shall include the plural, the plural the singular, and the use of the masculine, feminine or neuter gender shall include all genders.

22.   Notice. Any notice to be given hereunder by a Party may be effected by overnight delivery in writing or by registered or certified United States mail, postage prepaid. Notices shall be addressed to the Parties at their following respective addresses or at such other address as a Party may designate by giving written notice in accordance with the provisions of this Paragraph.

TO: 1A Distribution:See below.   TO: Jeremy Burrowes   CONTRACTOR: See below.
        PO Box 2847   16660 Raymond ave.
        Fullerton, CA 92837   Fontana, CA 92336

23.   Reformation and Severability. If any provision of this Agreement shall be invalid, illegal or unenforceable, it shall to the extent possible, be modified in such a manner as to be valid, legal and enforceable but so as to most nearly retain the intent of the Parties, and if such modification is not possible, such provision shall be severed from this Agreement, and in either case the validity, legality and enforceability of the remaining provisions of this Agreement shall not in any way be affected or impaired thereby.

24.   Assignment.
        (a) Assignment by 1A Distribution: This Agreement shall be binding upon and inure to the benefit of the Parties to this Agreement and their assignees. 1A Distribution may assign this Agreement, without written confirmation from Vendor, to any corporation which controls 1A Distribution, is controlled by or under control of 1A Distribution, or to any corporation resulting from the merger of or consolidation with 1A Distribution.

25. Counterparts; Facsimile or Email Signatures. This Agreement may be executed in any number of counterparts and by different Parties on separate counterparts, each of which counterparts, when so executed and delivered, shall be deemed to be an original and all of which counterparts, taken together, shall constitute but one and the same Agreement. This Agreement shall become effective upon the execution and delivery of a counterpart hereof by each of the Parties hereto. Delivery by facsimile or by electronic or digital transmission in PDF or other format of an executed counterpart of a signature page to this Agreement or any notice, communication, agreement, certificate, document or other instrument in connection herewith shall be effective as delivery of an executed original counterpart thereof.

26. Constructions and Review. In the event of any ambiguity in any of the terms of this Agreement, including any exhibits hereto, such ambiguity shall not be construed for or against a Party on the basis that the Party did or did not author same. Each Party acknowledges and agrees that they (a) have had AN adequate opportunity OF AT LEAST THREE (3) DAYS to review the terms and conditions and to reflect upon and consider the terms and conditions of this Agreement, (b) have had the opportunity to consult with legal counsel regarding such terms, and (c) fully understand the terms of this Agreement and have voluntarily signed it.

SIGNATURE PAGE FOLLOWS

IN WITNESS WHEREOF, the Parties have executed this Agreement as of the day and year first above written.

1A DISTRIBUTION, INC.   VENDOR

                                                _____
                                                Insert Company Name if Applicable

By: _____   By: _____

Print Name Nikolay Kim   Print Name: Jeremy Burrowes

Title: General Manager   Title: Vendor

Date: 11/5/2017   Date: 11/5/2017

SCHEDULE A

VENDOR'S PROPOSAL FOR TRANSPORTATION SERVICES

Vendor acknowledges and agrees that Vendor has submitted this proposal to bid on the transportation services described below and is willing to provide such services for the amounts listed below subject to the deductions authorized by Vendor under the Agreement.

Proposed Scheduled Route Settlement:

$ 80.00 (ND route) Per trip

$ 80.00 (SD route) Per trip

1A Distribution Inc.
Arbitration Agreement and Waiver to Join A Class

This Arbitration Agreement and Waiver to Join A Class ("Agreement") is made and entered into as of the 5 day of November, 2017 (the "Effective Date") by and between 1A Distribution, Inc., a California corporation with an office located at P.O. Box 2847, Fullerton, CA 92837, and any of its parents, subsidiaries, affiliated companies, successors, assigns, and any shareholders, officers, directors, agents, members, and employees of the foregoing companies or entities (the "Company" and/or sometimes referred to as "1A Distribution"), and Jeremy Burrowes located at 16660 Raymond ave., Fontana, CA 92336 (the "Vendor" and/or sometimes referred to as "you"). The Company and the Vendor are sometimes individually referred to as a "Party" and collectively referred to herein as the "Parties".

WHEREAS, this Agreement is an essential element of the Vendor's continued independent contractual relationship with the Company; and

WHEREAS, the Parties desire to enter into this Agreement pursuant to an Independent Vendor Agreement for transportation services of even date herewith between the Company and the Vendor (the "Vendor Agreement").

NOW THEREFORE, the Parties agree as follows:

1. Intent of the Agreement. It is the intent of the Parties that this Agreement will govern all grievances, disputes, claims, causes of action and any other matters in question in any way arising out of or relating to the Vendor Agreement, or the transportation services provided thereunder or any relationship between the Parties, or the termination of such Vendor Agreement, transportation services, or relationship (hereinafter individually referred to as a "Claim" and collectively referred to as "Claims") that are asserted or pursued at any time after the Effective Date of this Agreement, and regardless of whether such Claims arose before the Effective Date of this Agreement. The Parties shall submit and resolve all such Claims in accordance with the provisions of this Agreement.

2. Final and Binding Arbitration. The Parties agree that any Claim that arises out of or relates in any way to the Vendor Agreement or the transportation services provided thereunder, or relationship between the Parties, or the termination of such Vendor Agreement, transportation services, or shall be submitted to and decided by binding arbitration in the county where the Vendor provided services pursuant to the Vendor Agreement (or as close thereto as possible, where the Administrator maintains an office location). The arbitration shall be administered by an Administrator (defined below). "Administrator" shall mean either the American Arbitration Association, www.adr.org, 800-778-7879 ("AAA"), or JAMS, www.jamsadr.com, 800-352-5267. Except as otherwise provided for in this Agreement, the arbitration shall be conducted in accordance with the commercial arbitration rules of the Administrator applicable at the time the arbitration is commenced. A copy of the current version of the rules of the Administrator can be obtained by contacting the Administrator. The Vendor can also call the Administrator if you have questions about the arbitration process. If the rules of the Administrator are inconsistent with the terms of this Agreement, the terms of this Agreement shall govern. The Arbitrator, and not any federal, state, or local court or agency, shall have exclusive authority to resolve any dispute relating to the enforceability or formation of this Agreement and the arbitrability of the dispute between the Parties. The Arbitrator's decision shall be final and binding upon the Company and Vendor.

3. Covered Claims. This Agreement to arbitrate covers all Claims that otherwise could be brought in a federal, state, or local court or agency under applicable federal, state, or local laws, arising out of or relating to the Vendor Agreement or the transportation services provided thereunder, the termination of that agreement, or any transportation services or any relationship between the Parties. The term "Claims" includes any Claims Vendor may have against the Company or against its officers, directors, supervisors, managers, employees, members, shareholders, Customers (defined below) or agents in their capacity as such or otherwise, or that the Company may have against Vendor. The Claims covered by this Agreement include, but are not limited to, claims for breach of any contract or covenant (express or implied), tort claims, claims for loss, damage or delay of freight, claims for settlement payments, claims for wages or other compensation due, claims for wrongful termination (constructive or actual), claims for discrimination or harassment

(including, but not limited to, harassment or discrimination based on race, age, color, sex, gender, national origin, alienage or citizenship status, creed, religion, marital status, partnership status, military status, predisposing genetic characteristics, medical condition, psychological condition, mental condition, criminal accusations and convictions, disability, sexual orientation, or any other trait or characteristic protected by federal, state, or local law), claims for violation of any federal, state, local or other governmental law, statute, regulation, or ordinance, including, but not limited to, all claims arising under Title VII of the Civil Rights Act, as amended, the Americans with Disabilities Act, as amended, the Family and Medical Leave Act, as amended, the Fair Labor Standards Act, as amended, the Equal Pay Act, as amended, the Vendor Retirement Income Security Act, as amended, the Civil Rights Act of 1991, as amended, Section 1981 of U.S.C. Title 42, the Sarbanes-Oxley Act of 2002, as amended, the Worker Adjustment and Retraining Notification Act, as amended, the Age Discrimination in Employment Act, as amended, the Uniform Services Employment and Reemployment Rights Act, as amended, the Genetic Information Nondiscrimination Act, the California Human Rights Law, the California Labor Law, the California Civil Rights Law, the Rehabilitation Act of 1973, the California Whistleblower Law, California Anti-Retaliation and Anti-Discrimination Laws, the Older Workers' Benefit Protection Act, the U.S. Constitution, the Constitution of the State of California, all of their respective implementing regulations and any other federal, state, local, or foreign law (statutory, regulatory, or otherwise). Claims are covered by this Agreement regardless of whether they have already accrued or will accrue in the future.

4. Claims Not Covered. Claims not covered by this Agreement are claims for unemployment compensation benefits, claims for workers' compensation benefits except that claims for interference with or retaliation for filing a workers' compensation claim shall be considered Claims subject to arbitration under this Agreement, or any other claims that, as a matter of law, the Parties cannot agree to arbitrate. Nothing in this Agreement shall be interpreted to mean that Vendor is precluded from filing complaints with the California Division of Human Rights, and/or the federal Equal Employment Opportunity Commission, however, the Vendor understands and agrees that the Vendor cannot obtain any monetary relief or recovery from such complaints filed with the EEOC, or the California State Division of Human Rights. The Parties agree that any demand for arbitration by either Party shall be filed within the statute of limitation that is applicable to the Claim upon which arbitration is sought.

5. WAIVER OF CLASS ACTION AND REPRESENTATIVE ACTION CLAIMS. THE PARTIES EXPRESSLY INTEND AND AGREE THAT: (A) CLASS ACTION, COLLECTIVE ACTION, MULTIPLE PLAINTIFF ACTION, AND REPRESENTATIVE ACTION PROCEDURES SHALL NOT BE ASSERTED, NOR WILL THEY APPLY, IN ANY ARBITRATION PURSUANT TO THIS AGREEMENT; (B) EACH WILL NOT ASSERT CLASS ACTION, COLLECTIVE ACTION, MULTIPLE PLAINTIFF ACTION OR REPRESENTATIVE ACTION CLAIMS AGAINST THE OTHER IN ARBITRATION OR OTHERWISE; AND (C) THE PARTIES SHALL ONLY SUBMIT THEIR OWN, INDIVIDUAL CLAIMS IN ARBITRATION AND WILL NOT SEEK TO REPRESENT THE INTERESTS OF ANY OTHER PERSON. FURTHER, THE PARTIES EXPRESSLY INTEND AND AGREE THAT ANY CLAIMS BY THE VENDOR WILL NOT BE JOINED, CONSOLIDATED, OR HEARD TOGETHER WITH CLAIMS OF ANY OTHER INDEPENDENT CONTRACTOR, PERSON, OR ENTITY WHO OR WHICH MAY BE SIMILARLY SITUATED OR HAVE SIMILAR DISPUTES. NOTWITHSTANDING ANYTHING TO THE CONTRARY IN THE RULES OF THE ADMINISTRATOR, AND THE GENERAL GRANT OF AUTHORITY TO THE ARBITRATOR IN SECTIONS 1 AND 2 OF THIS AGREEMENT, THE ARBITRATOR SHALL HAVE NO JURISDICTION OR AUTHORITY TO COMPEL ANY CLASS OR COLLECTIVE CLAIM OR REPRESENTATIVE ACTION, TO CONSOLIDATE DIFFERENT ARBITRATION PROCEEDINGS OR TO JOIN ANY OTHER PARTY TO AN ARBITRATION BETWEEN THE COMPANY AND THE VENDOR. THE VALIDITY AND EFFECT OF THIS SECTION 5 SHALL BE DETERMINED EXCLUSIVELY BY A COURT AND NOT BY AN ARBITRATOR. IF FOR ANY REASON THE WAIVER SET FORTH IN THIS SECTION 5 IS FOUND TO BE VOID OR UNENFORCEABLE, THE CLASS, COLLECTIVE, OR REPRESENTATIVE OR JOINT ACTION MAY ONLY PROCEED IN COURT AND MAY NOT BE ARBITRATED UNDER THIS AGREEMENT.

VENDOR SHALL HAVE THE RIGHT TO OPT OUT OF THIS WAIVER OF CLASS ACTION AND REPRESENTATIVE ACTION CLAIMS BY SENDING A LETTER REQUESTING AN OPT OUT OF THIS WAIVER TO THE COMPANY AT ITS ADDRESS LISTED ABOVE (OR THE COMPANY'S THEN CURRENT ADDRESS) WITHIN SIXTY (60) DAYS OF SIGNING THIS AGREEMENT. VENDOR SHALL SEND SUCH LETTER TO THE COMPANY BY CERTIFIED OR REGISTERED MAIL, RETURN RECEIPT REQUESTED.

6. WAIVER OF TRIAL BY JURY. THE PARTIES UNDERSTAND AND FULLY AGREE THAT BY ENTERING INTO THIS AGREEMENT TO ARBITRATE; THEY ARE GIVING UP THEIR CONSTITUTIONAL RIGHT TO HAVE A TRIAL BY JURY, AND ARE GIVING UP THEIR NORMAL RIGHTS OF APPEAL FOLLOWING THE RENDERING OF THE ARBITRATOR'S AWARD EXCEPT AS APPLICABLE LAW PROVIDES FOR JUDICIAL REVIEW OF ARBITRATION PROCEEDINGS.

7. Claims Procedure. Arbitration shall be initiated upon the express written notice of either Party. The aggrieved Party must give written notice of any claim to the other Party. Written notice of a Vendor's claim shall be mailed by certified or registered mail, return receipt requested, or by overnight courier with signature requested to 1A Distribution Inc., P.O. Box 2847, Fullerton, California 92837 and/or to the Customer at the address first set forth above. Written notice of the Company's claim will be mailed by certified mail return receipt requested or by overnight courier with signature requested to the last known address of Vendor. The written notice shall identify and describe the nature of all claims asserted and the facts upon which such claims are based. Written notice of arbitration shall be initiated within the same time limitations that California law applies to those claim(s).

8. Arbitrator Selections and Authority. Any Arbitration shall be conducted before a single arbitrator selected from a list of potential arbitrators provided by the Administrator. The arbitrator shall be a former judge or lawyer with at least ten years of experience. The Parties agree that the arbitrator shall be authorized to award all remedies available under the substantive law applicable to the Claim except as otherwise set forth in this Agreement. The arbitrator's award shall include a written explanation of the factual findings and legal conclusions reached in issuing the award. The arbitrator's award will be final and binding.

9. Discovery. The Arbitrator shall have the authority to set deadlines for completion of discovery. The Arbitrator shall decide all discovery disputes. Each Party shall be entitled to draft and serve upon the other Party one set of no more than twenty-five interrogatories and one set of no more than twenty requests for production of documents in a form consistent with the Federal Rules of Civil Procedure. In addition, each Party shall be entitled to take no more than three depositions, each of which must be concluded within a period not exceeding four hours. The Vendor's deposition shall be scheduled and completed before any other depositions may be conducted. To be used as evidence, depositions must be recorded by a licensed court reporter at the cost of the Party taking the deposition. Parties wishing to obtain copies of deposition transcripts must pay the cost of such copies.

10. Federal Arbitration Act. The Parties agree that arbitration proceedings filed under this Agreement shall be controlled and governed by the provisions of the Federal Arbitration Act ("FAA"). And not by any state law concerning arbitration. The Parties acknowledge and agree that the Vendor Agreement and the relationship between the Parties evidence a transaction in the interstate commerce and as a result, the FAA governs the interpretation and enforcement of this Agreement.

11. Motions. The Arbitrator shall have jurisdiction to hear and rule on prehearing disputes and is authorized to hold prehearing conferences by telephone or in person as the Arbitrator deems necessary. The Arbitrator shall have the authority to set deadlines for filing motions for summary judgment, and to set briefing schedules for any motions. The Arbitrator may allow the filing of a dispositive motion if the Arbitrator determines that the moving Party has shown substantial cause that the motion is likely to succeed and dispose of or narrow the issues in the case. The Arbitrator shall have the authority to adjudicate any cause of action, or the entire claim, pursuant to a motion for summary adjudication and in deciding the motion, shall apply the substantive law applicable to the cause of action.

12. Compelling Arbitration/Enforcing Award. Either Party may ask a court to stay any court proceeding, to compel arbitration under this Agreement and to confirm, vacate, or enforce an arbitration award. Judgment on the award rendered by the arbitrator may be entered in any court having jurisdiction thereof.

13. Arbitration Fees and Costs. Company shall be responsible for the arbitrator's fees and expenses. Each Party shall pay its own costs and attorneys' fees, if any. However, if any Party prevails on a statutory claim that affords the prevailing Party attorneys' fees and costs, or if there is a written agreement providing for attorneys' fees and costs, the Arbitrator may award reasonable attorneys' fees in accordance with the applicable statute or written agreement. The Arbitrator shall resolve any dispute as to the reasonableness of any fee or cost that may be awarded under this Section.

14. Term of Agreement. This Agreement to arbitrate shall survive the termination of the Vendor Agreement. It can only be revoked or modified in writing signed by both Parties hereto.

15. Severability. Except as otherwise provided in Section 5 or elsewhere herein, if any provision of this Agreement to arbitrate is adjudged to be void or otherwise unenforceable, in whole or in part, the void or unenforceable provision shall be severed and such adjudication shall not affect the validity of the remainder of this Agreement to arbitrate.

16. Entire Agreement. This Agreement is the complete agreement of the Parties on the subject of arbitration of disputes and supersedes any prior or contemporaneous oral or written understanding on the subject.

17. Third Party Beneficiaries. The Parties acknowledge and agree that the following Customers of the Company are hereby intended to be third party beneficiaries of this Agreement and that any Claim filed against such Customers shall be submitted to Arbitration in accordance with this Agreement. The term "Customer" shall mean Amazon.com, Inc. and Dynamex, Inc.

18. VOLUNTARY AGREEMENT. BY EXECUTING THIS AGREEMENT THE PARTIES REPRESENT THAT THEY HAVE BEEN GIVEN THE OPPORTUNITY TO FULLY REVIEW, AND COMPREHEND THE TERMS OF THIS AGREEMENT. THE PARTIES UNDERSTAND THE TERMS OF THIS AGREEMENT AND FREELY AND VOLUNTARILY SIGN THIS AGREEMENT. THE VENDOR FURTHER ACKNOWLEDGES THAT VENDOR HAS BEEN GIVEN THE OPPORTUNITY TO AND HAS BEEN ADVISED TO DISCUSS THIS AGREEMENT WITH VENDOR'S PRIVATE LEGAL COUNSEL AND HAS AVAILED ITSELF OF THAT OPPORTUNITY TO THE EXTENT IT WISHES TO DO SO.

[SIGNATURE PAGE FOLLOWS]

IN WITNESS WHEREOF, the Parties have executed this Agreement as of the Effective Date above.

1A DISTRIBUTION, INC.

By _N. _____

Name: Nikolay Kim

Title: General Manager
Date: 11/5/2017

VENDOR

By _____

Print Name: Jeremy Burrowes

Date: 11/5/2017

TAB 'S'

Respondent's W-2s and Income Tax Returns (2007, 2011-2012, 2017)

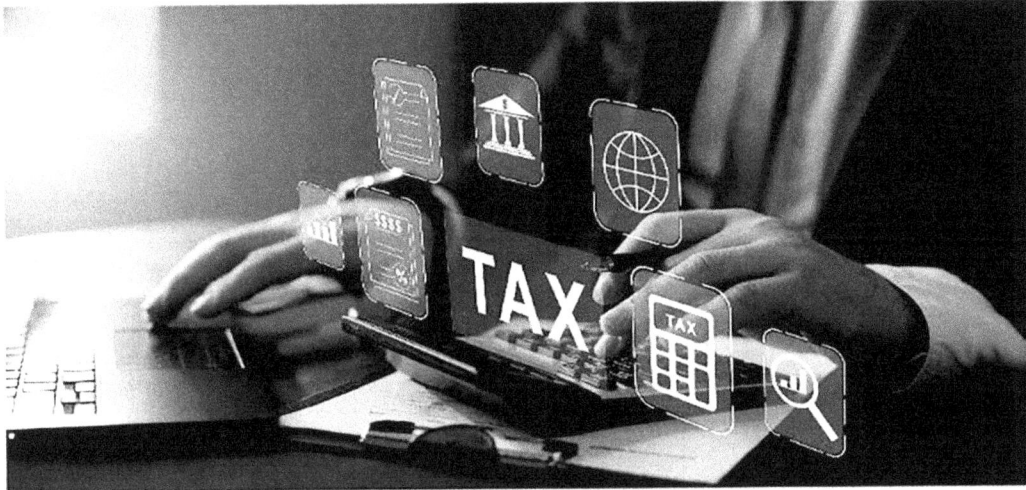

Department of the Treasury — Internal Revenue Service

Form **1040A** U.S. Individual Income Tax Return **2007** IRS Use Only — Do not write or staple in this space.

OMB No. 1545-0074

Label (See instructions.)

Your first name and initial   Last name

Your social security number

If a joint return, spouse's first name and initial

Spouse's social security number

Use the IRS label. Otherwise, please print or type.

Home address (number and street). If you have a P.O. box, see instructions.   Apartment no.

▲ You must enter ▲ your SSN(s) above

City, town or post office. If you have a foreign address, see instructions.   State   ZIP code

NORWALK

Checking a box below will not change your tax or refund

Presidential Election Campaign

► Check here if you, or your spouse if filing jointly, want $3 to go to this fund (see instructions) ... ► ☐ You ☐ Spouse

Filing status

Check only one box.

1 ☒ Single

2 ☐ Married filing jointly (even if only one had income)

3 ☐ Married filing separately. Enter spouse's SSN above and full name here ►

4 ☐ Head of household (with qualifying person). (See instructions.) If the qualifying person is a child but not your dependent, enter this child's name here ►

5 ☐ Qualifying widow(er) with dependent child (see instructions)

Exemptions

6a ☒ Yourself. If someone can claim you as a dependent, do not check box 6a ....

b ☐ Spouse ....

c Dependents:	(2) Dependent's social security number	(3) Dependent's relationship to you	(4) ✓ if qualifying child for child tax credit
(1) First name Last name			

If more than six dependents, see instructions.

Boxes checked on 6a and 6b **1**

No. of children on 6c who:
• lived with you ....
• did not live with you due to divorce or separation (see instructions) ...

Dependents on 6c not entered above ...

Add numbers on lines above ► **1**

d Total number of exemptions claimed ....

Income

Attach Form(s) W-2 here. Also attach Form(s) 1099-R if tax was withheld.

If you did not get a W-2, see instructions.

Enclose, but do not attach, any payment.

7 Wages, salaries, tips, etc. Attach Form(s) W-2 .... | 7 | 28,307.

8a Taxable interest. Attach Schedule 1 if required .... | 8a |

b Tax-exempt interest. Do not include on line 8a .... | 8b |

9a Ordinary dividends. Attach Schedule 1 if required .... | 9a |

b Qualified dividends (see instructions) .... | 9b |

10 Capital gain distributions (see instructions) .... | 10 |

11a IRA distributions .... | 11a | 11b Taxable amount ...... | 11b |

12a Pensions and annuities .... | 12a | 12b Taxable amount ...... | 12b |

13 Unemployment compensation and Alaska Permanent Fund dividends .... | 13 |

14a Social security benefits .... | 14a | 14b Taxable amount ...... | 14b |

15 Add lines 7 through 14b (far right column). This is your total income .... ► | 15 | 28,307.

Adjusted gross income

16 Educator expenses (see instructions) .... | 16 |

17 IRA deduction (see instructions) .... | 17 |

18 Student loan interest deduction (see instructions) .... | 18 |

19 Tuition and fees deduction. Attach Form 8917 .... | 19 |

20 Add lines 16 through 19. These are your total adjustments .... | 20 |

21 Subtract line 20 from line 15. This is your adjusted gross income .... ► | 21 | 28,307.

BAA For Disclosure, Privacy Act, and Paperwork Reduction Act Notice, see instructions.

Form 1040A (2007)

FDIA1312   11/14/07

Page 2

Tax, credits, and payments	22 Enter the amount from line 21 (adjusted gross income)	22	28,307.

23a Check if:
- You were born before January 2, 1943,
- Spouse was born before January 2, 1943,
- Blind
- Blind
Total boxes checked ► 23a

b If you are married filing separately and your spouse itemizes deductions, see instructions and check here .... ► 23b ☐

Standard Deduction for –
- People who checked any box on line 23a or 23b or who can be claimed as a dependent, see instructions.
- All others:
Single or Married filing separately, $5,350
Married filing jointly or Qualifying widow(er), $10,700
Head of Household, $7,850

24 Enter your standard deduction (see left margin) .... 24 — 5,350.
25 Subtract line 24 from line 22. If line 24 is more than line 22, enter -0- .... 25 — 22,957.
26 If line 22 is $117,300 or less, multiply $3,400 by the total number of exemptions claimed on line 6d. If line 22 is over $117,300, see the instructions .... 26 — 3,400.
27 Subtract line 26 from line 25. If line 26 is more than line 25, enter -0-. This is your taxable income .... ► 27 — 19,557.
28 Tax, including any alternative minimum tax (see instructions) .... 28 — 2,545.

29 Credit for child and dependent care expenses. Attach Schedule 2 29
30 Credit for the elderly or the disabled. Attach Schedule 3 ... 30
31 Education credits. Attach Form 8863 31
32 Child tax credit (see instructions). Attach Form 8901 if required 32
33 Retirement savings contributions credit. Attach Form 8880 ... 33
34 Add lines 29 through 33. These are your total credits 34
35 Subtract line 34 from line 28. If line 34 is more than line 28, enter -0- .... 35 — 2,545.
36 Advance earned income credit payments from Form(s) W-2, box 9 36
37 Add lines 35 and 36. This is your total tax .... ► 37 — 2,545.
38 Federal income tax withheld from Forms W-2 and 1099 ...... 38 — 3,463.

If you have a qualifying child, attach Schedule EIC.
39 2007 estimated tax payments and amount applied from 2006 return 39
40a Earned income credit (EIC) 40a
b Nontaxable combat pay election. 40b
41 Additional child tax credit. Attach Form 8812 41
42 Add lines 38, 39, 40a, and 41. These are your total payments .... ► 42 — 3,463.

Refund
43 If line 42 is more than line 37, subtract line 37 from line 42. This is the amount you overpaid .... 43 — 918.
44a Amount of line 43 you want refunded to you. If Form 8888 is attached, check here . ► ☐ 44a — 918.

Direct deposit? See Instructions and fill in 44b, 44c, and 44d or Form 8888.
► b Routing number 122000661   ► c Type: ☒ Checking ☐ Savings
► d Account number 0501167349
45 Amount of line 43 you want applied to your 2008 estimated tax 45

Amount you owe
46 Amount you owe. Subtract line 42 from line 37. For details on how to pay, see instructions .... ► 46
47 Estimated tax penalty (see instructions) 47

Third party designee
Do you want to allow another person to discuss this return with the IRS (see instructions)? .... ☒ Yes. Complete the following. ☐ No
Designee's name ► Preparer   Phone no. ►   Personal identification number (PIN) ►

Sign here
Under penalties of perjury, I declare that I have examined this return and accompanying schedules and statements, and to the best of my knowledge and belief, they are true, correct, and accurately list all amounts and sources of income I received during the tax year. Declaration of preparer (other than the taxpayer) is based on all information of which the preparer has any knowledge.

Joint return? See instructions.
Keep a copy for your records.

Your signature | Date | Your occupation FORK LIFT OPER | Daytime phone number
Spouse's signature. If a joint return, both must sign. | Date | Spouse's occupation |

Paid preparer's use only
Preparer's signature ► | Date 02/11/2008 | Check if self-employed ☒ | Preparer's SSN or PTIN P00055756
Firm's name (or yours if self-employed), address, and ZIP code ► ALBA RAPID TAX & SERVICES 15700 PIONEER BLVD NORWALK CA 90650-6533 | | EIN 95-4638210 Phone no. (562) 868-3518 |

FDIA1312   11/14/07
Form 1040A (2007)

For Privacy Notice, get form FTB 1131.

California Resident Income Tax Return 2007

FORM
540 2EZ C1 Side 1
CA/A4612 12/05/07

07

P
AC
A
R
RP

Filing Status

Check the box for your filing status. See instructions.

1 [X] Single
2 Married/RDP filing jointly (even if only one spouse/RDP had income)
4 Head of household. STOP! See instructions.
5 Qualifying widow(er) with dependent child. Year spouse/RDP died _____. ● □
If your California filing status is different from your federal filing status, check the box here.................

Exemptions

6 If another person can claim you (or your spouse/RDP) as a dependent on his or her tax return, even if he
    or she chooses not to, you must see instructions .... ● 6 □
7 Senior: If you (or your spouse/RDP) are 65 or older, enter 1; if both are 65 or older, enter 2 .... ● 7
8 Number of dependents. Enter name and relationship (Do not include yourself or your spouse/RDP) ..... ● 8

Dependent Exemptions

Taxable Income and Credits

9 Total wages (federal Form W-2, box 16 or CA Sch W-2CG, line C).
    See instructions .... ● 9 _____28,307._

10 Total interest income (Form 1099-INT, box 1) See instructions .... ● 10 _____

11 Total dividend income (Form 1099-DIV, box 1). See instructions......................... ● 11 _____

12 Total Pensions _____ See Instructions. Taxable amount .... ● 12 _____

Enclose, but do not staple, any payment.

13 Total capital gains distributions from mutual funds (Form 1099-DIV, box 2a).
    See instructions .... ● 13 _____

14 Unemployment compensation .... 14 _____

15 U.S. social security or railroad retirement .... 15 _____

Attach a copy of your Form(s) W-2 or complete CA Sch W-2CG.

16 Add line 9, line 10, line 11, line 12, and line 13. Caution: Do not include line 14 and
    line 15... ● 16 _____28,307._

17 Using the 2EZ Table for your filing status, enter the tax for the amount on line 16
    Caution: If you checked the box on line 6, STOP. See instructions. Dependent
    Tax Worksheet... 17 _____506._

18 Senior Exemption: See instructions. If you are 65 and entered 1 in the box on line 7,
    enter $94. If you entered 2 in the box on line 7, enter $188 .... 18 _____

19 Nonrefundable renter's credit. See instructions... ● 19 _____60._

20 Credits. Add line 18 and line 19... 20 _____60._

21 Tax. Subtract line 20 from line 17. If zero or less, enter -0- .... ● 21 _____446._

051   3111074

Your Name: JEREMY E. BURROWES   Your SSN or ITIN: 620-38-8827

Overpaid Tax/ Tax Due	22	Total tax withheld (federal Form W-2, box 17 or CA Sch W-2CG, box 17 and/or Form 1099-R, box 10)	● 22	640.
	23	Overpaid tax. If line 22 is more than line 21, subtract line 21 from line 22	● 23	194.
	24	Tax due. If line 22 is less than line 21, subtract line 22 from line 21. See instructions	24	0.

Use Tax	25	Use tax. This is not a total line. See instructions	● 25	

Contributions   Voluntary Contributions.

	Code	Amount
California Seniors Special Fund. See Instructions	● 50	
Alzheimer's Disease/Related Disorders Fund	● 51	
California Fund for Senior Citizens	● 52	
Rare and Endangered Species Preservation Program	● 53	
State Children's Trust Fund for the Prevention of Child Abuse	● 54	
California Breast Cancer Research Fund	● 55	
California Firefighters' Memorial Fund	● 56	
Emergency Food Assistance Program Fund	● 57	
California Peace Officer Memorial Foundation Fund	● 58	
California Military Family Relief Fund	● 59	
California Sea Otter Fund	● 60	

	26	Add line 50 through line 60. These are your total contributions	● 26	

Amount You Owe	27	AMOUNT YOU OWE. Add line 24, line 25, and line 26. If line 23 is less than line 25 and line 26, enter the difference here. See instructions. (Do Not Send Cash) Mail to: FRANCHISE TAX BOARD, PO BOX 942867, SACRAMENTO CA 94267-0001	● 27	

Direct Deposit (Refund Only)   Pay Online -- Go to our Website at www.ftb.ca.gov and search for **Web Pay**

	28	REFUND OR NO AMOUNT DUE. Subtract line 25 and line 26 from line 23. See instructions. Mail to: FRANCHISE TAX BOARD, PO BOX 942840, SACRAMENTO CA 94240-0002	● 28	194.

Complete this section to authorize direct deposit of your refund into one or two accounts. Do not attach a voided check or a deposit slip. Have you verified the routing and account numbers? Use whole dollars only.

All or the following amount of my refund (line 28) is authorized for direct deposit into the account shown below:

[X] Checking

████████████████████   194.

● Routing number	● Type	● Account number	● 29 Direct Deposit Amount

The remaining amount of my refund (line 28) is authorized for direct deposit into the account shown below:

[ ] Checking
[ ] Savings

● Routing number	● Type	● Account number	● 30 Direct Deposit Amount

Under penalties of perjury, I declare that, to the best of my knowledge and belief, the information on this return is true, correct, and complete.

Sign Here	Your signature	Spouse's/RDP's signature (if filing jointly, both must sign)	Daytime phone number (optional)
It is unlawful to forge a spouse's/RDP's signature.			
Joint return? See Instructions.			Date
	X	X	

Paid preparer's signature (declaration of preparer is based on all information of which preparer has any knowledge)		Paid Preparer's SSN/PTIN
[signature] 02/11/08		● P00055756
Firm's name (or yours if self-employed)	Firm's address	FEIN
ALBA RAPID TAX & SERVICES 15700 PIONEER BLVD		
NORWALK	CA 90650-6533	● 95-4638210

10791.80	1254.60
1. Wages, tips, other comp.	2. Fed. income tax withheld
10791.80	453.25
3. Social security wages	4. Soc. sec. tax withheld
10791.80	156.48
5. Medicare wages and tips	6. Medicare tax withheld

Employer's name, address, and ZIP code
Sacramento Overnight SoCal, LLC
1841 Monetary Lane Suite 130
Carrollton TX 75006

Employer ID no. (EIN)	11 Nonqualified plans
27-1257868	

Employee's SSN	12a
███████████	12b
7 Social security tips	12c
	12d
8 Allocated tips	13 Statutory employee / Retirement plan / Third-party sick pay
9	14
	CASDI 129.49
10 Dependent care benefits	
003500000740038	

Jeremy Burrowes
13038 Roseton Ave.
Norwalk CA 90650.

Employee's name, address, and ZIP code

15 State Employer's state ID number	16 State wages, tips, etc.	17 State income tax
CA 305-8518-6	10791.80	192.91
18 Local wages, tips, etc.	19 Local income tax	20 Locality name

Form **W-2** Wage and Tax Statement
Copy B— 2011
To Be Filed With Employee's
FEDERAL Tax Return.
This information is being furnished to the IRS.
OMB No. 1545-0008
Department of the Treasury -
Internal Revenue Service

1 W2PUA N17 2878367

Form **1040EZ**
Department of the Treasury — Internal Revenue Service
Income Tax Return for Single and Joint Filers With No Dependents (99) **2011**

OMB No. 1545-0074

Your first name	MI	Last name	Your social security number
▮	E	▮	▮
If a joint return, spouse's first name	MI	Last name	Spouse's social security number

Home address (number and street). If you have a P.O. box, see instructions.   Apt no.

City, town or post office. If you have a foreign address, also complete spaces below (see instructions).   State   ZIP code

CA   90650

Foreign country name   Foreign province/county   Foreign postal code

△ Make sure the SSN(s) above are correct. △

Presidential Election Campaign
Check here if you, or your spouse if filing jointly, want $3 to go to this fund. Checking a box below will not change your tax or refund.

[X] You   [ ] Spouse

Income

Attach Form(s) W-2 here.

Enclose, but do not attach, any payment.

1	Wages, salaries, and tips. This should be shown in box 1 of your Form(s) W-2. Attach your Form(s) W-2.	1 10,792.
2	Taxable interest. If the total is over $1,500, you cannot use Form 1040EZ.	2
3	Unemployment compensation and Alaska Permanent Fund dividends (see instructions).	3
4	Add lines 1, 2, and 3. This is your adjusted gross income.	4 10,792.
5	If someone can claim you (or your spouse if a joint return) as a dependent, check the applicable box(es) below and enter the amount from the worksheet. [ ] You [ ] Spouse. If no one can claim you (or your spouse if a joint return), enter $9,500 if single; $19,000 if married filing jointly. See instructions for explanation.	5 9,500.
6	Subtract line 5 from line 4. If line 5 is larger than line 4, enter -0-. This is your taxable income. ►	6 1,292.

Payments, Credits, and Tax

7	Federal income tax withheld from Form(s) W-2 and 1099.	7 1,255.
8a	Earned income credit (EIC) (see instructions).	8a 221.
b	Nontaxable combat pay election. 8b	
9	Add lines 7 and 8a. These are your total payments and credits. ►	9 1,476.
10	Tax. Use the amount on line 6 above to find your tax in the tax table in the instructions. Then, enter the tax from the table on this line.	10 129.

Refund

Have it directly deposited! See instructions and fill in 11b, 11c, and 11d or Form 8888.

11a	If line 9 is larger than line 10, subtract line 10 from line 9. This is your refund. If Form 8888 is attached, check here ► [ ] ►	11a 1,347.
b	Routing number ▮	► c Type: [X] Checking [ ] Savings
d	Account number ▮	

Amount You Owe

12	If line 10 is larger than line 9, subtract line 9 from line 10. This is the amount you owe. For details on how to pay, see instructions. ►	12

Third Party Designee

Do you want to allow another person to discuss this return with the IRS (see instructions)? .. [X] Yes. Complete below. [ ] No

Designee's name ► J. ALEXANDER ALBA, EA   Phone no. ► (562) 868-3518   Personal ID no. (PIN) ► 20176

Sign Here

Joint return? See instructions.

Keep a copy for your records.

Under penalties of perjury, I declare that I have examined this return and, to the best of my knowledge and belief, it is true, correct, and accurately lists all amounts and sources of income I received during the tax year. Declaration of preparer (other than the taxpayer) is based on all information of which the preparer has any knowledge.

Your signature	Date	Your occupation	Daytime phone number
		WAREHOUSE WORKER	(562) 522-7298
Spouse's signature. If a joint return, both must sign.	Date	Spouse's occupation	If the IRS sent you an Identity Protection PIN, enter it here (see inst.)

Paid Preparer Use Only

Print/Type preparer's name	Preparer's signature	Date	Check [X] if self-employed	PTIN
J. ALEXANDER ALBA, EA		02/07/2012		P00055756
Firm's name ► ALBA RAPID TAX & SERVICES				
Firm's address ► 15700 PIONEER BLVD			Firm's EIN ► 95-4638210	
NORWALK CA 90650-6533			Phone no. (562) 868-3518	

BAA For Disclosure, Privacy Act, and Paperwork Reduction Act Notice, see instructions.   FDIA0201   10/17/11   Form **1040EZ** (2011)

Form **8867**

Department of the Treasury
Internal Revenue Service

Paid Preparer's Earned Income Credit Checklist

► For more information about Form 8867, see www.irs.gov/form8867
► To be completed by preparer and filed with Form 1040, 1040A, or 1040EZ.

OMB No. 1545-1629

2011

Attachment
Sequence No. 177

Taxpayer name's shown on return

Taxpayer's social security number

For the definitions of the following terms, see Pub 596.
• Investment Income • Qualifying Child • Earned Income • Full-time Student

Part I	All Taxpayers

1 Enter preparer's name and PTIN ► ANA LAURA SANCHEZ
     P01203843

2 Is the taxpayer's filing status married filing separately?..................................... ☐ Yes ☒ No

► If you checked 'Yes' on line 2, stop; the taxpayer cannot take the EIC. Otherwise, continue.

3 Does the taxpayer (and the taxpayer's spouse if filing jointly) have a social security number (SSN) that allows him or her to work or is valid for EIC purposes? See the instructions before answering..... ☒ Yes ☐ No

► If you checked 'No' on line 3, stop; the taxpayer cannot take the EIC. Otherwise, continue.

4 Is the taxpayer filing Form 2555 or Form 2555-EZ (relating to the exclusion of foreign earned income)?..... ☐ Yes ☒ No

► If you checked 'Yes' on line 4, stop; the taxpayer cannot take the EIC. Otherwise, continue.

5a Was the taxpayer a nonresident alien for any part of 2011?..................................... ☐ Yes ☒ No

· ► If you checked 'Yes on line 5a, go to line 5b. Otherwise, skip line 5b and go to line 6.

b Is the taxpayer's filing status married filing jointly?..................................... ☐ Yes ☐ No

► If you checked 'Yes' on line 5a and 'No' on line 5b, stop the taxpayer cannot take the EIC. Otherwise, continue.

6 Is the taxpayer's investment income more than $3,150? See Rule 6 in Pub 596 before answering................. ☐ Yes ☒ No

► If you checked 'Yes' on line 6, stop the taxpayer cannot take the EIC. Otherwise, continue.

7 Could the taxpayer, or the taxpayer's spouse if filing jointly, be a qualifying child of another person for 2011? If the taxpayer's filing status is married filing jointly, check 'No.' Otherwise, see Rule 10 (Rule 13 if the taxpayer does not have a qualifying child) in Pub 596 before answering................................... ☐ Yes ☒ No

► If you checked 'Yes' on line 7, stop the taxpayer cannot take the EIC. Otherwise, go to Part II or Part III, whichever applies.

BAA For Paperwork Reduction Act Notice, see instructions.

Form 8867 (2011)

FDIA4312 01/00/12

Part II Taxpayers With a Child	Child 1	Child 2	Child 3
Caution. If there is more than one child, complete lines 8 through 14 for one child before going to the next column.			
8 Child's name			
9 Is the child the taxpayer's son, daughter, stepchild, foster child, brother, sister, stepbrother, stepsister, half brother, half sister, or a descendant of any of them?	☐ Yes ☐ No	☐ Yes ☐ No	☐ Yes ☐ No
10 Is either of the following true? • The child is unmarried, or • The child is married, can be claimed as the taxpayer's dependent, and is not filing a joint return (or is filing it only as a claim for refund)	☐ Yes ☐ No	☐ Yes ☐ No	☐ Yes ☐ No
11 Did the child live with the taxpayer in the United States for over half of the year? See the instructions before answering.................	☐ Yes ☐ No	☐ Yes ☐ No	☐ Yes ☐ No
12 Was the child (at the end of 2011) — • Under age 19 and younger than the taxpayer (or the taxpayer's spouse if the taxpayer files jointly), • Under age 24, a full-time student, and younger than the taxpayer (or the taxpayer's spouse if the taxpayer files jointly), or • Any age and permanently and totally disabled?............. ► If you checked 'Yes' on lines 9, 10, 11, and 12, the child is the taxpayer's qualifying child; go to line 13a. If you checked 'No' on line 9, 10, 11, or 12, the child is not the taxpayer's qualifying child; see the instructions for line 12.	☐ Yes ☐ No	☐ Yes ☐ No	☐ Yes ☐ No
13a Could any other person check 'Yes' on lines 9, 10, 11, and 12 for the child?	☐ Yes ☐ No	☐ Yes ☐ No	☐ Yes ☐ No
► If you checked 'No' on line 13a, go to line 14. Otherwise, go to line 13b. b Enter the child's relationship to the other person(s).............			
c Under the tiebreaker rules, is the child treated as the taxpayer's qualifying child? See the instructions before answering.........	☐ Yes ☐ No ☐ Don't know	☐ Yes ☐ No ☐ Don't know	☐ Yes ☐ No ☐ Don't know
► If you checked 'Yes' on line 13c, go to line 14. If you checked 'No,' the taxpayer cannot take the EIC based on this child and cannot take the EIC for taxpayers who do not have a qualifying child. If there is more than one child, see the Note at the bottom of this page. If you checked 'Don't know,' explain to the taxpayer that, under the tiebreaker rules, the taxpayer's EIC and other tax benefits may be disallowed. Then, if the taxpayer wants to take the EIC based on this child, complete lines 14 and 15. If not, and there are no other qualifying children, the taxpayer cannot take the EIC, including the EIC for taxpayers without a qualifying child; do not complete Part III. If there is more than one child, see the Note at the bottom of this page.			
14 Does the qualifying child have an SSN that allows him or her to work or is valid for EIC purposes? See the instructions before answering	☐ Yes ☐ No	☐ Yes ☐ No	☐ Yes ☐ No
► If you checked 'No' on line 14, the taxpayer cannot take the EIC based on this child and cannot take the EIC for taxpayers who do not have a qualifying child. If there is more than one child, see the Note at the bottom of this page. If you checked 'Yes' on line 14, continue.			
15 Are the taxpayer's earned income and adjusted gross income each less than the limit that applies to the taxpayer for 2011? See Pub 596 for the limit...			☐ Yes ☐ No
► If you checked 'No' on line 15, stop; the taxpayer cannot take the EIC. If you checked 'Yes' on line 15, the taxpayer can take the EIC. Complete Schedule EIC and attach it to the taxpayer's return. If there are two or three qualifying children with valid SSNs, list them on Schedule EIC in the same order as they are listed here. If the taxpayer's EIC was reduced or disallowed for a year after 1996, see Pub 596 to see if Form 8862 must be filed. Go to line 20. Note. If you checked 'No' on line 13c or 14 but there is more than one child, complete lines 8 through 14 for the other child(ren) (but for no more than three qualifying children). Also do this if you checked 'Don't know' on line 13c and the taxpayer is not taking the EIC based on this child.			

Part III   Taxpayers Without a Qualifying Child

16   Was the taxpayer's main home, and the main home of the taxpayer's spouse if filing jointly, in the United States for more than half the year? (Military personnel on extended active duty outside the United States are considered to be living in the United States during that duty period. See Pub 596.) ....   [X] Yes   [ ] No

     ▸ If you checked 'No' on line 16, stop; the taxpayer cannot take the EIC. Otherwise, continue.

17   Was the taxpayer, or the taxpayer's spouse if filing jointly, at least age 25 but under age 65 at the end of 2011?   [X] Yes   [ ] No

     ▸ If you checked 'No' on line 17, stop; the taxpayer cannot take the EIC. Otherwise, continue.

18   Is the taxpayer, or the taxpayer's spouse if filing jointly, eligible to be claimed as a dependent on anyone else's federal income tax return for 2011? If the taxpayer's filing status is married filing jointly, check 'No'. ....   [ ] Yes   [X] No

     ▸ If you checked 'Yes' on line 18, stop; the taxpayer cannot take the EIC. Otherwise, continue.

19   Are the taxpayer's earned income and adjusted gross income each less than the limit that applies to the taxpayer for 2011? See Pub 596 for the limit. ....   [X] Yes   [ ] No

     ▸ If you checked 'No' on line 19, stop; the taxpayer cannot take the EIC. If you checked 'Yes' on line 19, the taxpayer can take the EIC. If the taxpayer's EIC was reduced or disallowed for a year after 1996, see Pub 596 to find out if Form 8862 must be filed. Go to line 20.

Part IV   Due Diligence Requirements

20   Did you complete Form 8867 based on information provided by the taxpayer or reasonably obtained by you? ....   [X] Yes   [ ] No

21   Did you complete the EIC worksheet found in the Form 1040, 1040A, or 1040EZ instructions (or your own worksheet that provides the same information as the 1040, 1040A, or 1040EZ worksheet)? ....   [X] Yes   [ ] No

22   Did you comply with the knowledge requirements? (To comply with the knowledge requirements, you must not know or have reason to know that any information used to determine the taxpayer's eligibility for, and the amount of, the EIC is incorrect. You may not ignore the implications of information furnished to or known by you, and you must make reasonable inquiries if the information furnished appears to be incorrect, inconsistent, or incomplete. At the time you make these inquiries, you must document in your files the inquiries you made and the responses you received.) ....   [X] Yes   [ ] No

23   Did you keep the following records?
- Form 8867,
- The EIC worksheet(s) or your own worksheet(s),
- A record of how, when, and from whom the information used to prepare the form and worksheet(s) was obtained, and
- Copies of any documents provided by the taxpayer and on which you relied to complete the form and the worksheet ....   [X] Yes   [ ] No

     ▸ If you checked 'Yes' on lines 20, 21, 22, and 23, submit Form 8867 in the manner required, and keep the records described on line 23 for 3 years (see instructions), you have complied with all the due diligence requirements.

     ▸ If you checked 'No' on line 20, 21, 22, or 23, you have not complied with all the due diligence requirements and may have to pay a $500 penalty for each failure to comply.

Form W-2 Wage and Tax Statement 2012

a Control number 0480-8592 0000000740-000003	Void	c Employer's name, address, and ZIP code SO CAL REGION OVERNIGHT INC 12858 FLORENCE AVE SANTA FE SPGS CA 90670	Department of the Treasury - Internal Revenue Service OMB No. 1545-0008	
b Employer's identification number 45-3944307	e Employee's social security number 620-38-8827		1 Wages, tips, other compensation 9069.80	2 Federal income tax withheld 1044.87
			3 Social security wages 9069.80	4 Social security tax withheld 380.93
13 Statutory employee	Retirement plan	Third party sick pay	5 Medicare wages and tips 9069.80	6 Medicare tax withheld 131.51
12 See Instrs. for Box 12	14 Other CASDI 90.70	e Employee's name, address, and ZIP code	7 Social security tips	8 Allocated tips
			9 Advance EIC payment	10 Dependent care benefits
			11 Nonqualified plans	
15 State CA	Employer's state ID No. 305-8518-6	16 State wages, tips, etc. 9069.80	17 State income tax 145.66	18 Local wages, tips, etc.	19 Local income tax	20 Locality name

This information is being furnished to the Internal Revenue Service. If you are required to file a tax return, a negligence penalty or other sanction may be imposed on you if this income is taxable and you fail to report it.

Form W-2 Wage and Tax Statement 2012

a Control number 0480-8592 0000000740-000003	Void	c Employer's name, address, and ZIP code SO CAL REGION OVERNIGHT INC 12858 FLORENCE AVE SANTA FE SPGS CA 90670	Department of the Treasury - Internal Revenue Service OMB No. 1545-0008	
b Employer's identification number 45-3944307	e Employee's social security number 620-38-8827		1 Wages, tips, other compensation 9069.80	2 Federal income tax withheld 1044.87
			3 Social security wages 9069.80	4 Social security tax withheld 380.93
13 Statutory employee	Retirement plan	Third party sick pay	5 Medicare wages and tips 9069.80	6 Medicare tax withheld 131.51
12 See Instrs. for Box 12	14 Other CASDI 90.70	e Employee's name, address, and ZIP code	7 Social security tips	8 Allocated tips
			9 Advance EIC payment	10 Dependent care benefits
			11 Nonqualified plans	
15 State CA	Employer's state ID No. 305-8518-6	16 State wages, tips, etc. 9069.80	17 State income tax 145.66	18 Local wages, tips, etc.	19 Local income tax	20 Locality name

This information is being furnished to the Internal Revenue Service. If you are required to file a tax return, a negligence penalty or other sanction may be imposed on you if this income is taxable and you fail to report it.

Form W-2 Wage and Tax Statement 2012

a Control number	Void X	c Employer's name, address, and ZIP code	Department of the Treasury - Internal Revenue Service OMB No. 1545-0008	
b Employer's identification number	e Employee's social security number		1 Wages, tips, other compensation	2 Federal income tax withheld
			3 Social security wages	4 Social security tax withheld
13 Statutory employee	Retirement plan	Third party sick pay	5 Medicare wages and tips	6 Medicare tax withheld
12 See Instrs. for Box 12	14 Other	e Employee's name, address, and ZIP code	7 Social security tips	8 Allocated tips
			9 Advance EIC payment	10 Dependent care benefits
			11 Nonqualified plans	
15 State	Employer's state ID No.	16 State wages, tips, etc.	17 State income tax	18 Local wages, tips, etc.	19 Local income tax	20 Locality name

This information is being furnished to the Internal Revenue Service. If you are required to file a tax return, a negligence penalty or other sanction may be imposed on you if this income is taxable and you fail to report it.

Form **1040EZ**	Department of the Treasury — Internal Revenue Service **Income Tax Return for Single and Joint Filers With No Dependents** (99) **2012**	OMB No. 1545-0074

Your first name ▮ MI ▮ Last name ▮ E   Your social security number ▮

If a joint return, spouse's first name ▮ MI ▮ Last name   Spouse's social security number ▮

Home address (number and street). If you have a P.O. box, see instructions. ▮   Apt. no.   ⚠ Make sure the SSN(s) above are correct. ⚠

City, town or post office. If you have a foreign address, also complete spaces below (see instructions). ▮   State ZIP code CA 90650

NORWALK

Foreign country name   Foreign province/state/county   Foreign postal code

Presidential Election Campaign
Check here if you, or your spouse if filing jointly, want $3 to go to this fund. Checking a box below will not change your tax or refund.
☐ You   ☐ Spouse

Income	1	Wages, salaries, and tips. This should be shown in box 1 of your Form(s) W-2. Attach your Form(s) W-2	1	9,070.
Attach Form(s) W-2 here. Enclose, but do not attach, any payment.	2	Taxable interest. If the total is over $1,500, you cannot use Form 1040EZ	2	
	3	Unemployment compensation and Alaska Permanent Fund dividends (see instructions)	3	
	4	Add lines 1, 2, and 3. This is your adjusted gross income	4	9,070.
	5	If someone can claim you (or your spouse if a joint return) as a dependent, check the applicable box(es) below and enter the amount from the worksheet. ☐ You ☐ Spouse		
		If no one can claim you (or your spouse if a joint return), enter $9,750 if single; $19,500 if married filing jointly. See instructions for explanation.	5	9,750.
	6	Subtract line 5 from line 4. If line 5 is larger than line 4, enter -0-. This is your taxable income	▶ 6	0.
Payments, Credits, and Tax	7	Federal income tax withheld from Form(s) W-2 and 1099	7	1,045.
	8a	Earned income credit (EIC) (see instructions)	8a	375.
	b	Nontaxable combat pay election	8b	
	9	Add lines 7 and 8a. These are your total payments and credits	▶ 9	1,420.
	10	Tax. Use the amount on line 6 above to find your tax in the tax table in the instructions. Then, enter the tax from the table on this line	10	0.
Refund Have it directly deposited! See instructions and fill in 11b, 11c, and 11d or Form 8888.	11a	If line 9 is larger than line 10, subtract line 10 from line 9. This is your refund. If Form 8888 is attached, check here ▶ ☐	11a	1,420.
	▶ b	Routing number ▮	▶ c Type: ☒ Checking ☐ Savings	
	▶ d	Account number ▮		
Amount You Owe	12	If line 10 is larger than line 9, subtract line 9 from line 10. This is the amount you owe. For details on how to pay, see instructions	▶ 12	

Third Party Designee	Do you want to allow another person to discuss this return with the IRS (see instructions)? ☒ Yes. Complete below. ☐ No		
	Designee's name ▶ J. ALEXANDER ALBA, EA	Phone no. ▮	Personal ID no. (PIN) ▶ 20176

Sign Here
Joint return? See instructions.
Keep a copy for your records.

Under penalties of perjury, I declare that I have examined this return and, to the best of my knowledge and belief, it is true, correct, and accurately lists all amounts and sources of income I received during the tax year. Declaration of preparer (other than the taxpayer) is based on all information of which the preparer has any knowledge.

Your signature	Date	Your occupation WAREHOUSE	Daytime phone number
Spouse's signature. If a joint return, both must sign.	Date	Spouse's occupation	If the IRS sent you an Identity Protection PIN, enter it here (see instrs.)

Paid Preparer Use Only	Print/Type preparer's name J. ALEXANDER ALBA, EA	Preparer's signature	Date 02/20/2013	Check ☒ if self-employed	PTIN P00055756
	Firm's name ▶ ALBA RAPID TAX & SERVICES			Firm's EIN ▶ 95-4638210	
	Firm's address ▶ 15700 PIONEER BLVD NORWALK CA 90650-6533			Phone no. (562) 868-3518	

BAA For Disclosure, Privacy Act, and Paperwork Reduction Act Notice, see instructions.   FDIA0201   10/22/12   Form **1040EZ** (2012)

Form **8867**	Paid Preparer's Earned Income Credit Checklist	OMB No. 1545-1629
	▶ To be completed by preparer and filed with Form 1040, 1040A, or 1040EZ.	**2012**
Department of the Treasury Internal Revenue Service	▶ Information about Form 8867 and its separate instructions is at *www.irs.gov/form8867*.	Attachment Sequence No. **177**

Taxpayer name(s) shown on return	Taxpayer's social security number
██████████████	████████

For the definitions of the following terms, see Pub 596.
- Investment Income • Qualifying Child • Earned Income • Full-time Student

Part I   All Taxpayers

1 Enter preparer's name and PTIN ▶ ████████████████

2 Is the taxpayer's filing status married filing separately? .... ☐ Yes ☒ No

▶ If you checked 'Yes' on line 2, stop; the taxpayer cannot take the EIC. Otherwise, continue.

3 Does the taxpayer (and the taxpayer's spouse if filing jointly) have a social security number (SSN) that allows him or her to work or is valid for EIC purposes? See the instructions before answering .... ☒ Yes ☐ No

▶ If you checked 'No' on line 3, stop; the taxpayer cannot take the EIC. Otherwise, continue.

4 Is the taxpayer filing Form 2555 or Form 2555 EZ (relating to the exclusion of foreign earned income)? .... ☐ Yes ☒ No

▶ If you checked 'Yes' on line 4, stop; the taxpayer cannot take the EIC. Otherwise, continue.

5a Was the taxpayer a nonresident alien for any part of 2012? .... ☐ Yes ☒ No

▶ If you checked 'Yes' on line 5a, go to line 5b. Otherwise, skip line 5b and go to line 6.

b Is the taxpayer's filing status married filing jointly? .... ☐ Yes ☐ No

▶ If you checked 'Yes' on line 5a and 'No' on line 5b stop; the taxpayer cannot take the EIC. Otherwise, continue.

6 Is the taxpayer's investment income more than $3,200? See Rule 6 in Pub 596 before answering .... ☐ Yes ☒ No

▶ If you checked 'Yes' on line 6, stop the taxpayer cannot take the EIC. Otherwise, continue.

7 Could the taxpayer, or the taxpayer's spouse if filing jointly, be a qualifying child of another person for 2012? If the taxpayer's filing status is married filing jointly, check 'No.' Otherwise, see Rule 10 (Rule 13 if the taxpayer does not have a qualifying child) in Pub 596 before answering .... ☐ Yes ☒ No

▶ If you checked 'Yes' on line 7, stop; the taxpayer cannot take the EIC. Otherwise, go to Part II or Part III, whichever applies.

BAA For Paperwork Reduction Act Notice, see instructions.   Form 8867 (2012)

FDIA4312   04/11/12

Part II	Taxpayers With a Child	Child 1	Child 2	Child 3
	Caution. If there is more than one child, complete lines 8 through 14 for one child before going to the next column.			
8	Child's name			
9	Is the child the taxpayer's son, daughter, stepchild, foster child, brother, sister, stepbrother, stepsister, half brother, half sister, or a descendant of any of them?	☐Yes ☐No	☐Yes ☐No	☐Yes ☐No
10	Is either of the following true? • The child is unmarried, or • The child is married, can be claimed as the taxpayer's dependent, and is not filing a joint return (or is filing it only as a claim for refund)	☐Yes ☐No	☐Yes ☐No	☐Yes ☐No
11	Did the child live with the taxpayer in the United States for over half of the year? See the instructions before answering..............	☐Yes ☐No	☐Yes ☐No	☐Yes ☐No
12	Was the child (at the end of 2012) – • Under age 19 and younger than the taxpayer (or the taxpayer's spouse if the taxpayer files jointly), • Under age 24, a full-time student, and younger than the taxpayer (or the taxpayer's spouse if the taxpayer files jointly), or • Any age and permanently and totally disabled?.............. ► If you checked 'Yes' on lines 9, 10, 11, and 12, the child is the taxpayer's qualifying child; go to line 13a. If you checked 'No' on line 9, 10, 11, or 12, the child is not the taxpayer's qualifying child; see the instructions for line 12.	☐Yes ☐No	☐Yes ☐No	☐Yes ☐No
13a	Could any other person check 'Yes' on lines 9, 10, 11, and 12 for the child? .... ► If you checked 'No' on line 13a, go to line 14. Otherwise, go to line 13b.	☐Yes ☐No	☐Yes ☐No	☐Yes ☐No
b	Enter the child's relationship to the other person(s)			
c	Under the tiebreaker rules, is the child treated as the taxpayer's qualifying child? See the instructions before answering........... ► If you checked 'Yes' on line 13c, go to line 14. If you checked 'No,' the taxpayer cannot take the EIC based on this child and cannot take the EIC for taxpayers who do not have a qualifying child. If there is more than one child, see the Note at the bottom of this page. If you checked 'Don't know,' explain to the taxpayer that, under the tiebreaker rules, the taxpayer's EIC and other tax benefits may be disallowed. Then, if the taxpayer wants to take the EIC based on this child, complete lines 14 and 15. If not, and there are no other qualifying children, the taxpayer cannot take the EIC, including the EIC for taxpayers without a qualifying child; do not complete Part III. If there is more than one child, see the Note at the bottom of this page.	☐Yes ☐No ☐Don't know	☐Yes ☐No ☐Don't know	☐Yes ☐No ☐Don't know
14	Does the qualifying child have an SSN that allows him or her to work or is valid for EIC purposes? See the instructions before answering .... ► If you checked 'No' on line 14, the taxpayer cannot take the EIC based on this child and cannot take the EIC available to taxpayers without a qualifying child. If there is more than one child, see the Note at the bottom of this page. If you checked 'Yes' on line 14, continue.	☐Yes ☐No	☐Yes ☐No	☐Yes ☐No
15	Are the taxpayer's earned income and adjusted gross income each less than the limit that applies to the taxpayer for 2012? See Pub 596 for the limit................................... ► If you checked 'No' on line 15, stop; the taxpayer cannot take the EIC. If you checked 'Yes' on line 15, the taxpayer can take the EIC. Complete Schedule EIC and attach it to the taxpayer's return. If there are two or three qualifying children with valid SSNs, list them on Schedule EIC in the same order as they are listed here. If the taxpayer's EIC was reduced or disallowed for a year after 1996, see Pub 596 to see if Form 8862 must be filed. Go to line 20.			☐Yes ☐No

Note. If you checked 'No' on line 13c or 14 but there is more than one child, complete lines 8 through 14 for the other child(ren) (but for no more than three qualifying children). Also do this if you checked 'Don't know' on line 13c and the taxpayer is not taking the EIC based on this child.

Part III   Taxpayers Without a Qualifying Child

16 Was the taxpayer's main home, and the main home of the taxpayer's spouse if filing jointly, in the United States for more than half the year? (Military personnel on extended active duty outside the United States are considered to be living in the United States during that duty period. See Pub 596.) ....   [X] Yes   [ ] No

    ► If you checked 'No' on line 16, stop; the taxpayer cannot take the EIC. Otherwise, continue.

17 Was the taxpayer, or the taxpayer's spouse if filing jointly, at least age 25 but under age 65 at the end of 2012? See the instructions before answering..   [X] Yes   [ ] No

    ► If you checked 'No' on line 17, stop; the taxpayer cannot take the EIC. Otherwise, continue.

18 Is the taxpayer, or the taxpayer's spouse if filing jointly, eligible to be claimed as a dependent on anyone else's federal income tax return for 2012? If the taxpayer's filing status is married filing jointly, check 'No,' ....   [ ] Yes   [X] No

    ► If you checked 'Yes' on line 18, stop; the taxpayer cannot take the EIC. Otherwise, continue.

19 Are the taxpayer's earned income and adjusted gross income each less than the limit that applies to the taxpayer for 2012? See Pub 596 for the limit ....   [X] Yes   [ ] No

    ► If you checked 'No' on line 19, stop; the taxpayer cannot take the EIC. If you checked 'Yes' on line 19, the taxpayer can take the EIC. If the taxpayer's EIC was reduced or disallowed for a year after 1996, see Pub 596 to find out if Form 8862 must be filed. Go to line 20.

Part IV   Due Diligence Requirements

20 Did you complete Form 8867 based on information provided by the taxpayer or reasonably obtained by you? ......   [X] Yes   [ ] No

21 Did you complete the EIC worksheet found in the Form 1040, 1040A, or 1040EZ instructions (or your own worksheet that provides the same information as the 1040, 1040A, or 1040EZ worksheet)? ....   [X] Yes   [ ] No

22 If any qualifying child was not the taxpayer's son or daughter, did you ask why the parents were not claiming the child and document the answer?..   [ ] Yes   [ ] No   [X] Does not apply

23 If the answer to question 13a is 'Yes' (indicating that the child lived for more than half the year with someone else who could claim the child for the EIC), did you explain the tiebreaker rules and possible consequences of another person claiming your client's qualifying child?..................................   [ ] Yes   [ ] No   [X] Does not apply

24 Did you ask this taxpayer any additional questions that are necessary to meet your knowledge requirement? See the instructions before answering.......................................   [X] Yes   [ ] No   [ ] Does not apply

    To comply with the EIC knowledge requirement, you must not know or have reason to know that any information used to determine the taxpayer's eligibility for, and the amount of, the EIC is incorrect. You may not ignore the implications of information furnished to or known by you, and you must make reasonable inquiries if the information furnished appears to be incorrect, inconsistent, or incomplete. At the time you make these inquiries, you must document in your files the inquiries you made and the taxpayer's responses.

25 Did you document the additional questions you asked and your client's answers? ....   [X] Yes   [ ] No   [ ] Does not apply

BAA

Form 1040 Department of the Treasury—Internal Revenue Service (99)

U.S. Individual Income Tax Return **2017** OMB No. 1545-0074 | IRS Use Only—Do not write or staple in this space.

For the year Jan. 1–Dec. 31, 2017, or other tax year beginning , 2017, ending , 20

See separate instructions.

Your first name and initial | Last name | Your social security number

█████████ | ████████

If a joint return, spouse's first name and initial | Last name | Spouse's social security number

Home address (number and street). If you have a P.O. box, see instructions. | Apt. no. | ⚠ Make sure the SSN(s) above and on line 6c are correct.

█████████

City, town or post office, state, and ZIP code. If you have a foreign address, also complete spaces below (see instructions).

FONTANA CA 92336

Foreign country name | Foreign province/state/county | Foreign postal code

Presidential Election Campaign
Check here if you, or your spouse if filing jointly, want $3 to go to this fund. Checking a box below will not change your tax or refund. ☐ You ☐ Spouse

Filing Status
Check only one box.

1. ☒ Single
2. ☐ Married filing jointly (even if only one had income)
3. ☐ Married filing separately. Enter spouse's SSN above and full name here. ▶
4. ☐ Head of household (with qualifying person). (See instructions.) If the qualifying person is a child but not your dependent, enter this child's name here. ▶
5. ☐ Qualifying widow(er) (see instructions)

Exemptions

6a ☒ **Yourself.** If someone can claim you as a dependent, do not check box 6a
b ☐ **Spouse**

c Dependents:				Boxes checked on 6a and 6b	1
(1) First name Last name	(2) Dependent's social security number	(3) Dependent's relationship to you	(4) ✓ if child under age 17 qualifying for child tax credit (see instructions)	No. of children on 6c who:	
			☐	• lived with you	
			☐	• did not live with you due to divorce or separation (see instructions)	
			☐	Dependents on 6c not entered above	

If more than four dependents, see instructions and check here ▶ ☐

d Total number of exemptions claimed ... Add numbers on lines above ▶ | 01

Income

Attach Form(s) W-2 here. Also attach Forms W-2G and 1099-R if tax was withheld.

If you did not get a W-2, see instructions.

7	Wages, salaries, tips, etc. Attach Form(s) W-2	7	5,134
8a	Taxable interest. Attach Schedule B if required	8a	
b	Tax-exempt interest. Do not include on line 8a	8b	
9a	Ordinary dividends. Attach Schedule B if required	9a	
b	Qualified dividends	9b	
10	Taxable refunds, credits, or offsets of state and local income taxes	10	
11	Alimony received	11	
12	Business income or (loss). Attach Schedule C or C-EZ	12	
13	Capital gain or (loss). Attach Schedule D if required. If not required, check here ▶ ☐	13	
14	Other gains or (losses). Attach Form 4797	14	
15a	IRA distributions . 15a	b Taxable amount	15b	
16a	Pensions and annuities . 16a	b Taxable amount	16b	
17	Rental real estate, royalties, partnerships, S corporations, trusts, etc. Attach Schedule E	17	
18	Farm income or (loss). Attach Schedule F	18	
19	Unemployment compensation	19	
20a	Social security benefits . 20a	b Taxable amount	20b	
21	Other income. List type and amount SEE OTHER INCOME WKS	21	1,306
22	Combine the amounts in the far right column for lines 7 through 21. This is your total income ▶	22	6,440

Adjusted Gross Income

23	Educator expenses	23			
24	Certain business expenses of reservists, performing artists, and fee-basis government officials. Attach Form 2106 or 2106-EZ	24			
25	Health savings account deduction. Attach Form 8889	25			
26	Moving expenses. Attach Form 3903	26			
27	Deductible part of self-employment tax. Attach Schedule SE	27		93	
28	Self-employed SEP, SIMPLE, and qualified plans	28			
29	Self-employed health insurance deduction	29			
30	Penalty on early withdrawal of savings	30			
31a	Alimony paid b Recipient's SSN ▶	31a			
32	IRA deduction	32			
33	Student loan interest deduction	33			
34	Tuition and fees. Attach Form 8917	34			
35	Domestic production activities deduction. Attach Form 8903	35			
36	Add lines 23 through 35	36			93
37	Subtract line 36 from line 22. This is your adjusted gross income ▶	37			6,347

SPA   For Disclosure, Privacy Act, and Paperwork Reduction Act Notice, see separate instructions.   1037 PEI 7US011   Form **1040** (2017)

FONTANA Page 06

Tax and Credits	38	Amount from line 37 (adjusted gross income)				38	6,347
	39a	Check if: { You were born before January 2, 1953, ☐ Blind. Spouse was born before Jan. 2, 1953, ☐ Blind. } Total boxes checked + 39a ☐					
	b	If your spouse itemizes on a separate return or you were a dual-status alien, check here ▶ 39b ☐					
Standard Deduction for -	40	Itemized deductions (from Schedule A) or your standard deduction (see left margin)				40	6,350
•People who check any box on line 39a or 39b or who can be claimed as a dependent, see instructions.	41	Subtract line 40 from line 38				41	(3)
	42	Exemptions. If line 38 is $156,900 or less, multiply $4,050 by the number on line 6d. Otherwise, see inst.				42	4,050
	43	Taxable income. Subtract line 42 from line 41. If line 42 is more than line 41, enter -0-				43	
•All others:	44	Tax (see instructions). Check if any from: a ☐ Form(s) 8814 b ☐ Form 4972 c ☐				44	
Single or Married filing separately, $6,350	45	Alternative minimum tax (see instructions). Attach Form 6251				45	
	46	Excess advance premium tax credit repayment. Attach Form 8962				46	
Married filing jointly or Qualifying widow(er), $12,700	47	Add lines 44, 45, and 46			▶	47	
	48	Foreign tax credit. Attach Form 1116 if required	48				
	49	Credit for child and dependent care expenses. Attach Form 2441	49				
Head of household, $9,350	50	Education credits from Form 8863, line 19	50				
	51	Retirement savings contributions credit. Attach Form 8880	51				
	52	Child tax credit. Attach Schedule 8812, if required	52				
	53	Residential energy credits. Attach Form 5695	53				
	54	Other credits from Form a ☐ 3800 b ☐ 8801 c ☐	54				
	55	Add lines 48 through 54. These are your total credits				55	
	56	Subtract line 55 from line 47. If line 55 is more than line 47, enter -0-			▶	56	
Other Taxes	57	Self-employment tax. Attach Schedule SE				57	185
	58	Unreported social security and Medicare tax from Form: a ☐ 4137 b ☐ 8919				58	
	59	Additional tax on IRAs, other qualified retirement plans, etc. Attach Form 5329 if required				59	
	60a	Household employment taxes from Schedule H				60a	
	b	First-time homebuyer credit repayment. Attach Form 5405 if required				60b	
	61	Health care: individual responsibility (see instructions) Full-year coverage ☒				61	
	62	Taxes from: a ☐ Form 8959 b ☐ Form 8960 c ☐ Instructions; enter code(s)				62	
	63	Add lines 56 through 62. This is your total tax			▶	63	185
Payments	64	Federal income tax withheld from Forms W-2 and 1099	64	492			
	65	2017 estimated tax payments and amount applied from 2016 return	65				
If you have a qualifying child, attach Schedule EIC.	66a	Earned income credit (EIC)	66a	484			
	b	Nontaxable combat pay election	66b				
	67	Additional child tax credit. Attach Form 8812	67				
	68	American opportunity credit from Form 8863, line 8	68				
	69	Net premium tax credit. Attach Form 8962	69				
	70	Amount paid with request for extension to file	70				
	71	Excess social security and tier 1 RRTA tax withheld	71				
	72	Credit for federal tax on fuels. Attach Form 4136	72				
	73	Credits from Form: a ☐ 2439 b ☐ Reserved c ☐ 8885 d ☐	73				
	74	Add lines 64, 65, 66a, and 67 through 73. These are your total payments			▶	74	976
Refund	75	If line 74 is more than line 63, subtract line 63 from line 74. This is the amount you overpaid				75	791
Direct deposit? See instructions.	76a	Amount of line 75 you want refunded to you. If Form 8888 is attached, check here ▶ ☐				76a	791
	▶ b	Routing number ▶ c Type: ☒ Checking ☐ Savings					
	▶ d	Account number					
	77	Amount of line 75 you want applied to your 2018 estimated tax ▶ 77					
Amount You Owe	78	Amount you owe. Subtract line 74 from line 63. For details on how to pay, see instructions ▶				78	
	79	Estimated tax penalty (see instructions)	79				

Third Party Designee Do you want to allow another person to discuss this return with the IRS (see instructions)? ☐ Yes. Complete below. ☐ No

Designee's name ▶   Phone no. ▶   Personal Identification number (PIN) ▶

Sign Here
Under penalties of perjury, I declare that I have examined this return and accompanying schedules and statements, and to the best of my knowledge and belief, they are true, correct, and accurately list all amounts and sources of income I received during the tax year. Declaration of preparer (other than taxpayer) is based on all information of which preparer has any knowledge.

Joint return? See inst. Keep a copy for your records.

Your signature   XXXXXXXXXXXXXXXXX   Date   Your occupation CONTRACTOR   Daytime phone number

Spouse's signature. If a joint return, both must sign.   XXXXXXXXXXXXXXXXX   Date   Spouse's occupation   If the IRS sent you an Identity Protection PIN, enter it here (see inst.)

Paid preparer use only

Print/type preparer's name	Preparer's signature	Date		PTIN
THOMAS SNIPP (RTRP)	XXXXXXXXXXXXXXX	06/13/18	☒ Check if self-employed	P01546909

Firm's name ▶ SFS LLC DBA LYZETS TAX SERVICE   Firm's EIN ▶ 46-3783086

Firm's address ▶ 8275 SIERRA AVE SUITE 105 FONTANA CA 92335   Phone no. 909-822-5192

SPA Go to www.irs.gov/Form1040 for instructions and the latest information.   1037 FEI 7U5012   FONTANA   Form 1040 (2017)

SCHEDULE SE
(Form 1040)

Department of the Treasury
Internal Revenue Service (99)

Self-Employment Tax

▶ Go to www.irs.gov/ScheduleSE for Instructions and the latest information.
▶ Attach to Form 1040 or Form 1040NR.

OMB No. 1545-0074

2017

Attachment
Sequence No. **17**

Name of person with self-employment income (as shown on Form 1040 or Form 1040NR)

Social security number of person
with self-employment income ▶

Before you begin: To determine if you must file Schedule SE, see the instructions.

May I Use Short Schedule SE or Must I Use Long Schedule SE?

Note. Use this flowchart only if you must file Schedule SE. If unsure, see Who Must File Schedule SE in the instructions.

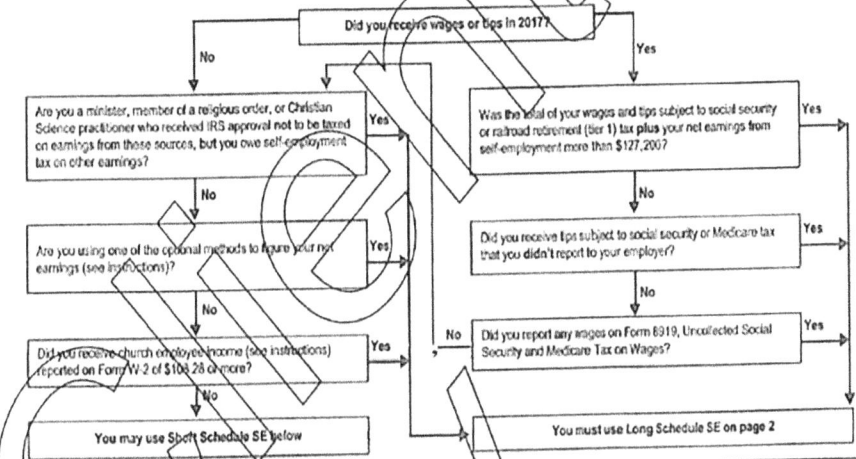

Did you receive wages or tips in 2017?

No / **Yes**

Are you a minister, member of a religious order, or Christian Science practitioner who received IRS approval not to be taxed on earnings from those sources, but you owe self-employment tax on other earnings? — **Yes**

Was the total of your wages and tips subject to social security or railroad retirement (tier 1) tax plus your net earnings from self-employment more than $127,200? — **Yes**

No

Are you using one of the optional methods to figure your net earnings (see instructions)? — **Yes**

No

Did you receive tips subject to social security or Medicare tax that you didn't report to your employer? — **Yes**

No

Did you receive church employee income (see instructions) reported on Form W-2 of $108.28 or more? — **Yes**

No

Did you report any wages on Form 8919, Uncollected Social Security and Medicare Tax on Wages? — **Yes**

No

You may use Short Schedule SE below

You must use Long Schedule SE on page 2

Section A - Short Schedule SE. Caution. Read above to see if you can use Short Schedule SE.

1a	Net farm profit or (loss) from Schedule F, line 34, and farm partnerships, Schedule K-1 (Form 1065), box 14, code A	**1a**	
b	If you received social security retirement or disability benefits, enter the amount of Conservation Reserve Program payments included on Schedule F, line 4b, or listed on Schedule K-1 (Form 1065), box 20, code Z	**1b**	( )
2	Net profit or (loss) from Schedule C, line 31; Schedule C-EZ, line 3; Schedule K-1 (Form 1065), box 14, code A (other than farming); and Schedule K-1 (Form 1065-B), box 9, code J1. Ministers and members of religious orders, see instructions for types of income to report on this line. See instructions for other income to report	**2**	1,306
3	Combine lines 1a, 1b, and 2	**3**	1,306
4	Multiply line 3 by 92.35% (0.9235). If less than $400, you don't owe self-employment tax; don't file this schedule unless you have an amount on line 1b . . . . ▶	**4**	1,206
	Note. If line 4 is less than $400 due to Conservation Reserve Program payments on line 1b, see instructions.		
5	Self-employment tax. If the amount on line 4 is: • $127,200 or less, multiply line 4 by 15.3% (0.153). Enter the result here and on Form 1040, line 57, or Form 1040NR, line 55 • More than $127,200, multiply line 4 by 2.9% (0.029). Then, add $15,772.80 to the result. Enter the total here and on Form 1040, line 57, or Form 1040NR, line 55	**5**	185
6	Deduction for one-half of self-employment tax. Multiply line 5 by 50% (0.50). Enter the result here and on Form 1040, line 27, or Form 1040NR, line 27 . . . . **6**	93	

SPA   For Paperwork Reduction Act Notice, see your tax return instructions.   1037 PEI 7US171   Schedule SE (Form 1040) 2017

EIC Checklist

Department of the Treasury
Internal Revenue Service

▶ To be completed by preparer and filed with Form 1040, 1040A, or 1040EZ.
▶ Information about Form 8867 and its separate instructions is at www.irs.gov/form8867.

Taxpayer name(s) shown on return	Taxpayer's social security number
▮▮▮▮▮	▮▮▮▮▮

For the definitions of **Qualifying Child** and **Earned Income**, see Pub. 596.

Part I   All Taxpayers

1 Enter preparer's name and PTIN ▶ ▮▮▮▮▮▮▮

2 Is the taxpayer's filing status married filing separately? . . . .   ☐ Yes   ☒ No

   ▶ If you checked "Yes" on line 2, **stop**; the taxpayer **cannot** take the EIC. Otherwise, continue.

3 Does the taxpayer (and the taxpayer's spouse if filing jointly) have a social security number (SSN) that allows him or her to work and is valid for EIC purposes? See the instructions before answering . . . .   ☒ Yes   ☐ No

   ▶ If you checked "No" on line 3, **stop**; the taxpayer **cannot** take the EIC. Otherwise, continue.

4 Is the taxpayer (or the taxpayer's spouse if filing jointly) filing Form 2555 or 2555-EZ (relating to the exclusion of foreign earned income)? . . . .   ☐ Yes   ☒ No

   ▶ If you checked "Yes" on line 4, **stop**; the taxpayer **cannot** take the EIC. Otherwise, continue.

5a Was the taxpayer (or the taxpayer's spouse) a nonresident alien for any part of 2017? . . . . .   ☐ Yes   ☒ No

   ▶ If you checked "Yes" on line 5a, go to line 5b. Otherwise, skip line 5b and go to line 6.

  b Is the taxpayer's filing status married filing jointly? . . . .   ☐ Yes   ☐ No

   ▶ If you checked "Yes" on line 5a and "No" on line 5b, **stop**; the taxpayer **cannot** take the EIC. Otherwise, continue.

6 Is the taxpayer's investment income more than $3,400? See the instructions before answering.   ☐ Yes   ☒ No

   ▶ If you checked "Yes" on line 6, **stop**; the taxpayer **cannot** take the EIC. Otherwise, continue.

7 Could the taxpayer be a **qualifying child** of another person for 2017? If the taxpayer's filing status is married filing jointly, check "No." Otherwise, see instructions before answering . . . .   ☐ Yes   ☒ No

   ▶ If you checked "Yes" on line 7, **stop**; the taxpayer **cannot** take the EIC. Otherwise, go to Part II or Part III, whichever applies.

SPA For Paperwork Reduction Act Notice, see separate Instructions.   1037 PEI 7USEII   Form **8867** (2017)

Part II   Taxpayers With a Child

	Child 1	Child 2	Child 3
Caution. If there is more than one child, complete lines 8 through 14 for one child before going to the next column.			
8 Child's name			
9 Is the child the taxpayer's son, daughter, stepchild, foster child, brother, sister, stepbrother, stepsister, half brother, half sister, or a descendant of any of them?	☐Yes ☐No	☐Yes ☐No	☐Yes ☐No
10 Was the child unmarried at the end of 2017? If the child was married at the end of 2017, see the instructions before answering	☐Yes ☐No	☐Yes ☐No	☐Yes ☐No
11 Did the child live with the taxpayer in the United States for over half of 2017? See the instructions before answering	☐Yes ☐No	☐Yes ☐No	☐Yes ☐No
12 Was the child (at the end of 2017)- § Under age 19 and younger than the taxpayer (or the taxpayer's spouse, if the taxpayer files jointly), § Under age 24, a student (defined in the instructions), and younger than the taxpayer (or the taxpayer's spouse, if the taxpayer files jointly), or § Any age and permanently and totally disabled? . . . . . . ▶ If you checked "Yes" on lines 9, 10, 11, and 12, the child is the taxpayer's qualifying child; go to line 13a. If you checked "No" on line 9, 10, 11, or 12, the child is not the taxpayer's qualifying child; see the instructions for line 12.	☐Yes ☐No	☐Yes ☐No	☐Yes ☐No
13a Do you or the taxpayer know of another person who could check "Yes" on lines 9, 10, 11, and 12 for the child? (If the only other person is the taxpayer's spouse, see the instructions before answering.) . . . . ▶ If you checked "No" on line 13a, go to line 14. Otherwise, go to line 13b.	☐Yes ☐No	☐Yes ☐No	☐Yes ☐No
b Enter the child's relationship to the other person(s)			
c Under the tiebreaker rules, is the child treated as the taxpayer's qualifying child? See the instructions before answering	☐Yes ☐No ☐Don't know	☐Yes ☐No ☐Don't know	☐Yes ☐No ☐Don't know
▶ If you checked "Yes" on line 13c, go to line 14. If you checked "No," the taxpayer **cannot** take the EIC based on this child and cannot take the EIC for taxpayers who do not have a qualifying child. If there is more than one child, see the Note at the bottom of this page. If you checked "Don't know," explain to the taxpayer that, under the tiebreaker rules, the taxpayer's EIC and other tax benefits may be disallowed. Then, if the taxpayer wants to take the EIC based on this child, complete lines 14 and 15. If not, and there are no other qualifying children, the taxpayer cannot take the EIC, including the EIC for taxpayers without a qualifying child; do not complete Part III. If there is more than one child, see the Note at the bottom of this page.			
14 Does the qualifying child have an SSN that allows him or her to work and is valid for EIC purposes? See the instructions before answering . . . . ▶ If you checked "No" on line 14, the taxpayer cannot take the EIC based on this child and cannot take the EIC available to taxpayers without a qualifying child. If there is more than one child, see the Note at the bottom of this page. If you checked "Yes" on line 14, continue.	☐Yes ☐No	☐Yes ☐No	☐Yes ☐No
15 Are the taxpayer's **earned income** and **adjusted gross income** each less than the limit that applies to the taxpayer for 2017? See instructions . .			☐Yes ☐No
▶ If you checked "No" on line 15, **stop**; the taxpayer **cannot** take the EIC. If you checked "Yes" on line 15, the taxpayer can take the EIC. Complete **Schedule EIC** and attach it to the taxpayer's return. If there are two or three qualifying children with valid SSNs, list them on Schedule EIC in the same order as they are listed here. If the taxpayer's EIC was reduced or disallowed for a year after 1996, see Pub. 596 to see if Form 8862 must be filed. Go to line 20.			
Note. If there is more than one child, complete lines 8 through 14 for the other child(ren) (but for no more than three qualifying children).			

SPA   1037 PEI 7USEI2

Part III Taxpayers Without a Qualifying Child

16 Was the taxpayer's main home, and the main home of the taxpayer's spouse if filing jointly, in the United States for more than half the year? (Military personnel on extended active duty outside the United States are considered to be living in the United States during that duty period.) See the instructions before answering. ☒Yes ☐No

  ▶ If you checked "No" on line 16, **stop**; the taxpayer **cannot** take the EIC. Otherwise, continue.

17 Was the taxpayer, or the taxpayer's spouse if filing jointly, at least age 25 but under age 65 at the end of 2017? See the instructions before answering . . . . ☒Yes ☐No

  ▶ If you checked "No" on line 17, **stop**; the taxpayer **cannot** take the EIC. Otherwise, continue.

18 Is the taxpayer eligible to be claimed as a dependent on anyone else's federal income tax return for 2017? If the taxpayer's filing status is married filing jointly, check "No" . . . . ☐Yes ☒No

  ▶ If you checked "Yes" on line 18, **stop**; the taxpayer **cannot** take the EIC. Otherwise, continue.

19 Are the taxpayer's **earned income** and **adjusted gross income** each less than the limit that applies to the taxpayer for 2017? See instructions . . . . ☒Yes ☐No

  ▶ If you checked "No" on line 19, **stop**; the taxpayer **cannot** take the EIC. If you checked "Yes" on line 19, the taxpayer can take the EIC. If the taxpayer's EIC was reduced or disallowed for a year after 1996, see Pub. 596 to find out if Form 8862 must be filed. Go to line 20.

SPA

1037 PEI 7USEI3

FONTANA Page 11

California Resident Income Tax Return

FORM
540

APE

ATTACH FEDERAL RETURN

A
R
RP

17

CA 92336-0000

12-07-1985

01	1	45	0	405	0	113	0
06	0	46	0	406	0	115	128
07	1	114	47	0	407	0	116	128
08	0	0	48	0	408	0	117	0
09	0	0	61	0	410	0	APE	0
10	0	0	62	0	413	0	3800	0
11	114	63	0	422	0	3803	0
12	5134	64	0	423	0	SCHG1	0
13	6347	71	78	424	0	5870A	0
14	0	72	0	425	0	5805 5805F	0
16	0	73	0	430	0	DESIGNEE	0
17	6347	74	0	431	0	TPIDP 01546909	
18	4236	75	90	432	0	FN 463783086	
19	2111	76	128	433	0	CCF	0
31	21	91	0	434	0	3805P	1
32	114	92	128	435	0	NQDC	0
33	0	93	0	436	0	3540	1
34	0	94	128	437	0	3554	0
35	0	95	0	438	0	3805Z	0
40	0	96	128	439	0	3807	0
43	0	97	0	440	0	3808	0
44	0	400	0	110	0	3809	0
		401	0	111	0	IRC453A	0
		409	0	112	0	IRC1341	0

jerito89@yahoo.com

(903) 237-8978

DDR1 122000247
3797459231
1

Filing Status

1 [X] Single

2 [ ] Married/RDP filing jointly. See inst.

3 [ ] Married/RDP filing separately. Enter spouse's/RDP's SSN or ITIN above and full name here

4 [ ] Head of household (with qualifying person). See instructions.

5 [ ] Qualifying widow(er) with dependent child. Enter year spouse/RDP died

If your California filing status is different from your federal filing status, check the box here .... [ ]

6 If someone can claim you (or your spouse/RDP) as a dependent, check the box here. See inst. .... 8 6 [ ]

068 3101176

Form 540 2017 Side 1

Your name: [redacted] Your SSN or ITIN: 620-38-8827

Whole dollars only

+ For line 7, line 8, line 9, and line 10: Multiply the amount you enter in the box by the pre-printed dollar amount for that line.

Exemptions

7 Personal: If you checked box 1, 3, or 4 above, enter 1 in the box. If you checked box 2 or 5, enter 2, in the box. If you checked the box on line 6, see instructions. ● 7 [1] X $114 = ● $ _____114._____

8 Blind: If you (or your spouse/RDP) are visually impaired, enter 1; if both are visually impaired, enter 2 .... ● 8 [ ] X $114 = ● $ _____

9 Senior: If you (or your spouse/RDP) are 65 or older, enter 1; if both are 65 or older, enter 2 .... ● 9 [ ] X $114 = ● $ _____

10 Dependents: Do not include yourself or your spouse/RDP.

	Dependent 1	Dependent 2	Dependent 3
First Name			
Last Name			
SSN			
Dependent's relationship to you			

Total dependent exemptions .... ● 10 [ ] X $353 = ● $ _____

11 Exemption amount: Add line 7 through line 10. Transfer this amount to line 32 .... ● 11 $ _____114._____

Taxable Income

12 State wages from your Form(s) W-2, box 16 .... ● 12 _____5,134._____

13 Enter federal adjusted gross income from Form 1040, line 37; 1040A, line 21; or 1040EZ, line 4 ... ● 13 _____6,347._____

14 California adjustments – subtractions. Enter the amount from Schedule CA (540), line 37, column B ... ● 14 _____

15 Subtract line 14 from line 13. If less than zero, enter the result in parentheses. See instructions .... 15 _____6,347._____

16 California adjustments – additions. Enter the amount from Schedule CA (540), line 37, column C ... ● 16 _____

17 California adjusted gross income. Combine line 15 and line 16 .... ● 17 _____6,347._____

18 Enter the larger of: Your California itemized deductions from Schedule CA (540), line 44; OR
   Your California standard deduction shown below for your filing status:
   ● Single or Married/RDP filing separately $4,236
   ● Married/RDP filing jointly, Head of household, or Qualifying widow(er) $8,472
   If Married/RDP filing separately or the box on line 6 is checked, STOP. See instructions . ● 18 _____4,236._____

19 Subtract line 18 from line 17. This is your taxable income. If less than zero, enter -0- .... ● 19 _____2,111._____

Tax

31 Tax. Check the box if from: [X] Tax Table   [ ] Tax Rate Schedule
   ● [ ] FTB 3800 ● [ ] FTB 3803 .... ● 31 _____21._____

32 Exemption credits. Enter the amount from line 11. If your federal AGI is more than $187,203 see instructions .... ● 32 _____114._____

33 Subtract line 32 from line 31. If less than zero, enter -0- .... ● 33 _____

34 Tax. See instructions. Check the box if from: ● [ ] Schedule G-1 ● [ ] FTB 5870A .... ● 34 _____

35 Add line 33 and line 34 .... ● 35 _____

Your name: [redacted]   Your SSN or ITIN: [redacted]

Special Credits

40 Nonrefundable Child and Dependent Care Expenses Credit. See instructions .... 8 40 _____

43 Enter credit name _____ code 8 ____ and amount .... 8 43 _____

44 Enter credit name _____ code 8 ____ and amount .... 8 44 _____

45 To claim more than two credits, see instructions. Attach Schedule P (540) .... 8 45 _____

46 Nonrefundable renter's credit. See instructions .... 8 46 _____

47 Add line 40 and line 43 through line 46. These are your total credits .... # 47 _____

48 Subtract line 47 from line 35. If less than zero, enter -0- .... # 48 _____

Other Taxes

61 Alternative minimum tax. Attach Schedule P (540) .... 8 61 _____

62 Mental Health Services Tax. See instructions .... 8 62 _____

63 Other taxes and credit recapture. See instructions .... 8 63 _____

64 Add line 48, line 61, line 62, and line 63. This is your total tax .... 8 64 _____

Payments

71 California income tax withheld. See instructions .... 8 71   38.

72 2017 CA estimated tax and other payments. See instructions .... 8 72 _____

73 Withholding (Form 592-B and/or 593). See instructions .... 8 73 _____

74 Excess SDI (or VPDI) withheld. See instructions .... 8 74 _____

75 Earned Income Tax Credit (EITC) .... 8 75   90.

76 Add lines 71 through 75. These are your total payments. See instructions .... # 76   128.

Use Tax

91 Use Tax. Do not leave blank. See instructions .... 8 91 _____

If line 91 is zero, check if: [X] No use tax is owed.

☐ You paid your use tax obligation directly to CDTFA.

Overpaid Tax/Tax Due

92 Payments balance. If line 76 is more than line 91, subtract line 91 from line 76 .... # 92   128.

93 Use Tax balance. If line 91 is more than line 76, subtract line 76 from line 91 .... # 93 _____

94 Overpaid tax. If line 92 is more than line 64, subtract line 64 from line 92 .... # 94   128.

95 Amount of line 94 you want applied to your 2018 estimated tax .... 8 95 _____

96 Overpaid tax available this year. Subtract line 95 from line 94 .... 8 96   128.

97 Tax due. If line 92 is less than line 64, subtract line 92 from line 64 .... # 97 _____

068   3103176   Form 540 2017 **Side 3**

FONTANA Page 17

Your name: ▮▮▮▮▮▮▮▮▮▮   Your SSN or ITIN: ▮▮▮▮▮▮▮

	Code	Amount
California Seniors Special Fund. See instructions	8 400	
Alzheimer's Disease/Related Disorders Fund	8 401	
Rare and Endangered Species Preservation Voluntary Tax Contribution Program	8 403	
California Breast Cancer Research Voluntary Tax Contribution Fund	8 405	
California Firefighters' Memorial Fund	8 406	
Emergency Food for Families Voluntary Tax Contribution Fund	8 407	
California Peace Officer Memorial Foundation Fund	8 408	
California Sea Otter Fund	8 410	
California Cancer Research Voluntary Tax Contribution Fund	8 413	
School Supplies for Homeless Children Fund	8 422	
State Parks Protection Fund/Parks Pass Purchase	8 423	
Protect Our Coast and Oceans Voluntary Tax Contribution Fund	8 424	
Keep Arts in Schools Voluntary Tax Contribution Fund	8 425	
State Children's Trust Fund for the Prevention of Child Abuse	8 430	
Prevention of Animal Homelessness and Cruelty Fund	8 431	
Revive the Salton Sea Fund	8 432	
California Domestic Violence Victims Fund	8 433	
Special Olympics Fund	8 434	
Type 1 Diabetes Research Fund	8 435	
California YMCA Youth and Government Voluntary Tax Contribution Fund	8 436	
Habitat for Humanity Voluntary Tax Contribution Fund	8 437	
California Senior Citizen Advocacy Voluntary Tax Contribution Fund	8 438	
Native California Wildlife Rehabilitation Voluntary Tax Contribution Fund	8 439	
Rape Backlog Kit Voluntary Tax Contribution Fund	8 440	
110 Add code 400 through code 440. This is your total contribution	8 110	

Your name: [REDACTED]   Your SSN or ITIN: [REDACTED]

Amount You Owe

111 **AMOUNT YOU OWE.** If you do not have an amount on line 96, add line 93, line 97, and line 110. See instructions. Do not send cash.
   Mail to: **FRANCHISE TAX BOARD**
      PO BOX 942867
      SACRAMENTO CA 94267-0001 .... ⑧ 111 _____
   Pay online -- Go to ftb.ca.gov/pay for more information.

Interest and Penalties

112 Interest, late return penalties, and late payment penalties .... 112 _____

113 Underpayment of estimated tax. Check the box: ⑧ ☐ FTB 5805 attached ⑧ ☐ FTB 5805F attached ⑧ 113 _____

114 Total amount due. See instructions. Enclose, but do not staple, any payment .... 114 _____

115 **REFUND OR NO AMOUNT DUE.** Subtract the sum of line 110, line 112 and line 113 from line 96. See instructions.
   Mail to: **FRANCHISE TAX BOARD**
      PO BOX 942840
      SACRAMENTO CA 94240-0001 .... ⑧ 115   128.

Refund and Direct Deposit

Fill in the information to authorize direct deposit of your refund into one or two accounts. Do not attach a voided check or a deposit slip. See instructions.

Have you verified the routing and account numbers? Use whole dollars only.

All or the following amount of my refund (line 115) is authorized for direct deposit into the account shown below:

⑧ Routing number ⑧ Type ☒ Checking ⑧ Account number   ⑧ 116 Direct deposit amount
[REDACTED]   ☐ Savings   [REDACTED]   128.

The remaining amount of my refund (line 115) is authorized for direct deposit into the account shown below:

⑧ Routing number ⑧ Type ☐ Checking ⑧ Account number   ⑧ 117 Direct deposit amount
                   ☐ Savings

IMPORTANT: See the instructions to find out if you should attach a copy of your complete federal tax return.

To learn about your privacy rights, how we may use your information, and the consequences for not providing the requested information, go to ftb.ca.gov/forms and search for 1131. To request this notice by mail, call 800.852.5711. Under penalties of perjury, I declare that I have examined this tax return, including accompanying schedules and statements, and to the best of my knowledge and belief, it is true, correct, and complete.

Your signature   Date   Spouse's/RDP's signature (if a joint tax return, both must sign)
X XXXXXXXXXXXXXXXXX   X XXXXXXXXXXXXXXX

✗ Your email address. Enter only one email address.   ✗ Preferred phone number
[REDACTED]   [REDACTED]

Sign Here

It is unlawful to forge a spouse's/RDP's signature.

Joint tax return? (See instructions)

Paid preparer's signature (declaration of preparer is based on all information of which preparer has any knowledge)
XXXXXXXXXXXXXXXX

Firm's name (or yours, if self-employed)   ⑧ PTIN
THOMAS SNIPP   [REDACTED]

Firm's address   ⑧ FEIN
8275 SIERRA AVE SUITE 105 FONTANA CA 92335   [REDACTED]

Do you want to allow another person to discuss this tax return with us? See instructions ...... ⑧ ☐ Yes ☒ No

Print Third Party Designee's Name   Telephone Number

068   3105176   Form 540 2017 Side 5

FONTANA Page 19

TAXABLE YEAR

2017 California Earned Income Tax Credit

FORM **3514**

Attach to your California Form 540, Form 540 2EZ or Long or Short Form 540NR

Name(s) as shown on tax return

SSN

▮▮▮▮▮▮▮▮▮

▮▮▮▮▮▮▮▮▮

Before you begin:

If you claim the EITC even though you know you are not eligible, you may not be allowed to take the credit for up to 10 years.

Follow Step 1 through Step 7 in the instructions to determine if you meet the requirements, to complete this form, and to figure the amount of the credit.

If you are claiming the California Earned Income Tax Credit (EITC), you must provide your date of birth (DOB), and spouse's/RDP's DOB if filing jointly, on your California Form 540, Form 540 2EZ, or Long or Short Form 540NR.

Part I   Qualifying Information   See the Specific Instructions.

1 a Has the Internal Revenue Service (IRS) previously disallowed your federal Earned Income Credit (EIC)? ..... ☐ Yes ☒ No

b Has the Franchise Tax Board (FTB) previously disallowed your California EITC? .... ☐ Yes ☒ No

2 Federal AGI (federal Form 1040, line 38; Form 1040A, line 22, or Form 1040EZ, line 4) .... < 2   6,347. 00

3 Federal EIC (federal Form 1040, line 66a; Form 1040A, line 42a; or Form 1040EZ, line 8a) .... < 3   484. 00

Part II   Investment Income Information

4 Investment Income. See instructions for Step 2 - Investment Income .... < 4   00

Part III   Qualifying Child Information

You must complete Part I and Part II before filling out Part III. If you are not claiming a qualifying child, skip Part III and go to Step 4 in the instructions.

Qualifying Child Information	Child 1	Child 2	Child 3
5 First name			
6 Last name			
7 SSN			
8 Date of birth (mm/dd/yyyy). If born after 1998 and the child is younger than you (or your spouse/RDP, if filing jointly), skip line 9a and line 9b; go to line 10			
9 a Was the child under age 24 at the end of 2017, a student, and younger than you (or your spouse/RDP, if filing jointly)? If yes, go to line 10. If no, go to line 9b. See instructions	☐ Yes ☐ No	☐ Yes ☐ No	☐ Yes ☐ No
b Was the child permanently and totally disabled during any part of 2017? If yes, go to line 10. If no, stop here. The child is not a qualifying child	☐ Yes ☐ No	☐ Yes ☐ No	☐ Yes ☐ No
10 Child's relationship to you. See instructions			
11 Number of days child lived with you in California during 2017. Do not enter more than 365 days. See instructions			

	Child 1	Child 2	Child 3
12 a Child's physical address during 2017 (number, street, and apt. no./ste. no.). See instructions	#	#	#
b City	#	#	#
c State	#	#	#
d ZIP code	#	#	#

Part IV California Earned Income

13 Wages, salaries, tips, and other employee compensation, subject to California withholding. See instructions ...	<13	5,134. 00
14 Prison inmate wages. See instructions	# 14	00
15 Pension or annuity from a nonqualified deferred compensation plan or a nongovernmental IRC Section 457 plan. See instructions	# 15	00
16 Subtract line 14 and line 15 from line 13	<16	5,134. 00
17 Nontaxable combat pay. See instructions	# 17	00
18 Business income or (loss). Enter amount from Worksheet 3, line 5. See instructions	# 18	00

a Business name	#
b Business address	#
City, state, and zip code	#
c Business license number	#
d SEIN	#
e Business code	#

19 California Earned Income. Add line 16, line 17, and line 18	<19	5,134. 00

Part V California Earned Income Tax Credit (Complete Step 6 in the instructions.)

20 California EITC. Enter amount from California Earned Income Tax Credit Worksheet, Part III, line 6. This amount should also be entered on Form 540, line 75; or Form 540 2EZ, Line 23	<20	90. 00

Part VI Nonresident or Part-Year Resident California Earned Income Tax Credit

21 CA Exemption Credit Percentage from Form 540NR (Long or Short), line 38	<21	
22 Nonresident or Part-Year Resident EITC. Multiply line 20 by line 21. This amount should also be entered on Form 540NR (Long or Short), line 85	<22	00

Side 2 FTB 3514 2017   068   8462174   2017 1037 PEI 7CA252

FONTANA Page 21

TAB 'T'

Respondent's Immunization Record

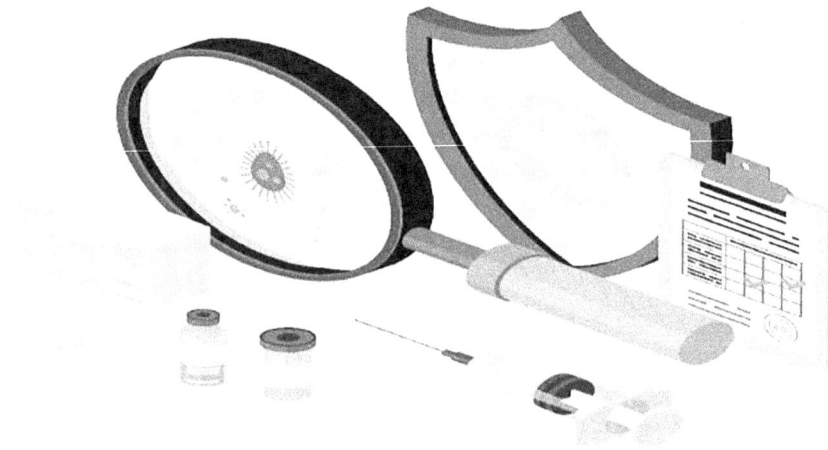

VACCINE	DATE GIVEN	DOCTOR OFFICE OR CLINIC	DATE NEXT DOSE DUE
Hep B 1 2 3	4/3/97		

TB SKIN TESTS Pruebas de la Tuberculosis	Type*	Date given		Date read	Read by	mm indur	Impression
	☒ PPD-Mantoux ☐ Other			9-17-96		00	☒ Pos ☐ Neg
	☒ PPD-Mantoux ☐ Other	9-12-96		9-16-96	CO		☒ Pos ☐ Neg
	☐ PPD-Mantoux ☐ Other	/ /		/ /			☐ Pos ☐ Neg

* If required for school entry, must be Mantoux unless exception granted by local health department.

CHEST X-RAY (Necessary if skin test positive.)	Film date: ___/___/___ Impression: ☐ normal ☐ abnormal Person is free of communicable tuberculosis: ☐ yes ☐ no
	Signature/Agency: _____

Parents: Your child must meet California's immunization requirements to be enrolled in school. Keep this Record as proof of immunization. Padres: Su niño debe cumplir con los requisitos de vacunas para ser admitido a la escuela. Mantega este Comprobante; lo necesitará.

IMMUNIZATION RECORD

Comprobante de Inmunizacion

Name
nombre

Birthdate
fecha de nacimiento   12.7.85

Allergies
alergias

Vaccine Reactions
reacciones a la vacuna

RETAIN THIS DOCUMENT — CONSERVE ESTA DOCUMENTO

TAB 'U'

Respondent's School/Education Awards and Certificates

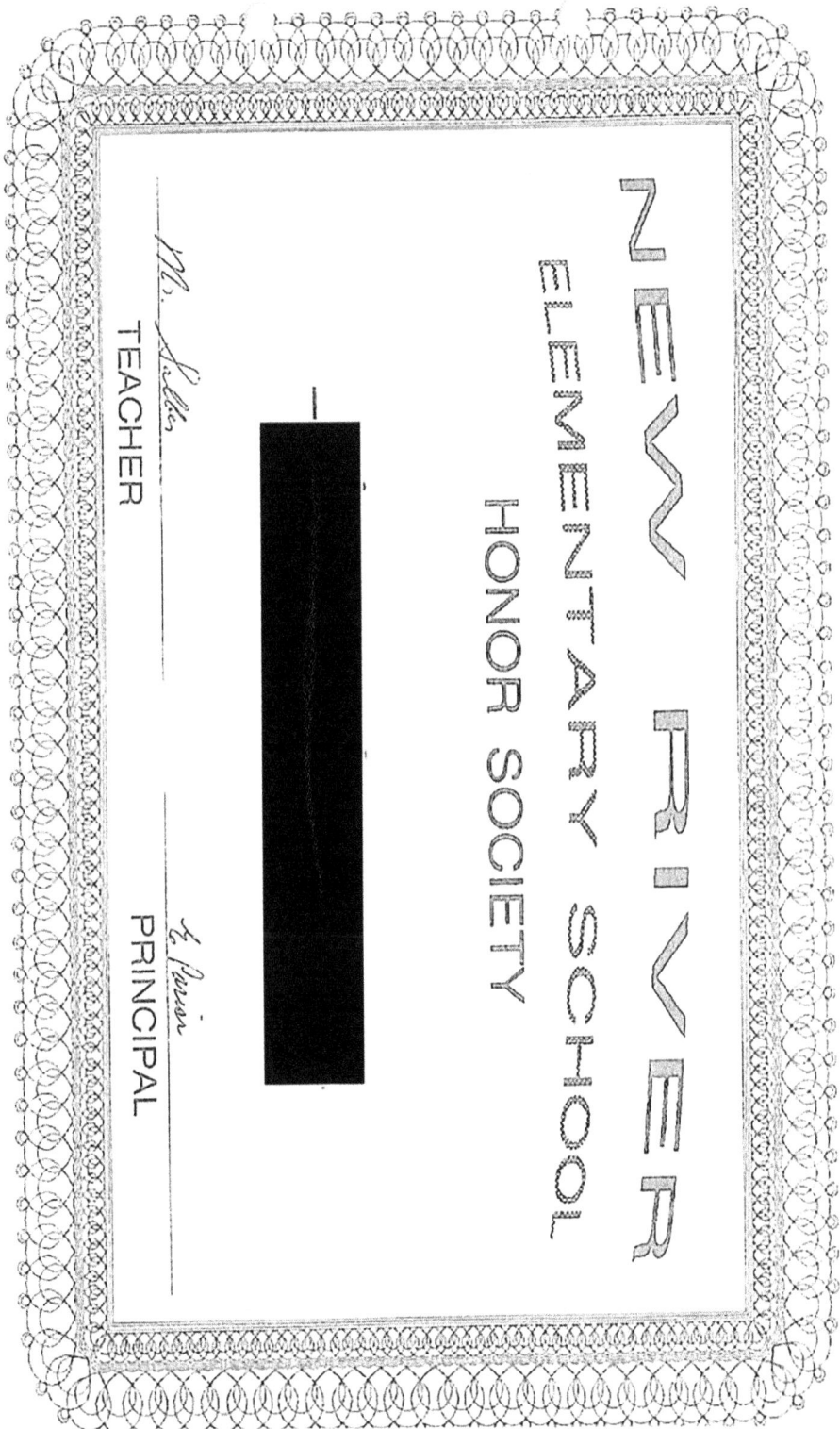

NEW RIVER

ELEMENTARY SCHOOL

HONOR SOCIETY

TEACHER

PRINCIPAL

STUDENT
OF THE
MONTH
IS
TO BELIEVE
"TO ACHIEVE"
NEW RIVER

...rivilege to select you as
THE MONTH. I encourage
...eep striving to be the best
...e. By doing so you are a
...o other students of what
excellence in education is

...naoshiro

TEACHER

Name

New River
School

May 26, 1995
Date

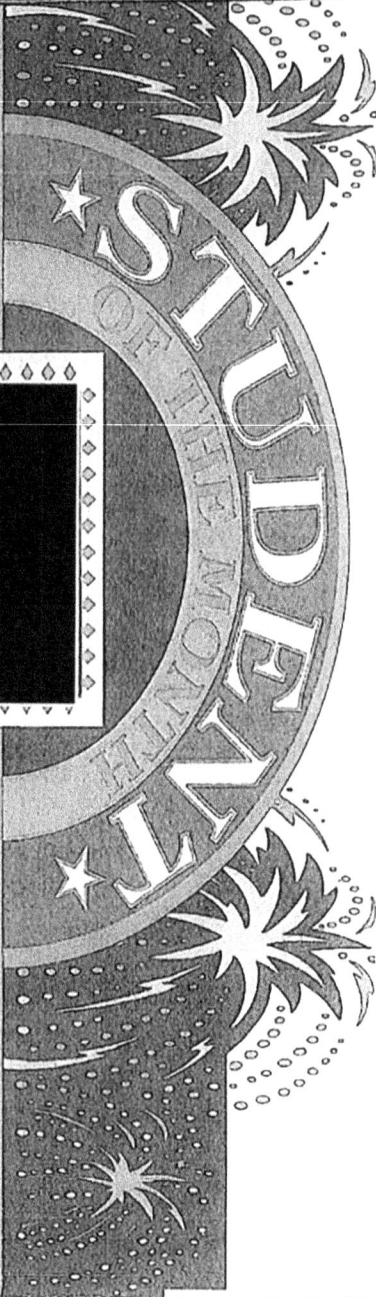

Congratulations for being selected
STUDENT OF THE MONTH. I understand
and appreciate all of the hard work it took
for you to achieve this honor. Your efforts
make our school and our world a better
place. Keep up the great work!

Lisa Moytirena-King
PRINCIPAL

PARTNERS IN
EDUCATION

Norwalk-La Mirada Unified School District

Alternative to Gangs Program

Achievement Award

Presented to _____ ▮▮▮▮▮▮▮▮▮▮

for taking the first step toward a successful life by not joining a gang.

Awarded this _28_ day of _May_ , 19 _96_

Ginger Shattuck
Superintendent

Patricie C. Cruz
President, Board of Education

David Plazo
Instructor

CERTIFICATE

CITIZENSHIP AWARD
SEPTEMBER 1996

Awarded to

In Acknowledgement of
Exceptional Efforts and Accomplishments
at New River School

_____
Principal

_____
Teacher

CERTIFICATE

HONOR SOCIETY
JUNE 1997

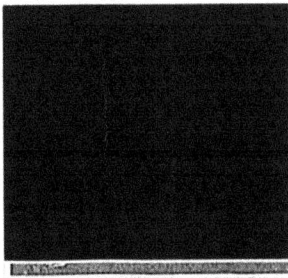

Awarded to

In Acknowledgement of
Exceptional Efforts and Accomplishments
at New River School

_____
Principal

_____
Teacher

Visual Artist Award

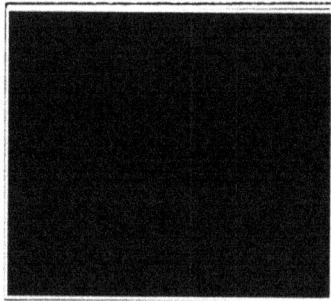

Awarded to

On this Eighteenth Day of December, 1997
In Acknowledgment for Outstanding Visual Arts
At Corvallis Middle School

Mrs. Michelle Mochen

Acunngham
Helene Cunningham, Principal

Mrs Bodas Hill
Teacher

Los Angeles County Sheriff's Department

Certificate
of
Completion

This certifies that

▮▮▮▮▮▮▮▮▮▮▮▮▮▮▮▮

has successfully completed a program in
Substance Abuse Narcotics Education
and is committed to a drug free life style

SANE

Mr. Salber

Teacher
Deputy Shepherd

Deputy
June 1997

Corvallis Middle School

Bulldog Football Team 1999

To be Acknowledged For Participation

Record 4-2

Coach Signature

Coach Signature

Principal Signature

Corvallis Middle School

Student of the Month

March

Trimester III
June 27, 2000

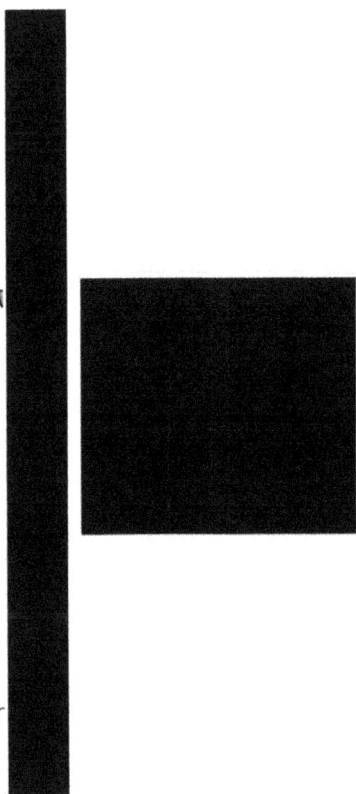

Teacher

CORVALLIS MIDDLE SCHOOL
PROMOTION CEREMONY

This Certificate of Achievement
is awarded to

For successfully meeting 8th grade standards of academic excellence.

Awarded on the 29th day of June in the year 2000

Principal

Norwalk High School

Athletic Award

Presented To

████████

In recognition of successful participation
in athletics and in the practice of
acceptable standards of scholarship & citizenship

Varsity Football

Sport

Harold Eggers
Coach

James Diaz
Director of Athletics

2001-2002
Date

Frank Zepeda
Principal

Norwalk High School

Athletic Award

Presented To

In recognition of successful participation
in athletics and in the practice of
acceptable standards of scholarship & citizenship

JV WRESTLING
Sport

2002-03
Year

Coach

Director of Athletics

Principal

VARSITY ATHLETIC AWARD

Norwalk High School

NHS
VARSITY AWARD

This is to certify that

has earned the Varsity Award
in the following sport

SPORT
FOOTBALL

YEAR
2003

PRINCIPAL

ATHLETIC DIRECTOR

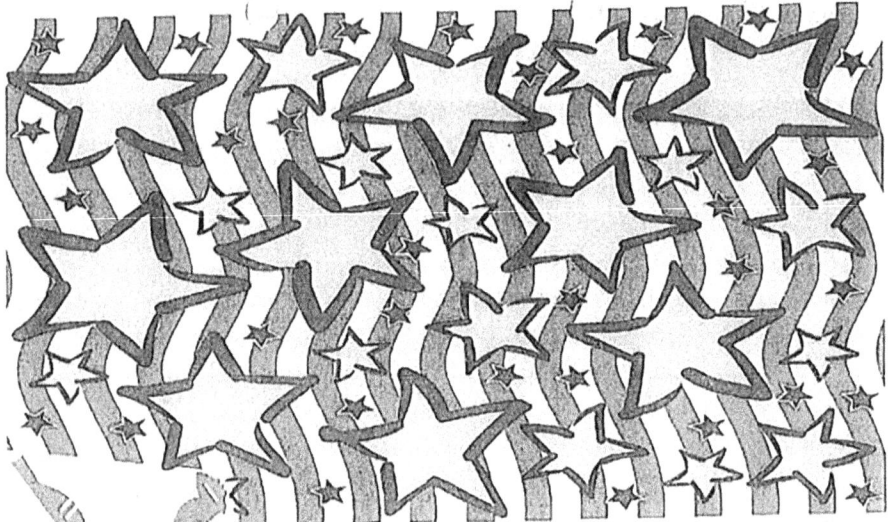

Norwalk-La Mirada Unified School District

Achievement in Excellence

Presented to

[REDACTED]

for excellence and outstanding
accomplishment

Awarded this 9th day of December, 2003

Stephen Hartick
Superintendent

Ernest Shryock
President, Board of Education

VARSITY ATHLETIC AWARD

Norwalk High School

NHS

VARSITY AWARD

This is to certify that

has earned the Varsity Award
in the following sport

SPORT: Wrestling

YEAR: 03-04

PRINCIPAL

ATHLETIC DIRECTOR

TAB 'V'

Criminal History Chart

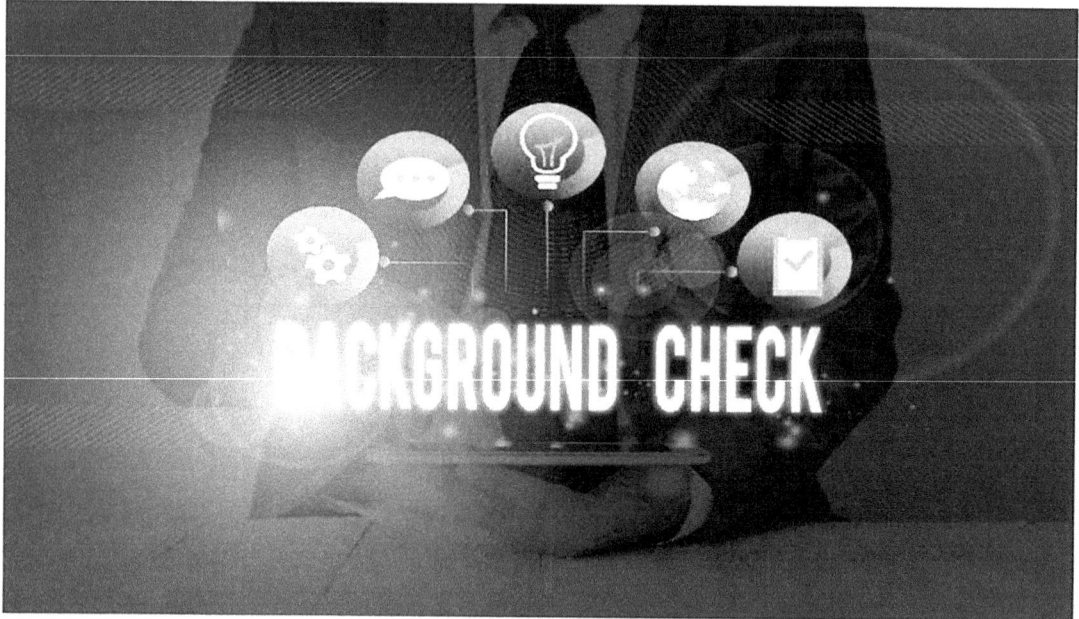

CRIMINAL HISTORY CHART

Date/Docket/Tab	Conviction	Sentence
02/21/2012 2JB01194 Tab L	VC 23152(b) – Misd DUI	3 Years Probation Fine

TAB 'W'

California Criminal History Information (CALDOJ)

State of California
DEPARTMENT OF JUSTICE

BUREAU OF CRIMINAL INFORMATION AND ANALYSIS
P.O. Box 903417
SACRAMENTO, CA 94203-4170

June 27, 2018

RE: California Criminal History Information

Dear Applicant:

This letter is in response to your record review request concerning the existence of information maintained in the California state summary criminal history files, as defined in subdivision (a) of Section 11105. Your fingerprints did identify to a record maintained in these files, and as such, a copy of that record is enclosed. If you wish to challenge the accuracy or completeness of your record, please complete and return the enclosed form (BCIA 8706) and supporting documentation to the address noted above.

Pursuant to California Penal Code section 11121, the purpose of a record review request is to afford an individual with a copy of their record and to refute any erroneous or inaccurate information contained therein. The intent is not to be used for licensing, certification or employment purposes.

Additionally, California Penal Code sections 11125, 11142, and 11143 does not allow for a person or agency to make a request to another person to provide them with a copy of an individual's criminal history or notification that a record does not exist; does not allow an authorized person to furnish the record to an unauthorized person; nor does it allow an unauthorized person to buy, receive or possess the record or information. A violation of these section codes is a misdemeanor.

Record Review and Challenge Program
Applicant Record and Certification Branch
Bureau of Criminal Information and Analysis

For XAVIER BECERRA
Attorney General

Enclosure(s)
BCIA 8711 (Rev. 02/17)

```
4CMTDP581124.IH
RE: QHY.CA0349400.32501955.AP  GR.      DATE:20180627 TIME:17   :04
RESTRICTED-DO NOT USE FOR EMF  .MENT,LICENSING OR CERTIFICATI(  PURPOSES
ATTN:APPUSR

** PALM PRINT ON FILE AT DOJ FOR ADDITIONAL INFORMATION PLEASE E-MAIL
PALM.PRINT@DOJ.CA.GOV
** III CALIFORNIA ONLY SOURCE RECORD
CII/A32501955
DOB/19851207    SEX/M RAC/HISPANIC
HGT/509 WGT/300  EYE/BRO  HAI/BLK  POB/BH
CTZ/BELIZE
██████████████████

FBI/418814ND3
SOC/620388827
OCC/PACKAGING
* * * *

ARR/DET/CITE:        NAM:001  DOB:19851207
20111227    CAPD GLENDORA

CNT:001      #2991752-33249569
  23152(A) VC-DUI ALCOHOL/DRUGS              TOC:M
   ARR BY:CAPD IRWINDALE

CNT:002
  23152(B) VC-DUI ALCOHOL/0.08 PERCENT       TOC:M

CNT:003
  12500(A) VC-DRIVE W/O LICENSE              TOC:M
   ADR:20111227 ██████████████████████      , )
   COM: PHOTO AVAILABLE
   SCN:L18E3610003
-- - - -
COURT:              NAM:001
20120221  CASC WEST COVINA

CNT:001      #CIT2JB0119401
  23152(A) VC-DUI ALCOHOL/DRUGS              TOC:M
DISPO:DISMISSED/FOJ/PLEA TO OTHER CHARGE

CNT:002
  12500(A) VC-DRIVE W/O LICENSE              TOC:M
DISPO:DISMISSED/FOJ/PLEA TO OTHER CHARGE

CNT:003
  23152(B) VC-DUI ALCOHOL/0.08 PERCENT       TOC:M
*DISPO:CONVICTED
  CONV STATUS:MISDEMEANOR
   SEN: 003 YEARS PROBATION, FINE, RESTN, WORK PROGRAM,
     IMP SEN SS

20120303
 DISPO:FOR CERT INFO SEE AUTOMATED ARCHIVE SYS
   COM: CONVICTION CERTIFIED BY JOHN A  CLARKE,EXECUTIVE
     OFFICER CLERK,CASCWEST COVINA
   DCN:P1000000651219000693

20160810
 DISPO:CONV SET ASIDE & DISM PER 1203.4 PC
    *    *    *    END OF MESSAGE    *    *    *
```

TAB 'X'

Letters of Support

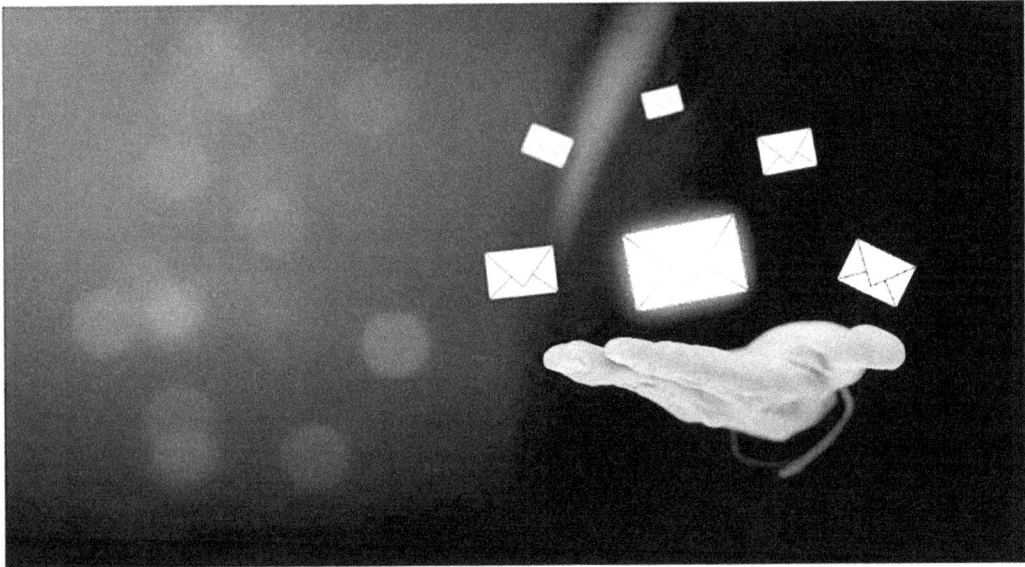

6/20/18

Dear Sir/Madam,

My name is ███████████████ I am the proud father of .████████████████████ I am currently employed with Boral Resources and have been for 5 years now. I became a United States Citizen in November 2016, before that I was a legal resident since 2003.

My son ████████████████; has been living in the United States since he was 4 years old. He has been and still is an exceptional person. He is the kindest, most loving and wonderful person any parent would want as a child. He has shown extreme patience over the years in trying to become a United States citizen, and I would be very appreciative if you can help my son achieve his dream of becoming a US citizen. The United States is the only place he knows and calls home.

████ is a hard working young man who is supporting his son Logan, who definitely needs his continued support both financially and emotionally, as he is still a young impressionable boy. Jeremy is a loving father, who adores Logan more than anything in this world. To separate a father and his son with this strong of a loving connection would devastate both him and his son. No one should ever have to separate from family, as family is the strongest bond anyone can have with another.

Sincerely,

Theodore Brown (signature)

████████████████

6/20/18

Dear Sir or Madam,

My name is ███████████ a born United States Citizen. I am writing on the behalf of ██████████, whom I have known for the past 6 years, in order to attest to his need for Citizenship in the United States.

I have been ██████ Step-mom and friend since 2013. I have met a lot of people, but none with the patience, kindness, determination, and loving spirit that Jeremy has and shows on a daily basis. In stressful situations, ██████ addresses it with a clear, open mind and graceful presence.

██████ immediate family members are all United States citizens. His son ██████ is ██████ world and to depart from that will devastate ███████████ ███████████ and ███████████ ██████ father and my husband) have both became U.S. Citizens. He also has two brothers and a sister with children who are all very close to him.

I know that ██████ is a hard working young man, and does and will continue to contribute to our wonderful country, given the opportunity.

With appreciation,

Jennifer Burrows

████████████

June 25, 2018

To Whom It May Concern:

I am writing this letter in regards to my younger brother, ████████████ My parents raised 4 children which consist of three boys and one girl. I was born in Belize and have been living in the United States for the past 28 years. I became a proud US citizen in 2016.

████ has always been the heart of our family. Although I love all my brothers dearly, I have always had a special connection to ████ because he has such a big and loving heart. He has always had a strong desire to help anyone in need. I can count on him for anything. There was a very difficult point in my life that if it wasn't for ████ I am not sure how I would have been able to be where I am today. In 2009, I was blessed and gave birth to two beautiful twin girls. When the girls were a year old I desperately needed to obtain a job working full time. I had anxiety wondering who I could trust to take care of my baby girls. Jeremy so kindly offered his help. I was able to go back to work full time while he cared for my babies. He took care of them for almost two years as if he was their father until they were able to attend Preschool. To this day my daughters, who are now 9 years old, are very much attached to Jeremy. They love their uncle very much and it brings me to tears to think of what would happen to not have such a strong male figure in their lives. Not only is he a wonderful uncle to my daughters he has another niece, two nephews and most importantly his son who all care for him dearly. All of the kids in my family light up when they see ████

I believe ████ would be a great addition to this country. He truly is the most helpful person I have ever met in my life. My parents are very hard working parents even up to this day. They raised a wonderful family and we are all supportive of each other. My father, mother, two other brothers and I are US citizens. ████ is that last person in our immediate family working on his immigration status. He was only 4 years old when he came to this country. He knows nothing else but the Unites States of America. I am proud to say ██████████ is honest, kind and the most loving person and I feel blessed to have him in my life. He is a great moral character to not only our family but to all the families he has come across.

Thank you for your consideration

Noelle Burrowes

June 1,2018

To Whom it may concern,

My name is ████████ and I am a US citizen. I am writing this letter regarding ████████████ ████████ and I have an eight-year-old son together, Logan Ramirez. To speak for my son, ████ <u>loves</u> his dad. I hate how I can't really express in a letter how happy and how loved my son is, by not just myself but by ████ as well. My son comes home from a weekend with his dad content and always excited to tell me about all the things they did with the time they spent together. ████ sees his dad as someone he wishes to be when he grows up. To ██ an our family and our situation is normal. He knows he has a mother who loves him and a father who loves him. He has never seen any negative from this situation. Last year my mother passed away, Logan and I were both dependent on her. As soon as ████ heard the news about my mom he showed me how caring he could be, not just towards ████ but to me as well. He showed me that him and I are family even though we are not in a typical family setting. He's been a lot more helpful with not just Logan but with me as well. I know that if I need help with anything such as moving. ████ will be there to help me. When my mother passed I was having a really hard time coping and I still do. Without ████████ would have been dealing with a mother who was sad. ████ took the time to make sure I was okay to ask how I was dealing with the loss of my mother, to ask if I needed help with anything and to take ████ for a day, a weekend, or a couple hours just so he wouldn't see his mom cry or sad. ████████████ happiness at a time of sadness. He made sure that our son was happy and that his sons mother was able to have the moments she needed to cope. I know that if ████ was not around ████ would be heart broken and how do you explain to an eight-year-old what this situation is. Life would be a lot more difficult for myself too, I need ████ here to help with our son. To help raise him, to help me when I need to take a moment for myself, to help financially, to help show my son how loved he is. A son needs his father, ████████████

Thank you

June 24, 2018

To Whom It May Concern:

████████████████

I am writing in support of ██████████████, and his application for California residency. I have known ████████████ for nearly 20 years. We were classmates from the time we were in middle school until high school graduation in 2004. We have remained fast friends and see one another frequently.

I can attest to ████████ character. When I first met ████████ I was the new kid in school being picked on. ████████ was respected throughout the campus and made sure that I was no longer bothered as a beginning middle school student. ████████ and I became good friends from that day on. We went on to play football and wrestle for the Junior Varsity and Varsity in high school.

████████ and I, along with others, were part of a group of volunteers that fed the homeless in Long Beach every Saturday for 3 years. ████████ is compassionate and sensitive to the needs of others less fortunate than he. This is only one example of his generosity and friendship.

████████ is a single father to his 9 year old son, Logan. He is involved in every aspect of his son's life. He currently lives with his mother and other family members and helps support the family. ████████████ is one of the best people I know.

I would not hesitate to support Mr. ████████████ petition to stay in the United States and would be only too glad to offer any additional information that you may require regarding Jeremey's character, work ethic, and family commitment.

Sincerely,

Jacob S. Fallert

████████████████████

June 15, 2018

To Whom It May Concern,

It is with great pleasure that I am able to provide this letter on behalf of one of my best friends, ███████████ My name is ███████████ and I reside at ███████████ San Diego, CA 92114. I was born in Long Beach California, and I was raised in Norwalk California where I first met █████. He has been my childhood friend since the sixth grade, and 21 years later I am proud to call █████ not only my friend but someone I consider a brother. He has always been there for the good times to make me laugh. He has always been the person I could depend on in hard times when I needed him the most. He has just always been there no matter what the situation. █████ deserves citizenship not only for being a good friend to me, but because he is a generally good person as a whole. ███████████ is someone I will standby not only because he is one of my best friends, but because he is the type of person you don't find every day, but wish you did.

Sincerely,

███████████

June 20, 2018

To Whom This May Concern,

My name is ████████ and I am proud to offer my recommendation of my good friend
████████ to whom I have personally known for 17 years. ████ is an amazing friend.
████ is someone that I have always been able to rely on no matter what. He is one of the
sweetest and most caring person I know. ████ is like a big brother to me, he helped me out in
so many ways as I was growing up. I was able to turn to him and he was always there, no matter
the time or the day. Jeremy would put me first as if I was his sister.

████ deserves citizenship as he is an amazing father, and caring person, and deserves to be
with his loving family.

My personal details are as follows:

Please feel free to contact me if you should require any further information.

Sincerely,

████████

6/24/2018

I have known ███████████ for over twenty years. We went to Corvallis Middle school and were friends from the moment we met. I have grown up with ██████ and watched him develop as a person. I don't know of a lot of people who work so hard to contribute to his family and society. It has been hard, with recent developments, not to worry about someone that I have spent such a considerable portion of my life, smiling and learning with.

███████ and I are a part of a good collection of local kids who grew up in Norwalk, California together. We played football, POGS, video games, talked about girls and in general lived as kids who weren't juvenile delinquents. From that young age, he displayed qualities that I didn't recognize are important in someone who represents and American. He would get mad when I made unfunny comments about his brothers or sisters, and would get mad at them if they did the same to me because family should respect each other. He has no aggressive bone in his body, instead separating fighters before kids would get in trouble, rather than being an instigator. I hope that his son picks up that quality, to run towards danger in an attempt to help and I see a man that wants to be near and nurturing as a father.

As long as I have known adult ██████ he has had a job and has given his income to his family to support them in the growing economic struggle that is Southern California. I haven't ever known him to be involved in any form of illicit activity. I truly believe you have a man that just wants to work, love his family, and be near his friends. I am glad that he has the opportunity that a lot of people don't have, to gather support from the people around him and prove that his presence in America has been uplifting.

To whom it may concern,

I, ████████████ a U.S. citizen and friend of ██████████████████ am writing this letter of recommendation.

I have known ██████ since we were 8 years old. We went to school together all the way through high school graduating in 2004. We also played 4 years of high school football together. ████████ is one of the few friends that I have managed to keep in touch with after high school. I consider his family my other family, so much so that I am often invited to family functions. ██████ is the kind of guy that would drop what he is doing if I were to need his assistance. He was kind enough to help my roommate and I move into our apartment and even gave us some furniture when we needed some. ██████ is a terrific father who loves and adores his son ██████ and he considers me to be his son's uncle a position I was honored with when we found out he was going to be a father. ██████ is an excellent human being that will contribute great things to society and I am lucky to be his friend for the last 24 years.

Sincerely,

████████████

Currently residing at:

████████████

TAB 'Y'

Photographs of Respondent and His Family

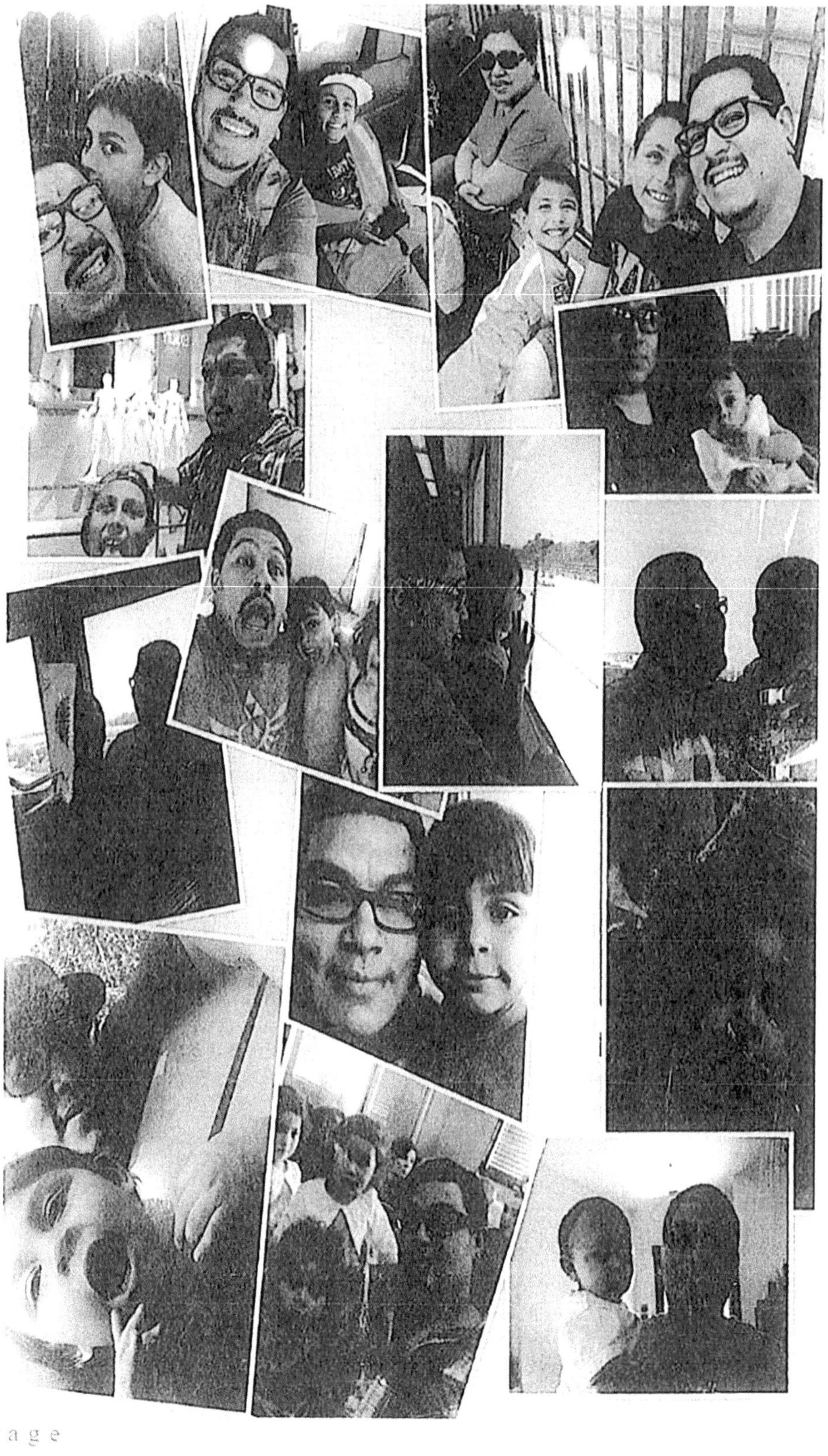

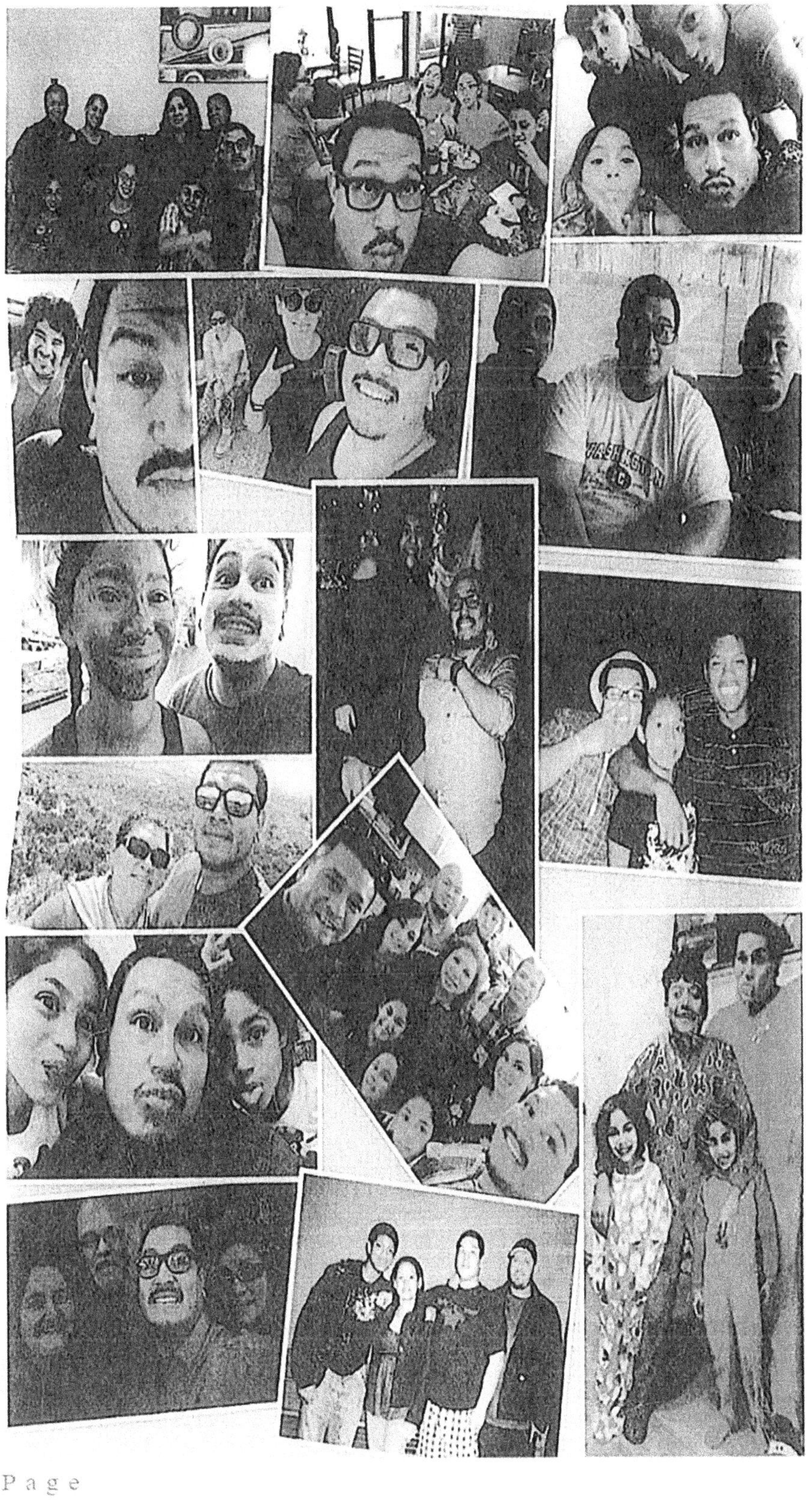

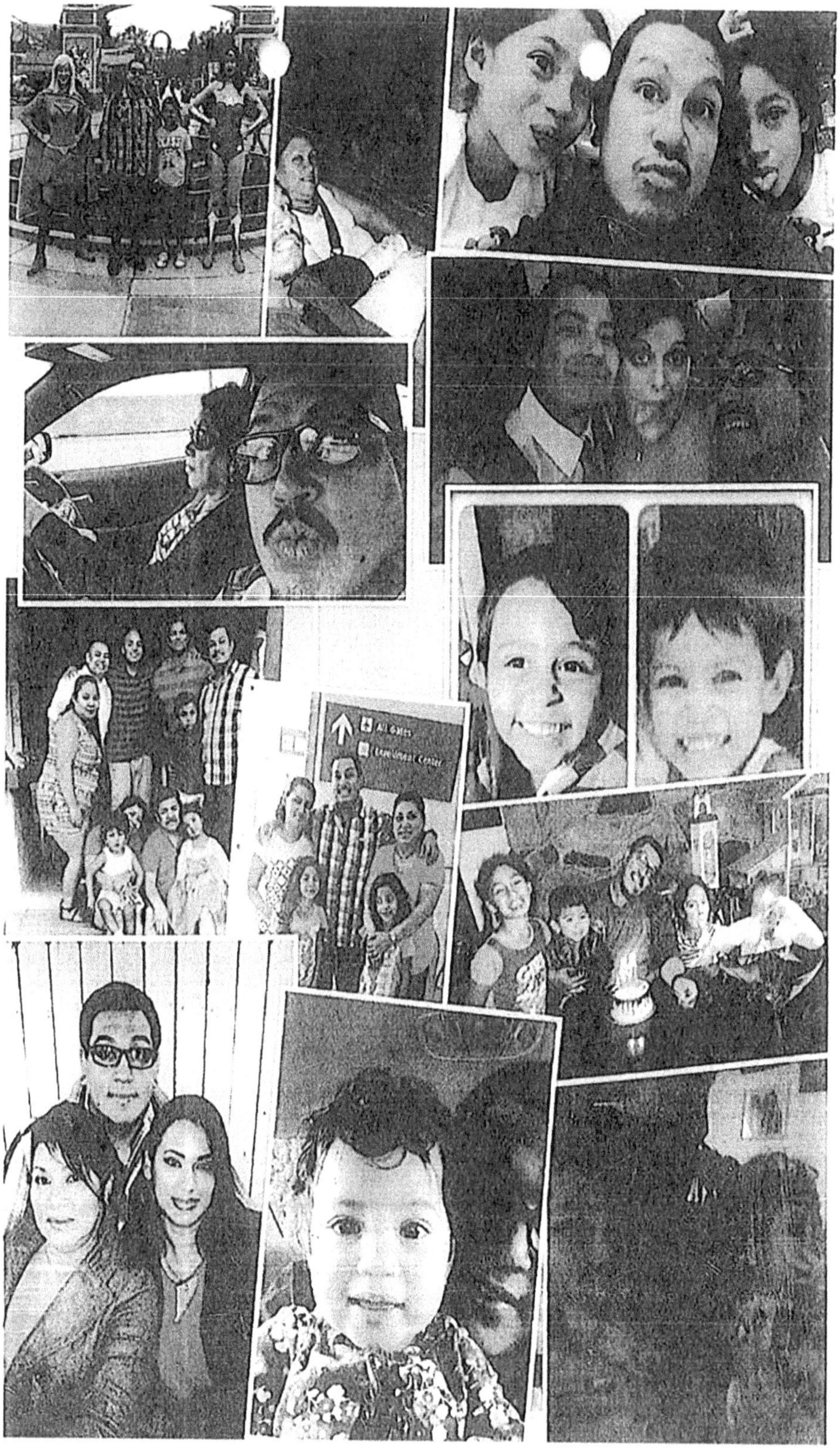

TAB 'Z'

Belize Profile – In Sight to Crime (11/10/2017)

Belize Profile

LAST UPDATE NOVEMBER 10, 2017

Belize

SHARE

🐦

f

in

G+

The small Central American nation of Belize has a remarkably high homicide rate. The main sources of violence in the country are domestic gangs that operate mainly in Belize City, engaging in local drug trafficking and robberies. However, as the country's role in the international drug trade has grown, Central American gangs and Mexican drug trafficking groups have also established a presence there.

Although the Belizean government has

noted that changes must be made to the country's security forces, most remain underfunded and officers are often poorly trained. Both the police force and justice system are widely regarded as corrupt and inefficient, and low levels of public confidence in these institutions mean that crimes often go unreported and perpetrators unpunished. While it is not overcrowded, according to the US State Department, Belize's only prison does not meet international standards.

- Geography
- History
- Criminal Groups
- Security Forces
- Judicial System
- Prisons

Geography

Belize, Central America's most sparsely populated country, shares borders with Mexico to the north and Guatemala to the south and west, while the eastern edge of the country consists of Caribbean coastline. This, combined with areas of heavy jungle, has rendered Belize an attractive destination for drug smugglers who use it as a gateway to Mexico.

Measuring roughly 23,000 square kilometers, Belize is approximately the size of New Jersey, although its many coastal and inland lagoons reduce its actual land area significantly. At the 2010 census, Belize's population stood at 324,528. Around one-quarter of the population lives in Belize City, the country's principal port and former capital. The nation's modern capital is Belmopan, the third largest settlement in the country and the smallest capital city in the Americas by population.

History

The former colony known as British Honduras changed its name to Belize in 1973, and gained full independence in 1981. Although crime rates in Belize are not as high as in Central America's "Northern Triangle" of El Salvador, Honduras and Guatemala, between 2000 and 2010 the homicide rate more than tripled, to 39 murders per 100,000 inhabitants. A rise in drug and arms seizures along the country's border with Mexico, and the Zetas' increasing presence in Belize saw the small nation added to the US watchlist of countries involved in the drug trade in 2011. The government of Belize and Belizean police have made several attempts to broker gang truces in the hope of reducing violence, but have so far had little success.

Criminal Groups

Belizean authorities have expressed concern in recent years that the violent Mexican drug gang, the Zetas, could be active along the border with Guatemala, another country where the group has a strong presence. Authorities have also noted that another Mexican criminal organization, the Sinaloa Cartel, has links to Belize. This was seemingly confirmed in August 2012 when the US Treasury Department placed sanctions on three alleged drug traffickers in Belize whom they believed to be "key associates" of the Sinaloa Cartel.

In addition to Mexican criminal groups, Central American gangs are involved in smuggling goods bought in the Corozal free trade zone to El Salvador, Guatemala, Mexico and Honduras, according to media reports. Officials from the National Gang Unit of US Immigration and Customs Enforcement (ICE) have confirmed this, pointing to reports of increasing numbers of MS13 members in the country.

Despite the presence of transnational criminal actors, the majority of violence in Belize is still driven by domestic gangs who engage in local drug trafficking and robberies, and violence is primarily concentrated in Belize City. Colonel George Lovell, the chief executive officer for the Ministry of National Security, stated in 2012 that 85 percent of all

139

hom' ·ides in Belize are a result of ~ng rivalries in Belize City, an area where 90 percent of all crimes in the country occur.

Belizean street gangs style themselves after the rival US street gangs the Bloods, and the Crips. Within these broad categories exist groups such as the George Street Bloods and the Brick City Bloods, and the Majestic-Alley Crips and Ghost Town Crips. These gangs are not as sophisticated as their Central American counterparts, and not considered to be well-organized.

Belize is a transit point for the regional arms trade, with traffickers exploiting weak border controls in the country to move weapons into neighboring Guatemala and Mexico, as well as Honduras. Experts have said that Belize may be a transshipment point for Mexico-bound weapons coming from the United States, due to the high concentration of law enforcement on the US/Mexico border.

The country is also known for providing opportunities for money laundering, in part because its currency is pegged to the US dollar.

Security Forces

The Belize Police Department (BPD), housed under the Ministry of National

Security, is the primary body charged with domestic law enforcement and has around 1,200 officers. The force has a reputation for being corrupt and inefficient. Low levels of confidence in the police mean that some crimes, particularly robberies and assault, often go unreported. Witness protection, or lack thereof, is a problem, with many scared to come forward for fear of reprisal.

The Belizean police force is under-resourced in areas, and poor training and limited oversight have fueled inefficiency and abuses. Low salaries for police officers make them susceptible to accepting bribes. According to the US State Department, the use of excessive force by security forces is a concern. The police force's Gang Suppression Unit (GSU) in particular has been involved in a number of incidents where suspects have been beaten with baseball bats, and/or shot at with rubber bullets.

In addition to managing the police, the National Security Ministry is responsible for the Belize Defense Force (BDF), which has a total of 1,029 personnel, split between ground and air forces. The BDF is primarily responsible for external security, although it does assist the BPD with domestic security on occasion, particularly in Belize City. However, it has limited powers in domestic law enforcement.

Beli. also has a Coast Guard, wh. . is separate from the BDF and works to counter maritime drug trafficking, among other responsibilities. The Coast Guard is under-resourced, with only six vessels at its disposal. Additionally, the country's Port Authority reportedly lacks the equipment to carry out nighttime searches, providing drug traffickers with an opportunity to move their product in the dark with little threat of being detected.

Judicial System

Due to Belize's colonial history, the country has an accusatory legal system based on British practice, with some variations. The judiciary is constitutionally independent and headed by the Supreme Court of Judicature, which is comprised of three Supreme Court judges and has unlimited jurisdiction over civil and criminal legal proceedings.

Below the Supreme Court are the Magistrates' Courts. Each of Belize's six districts has at least one Magistrate's Court, which can hand down rulings on less serious offenses. Appeals from both the Magistrates' Courts and the High Court are heard by the Court of Appeal. Final appellate jurisdiction rests with the

Caribbean Court of Justice (CCJ).

The attorney general acts as the government's legal advisor and is also part of the cabinet, and also serves as the foreign affairs minister. The principal prosecution authority is headed by the Director of Public Prosecutions (DPP). There is also an Ombudsman's Office which is an independent body and hears public complaints against the government for alleged injustices.

Belize's justice system suffers from inefficiency and corruption. Although the judicial branch is constitutionally independent from the executive and legislature, there are concerns surrounding political interference, according to the watchdog group Freedom House. Judges and lawyers are often poorly trained and there is a large case backlog with judges sometimes taking more than a year to hand down rulings. This backlog has helped to increase the number of pretrial detainees who, combined with prisoners on remand, accounted for around 30 percent of all inmates in 2012. Detainees sometimes spend years awaiting trial.

The 2011 Prosecutorial Reform Index (PRI) for Belize, carried out by the American Bar Association (ABA), found that the conviction rate for murder in

Beli: is 1 in every 10 cases. Furthe more, the DPP's office was found by the ABA to be lacking the resources required to effectively carry out its role.

Prisons

Belize's penitentiary system is overseen by the National Security Ministry. There is only one prison in the country, Belize Central Prison, which is managed by a local NGO, the Kolbe Foundation. Though overcrowding is not a problem — the prison was at approximately 67 percent capacity in 2012 — conditions in the prison do not meet international standards, according to the US State Department.

Moreover, according to the International Centre for Prison Studies, Belize has the world's 11th-highest prisoner-to-public ratio. International experts have also recommended that Belize use less punitive measures with regard to its youth detention practices.

What are your thoughts? Click here to send InSight Crime your comments.

top and bottom of the article. Check the Creative Commons website for more details of how to share our work, and please send us an email if you use an article.

SHARE 🐦 f in G+

The World Factbook: Belize (06/06/2018) - CIA

CENTRAL INTELLIGENCE AGENCY

(/)

Library

Library (/library)
Publications (/library/publications)
Center for the Study of Intelligence (/library/center-for-the-study-of-intelligence)
Freedom of Information Act Electronic Reading Room (/library/foia)
Kent Center Occasional Papers (/library/kent-center-occasional-papers)
Intelligence Literature (/library/intelligence-literature)
Reports (/library/reports)
Related Links (/library/related-links.html)
Video Center (/library/video-center)

THE WORLD FACTBOOK

Please select a country to view

Central America and Caribbean :: BELIZE

PAGE LAST UPDATED ON JUNE 06, 2018

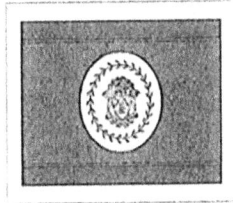

View **9 photos** of
BELIZE

147

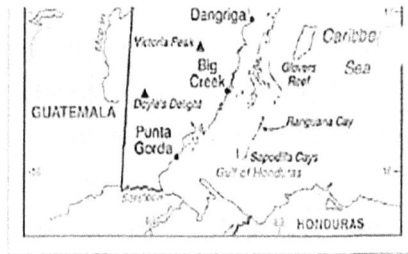

- Open All
- Close All

Introduction :: BELIZE

Background: (../docs/notesanddefs.html?fieldkey=2028&term=Background) (../fields/2028.html#bh)

Belize was the site of several Mayan city states until their decline at the end of the first millennium A.D. The British and Spanish disputed the region in the 17th and 18th centuries; it formally became the colony of British Honduras in 1862. Territorial disputes between the UK and Guatemala delayed the independence of Belize until 1981. Guatemala refused to recognize the new nation until 1992 and the two countries are involved in an ongoing border dispute. Tourism has become the mainstay of the economy. Current concerns include the country's heavy foreign debt burden, high unemployment, growing involvement in the Mexican and South American drug trade, high crime rates, and one of the highest HIV/AIDS prevalence rates in Central America.

Geography :: BELIZE

Location: (../docs/notesanddefs.html?fieldkey=2144&term=Location) (../fields/2144.html#bh)

Central America, bordering the Caribbean Sea, between Guatemala and Mexico

Geographic coordinates: (../docs/notesanddefs.html?fieldkey=2011&term=Geographic coordinates) (../fields/2011.html#bh)

17 15 N, 88 45 W

Map references: (../docs/notesanddefs.html?fieldkey=2145&term=Map references) (../fields/2145.html#bh)

Central America and the Caribbean

Area: (../docs/notesanddefs.html?fieldkey=2147&term=Area) (../fields/2147.html#bh)

total: 22,966 sq km

land: 22,806 sq km

water: 160 sq km

country comparison to the world: 152 (../rankorder/2147rank.html#bh)

Area - comparative: (../docs/notesanddefs.html?fieldkey=2023&term=Area - comparative) (../fields/2023.html#bh)

slightly smaller than Massachusetts

Land boundaries: (../docs/notesanddefs.html?fieldkey=2096&term=Land boundaries) (../fields/2096.html#bh)

total: 542 km

border countries (2): Guatemala 266 km, Mexico 276 km

Coastline: (../docs/notesanddefs.html?fieldkey=2060&term=Coastline) (../fields/2060.html#bh)

386 km

Maritime claims: (../docs/notesanddefs.html?fieldkey=2106&term=Maritime claims) (../fields/2106.html#bh)

territorial sea: 12 nm in the north, 3 nm in the south; note - from the mouth of the Sarstoon River to Ranguana Cay, Belize's territorial sea is 3 nm; according to Belize's Maritime Areas Act, 1992, the purpose of this limitation is to provide a framework for negotiating a definitive agreement on territorial differences with Guatemala

exclusive economic zone: 200 nm

Climate: (../docs/notesanddefs.html?fieldkey=2059&term=Climate) (../fields/2059.html#bh)

tropical; very hot and humid; rainy season (May to November); dry season (February to May)

Terrain: (../docs/notesanddefs.html?fieldkey=2125&term=Terrain) (../fields/2125.html#bh)

flat, swampy coastal plain; low mountains in south

Elevation: (../docs/notesanddefs.html?fieldkey=2020&term=Elevation) (../fields/2020.html#bh)

mean elevation: 173 m

elevation extremes: lowest point: Caribbean Sea 0 m

highest point: Doyle's Delight 1,124 m

Natural resources: (../docs/notesanddefs.html?fieldkey=2111&term=Natural resources) (../fields/2111.html#bh)

arable land potential, timber, fish, hydropower

Land use: (../docs/notesanddefs.html?fieldkey=2097&term=Land use) (../fields/2097.html#bh)

agricultural land: 6.9%

arable land 3.3%; permanent crops 1.4%; permanent pasture 2.2%

forest: 60.6%

other: 32.5% (2011 est.)

Irrigated land: (../docs/notesanddefs.html?f   :ey=2146&term=Irrigated land) (../fields/21   'ml#bh)

35 sq km (2012)

Population - distribution: (../docs/notesanddefs.html?fieldkey=2266&term=Population - distribution) (../fields/2266.html#bh)

approximately 25% to 30% of the population lives in the former capital, Belize City; over half of the overall population is rural; population density is slightly higher in the north and east

Natural hazards: (../docs/notesanddefs.html?fieldkey=2021&term=Natural hazards) (../fields/2021.html#bh)

frequent, devastating hurricanes (June to November) and coastal flooding (especially in south)

Environment - current issues: (../docs/notesanddefs.html?fieldkey=2032&term=Environment - current issues) (../fields/2032.html#bh)

deforestation; water pollution, including pollution of Belize's Barrier Reef System, from sewage, industrial effluents, agricultural runoff; inability to properly dispose of solid waste

Environment - international agreements: (../docs/notesanddefs.html?fieldkey=2033&term=Environment - international agreements) (../fields/2033.html#bh)

party to: Biodiversity, Climate Change, Climate Change-Kyoto Protocol, Desertification, Endangered Species, Hazardous Wastes, Law of the Sea, Ozone Layer Protection, Ship Pollution, Wetlands, Whaling

signed, but not ratified: none of the selected agreements

Geography - note: (../docs/notesanddefs.html?fieldkey=2113&term=Geography - note) (../fields/2113.html#bh)

only country in Central America without a coastline on the North Pacific Ocean

People and Society :: BELIZE

Population: (../docs/notesanddefs.html?fieldkey=2119&term=Population) (../fields/2119.html#bh)

360,346 (July 2017 est.)

country comparison to the world: 177 (../rankorder/2119rank.html#bh)

Nationality: (../docs/notesanddefs.html?fieldkey=2110&term=Nationality) (../fields/2110.html#bh)

noun: Belizean(s)

adjective: Belizean

Ethnic groups: (../docs/notesanddefs.html?fieldkey=2075&term=Ethnic groups) (../fields/2075.html#bh)

mestizo 52.9%, Creole 25.9%, Maya 11.3%, Garifuna 6.1%, East Indian 3.9%, Mennonite 3.6%, white 1.2%, Asian 1%, other 1.2%, unknown 0.3%

note: percentages add up to more than 100% because respondents were able to identify more than one ethnic origin (2010 est.)

Languages: (../docs/notesanddefs.html?fieldkey=2098&term=Languages) (../fields/2098.html#bh)

English 62.9% (official), Spanish 56.6%, Creole 44.6%, Maya 10.5%, German 3.2%, Garifuna 2.9%, other 1.8%, unknown 0.3%, none 0.2% (cannot speak)

note: shares sum to more than 100% because some respondents gave more than one answer on the census (2010 est.)

Religions: (../docs/notesanddefs.html?fieldkey=2122&term=Religions) (../fields/2122.html#bh)

Roman Catholic 40.1%, Protestant 31.5% (includes Pentecostal 8.4%, Seventh Day Adventist 5.4%, Anglican 4.7%, Mennonite 3.7%, Baptist 3.6%, Methodist 2.9%, Nazarene 2.8%), Jehovah's Witness 1.7%, other 10.5% (includes Baha'i, Buddhist, Hindu, Mormon, Muslim, Rastafarian, Salvation Army), unspecified 0.6%, none 15.5% (2010 est.)

Demographic profile: (../docs/notesanddefs.html?fieldkey=2257&term=Demographic profile) (../fields/2257.html#bh)

Migration continues to transform Belize's population. About 16% of Belizeans live abroad, while immigrants constitute approximately 15% of Belize's population. Belizeans seeking job and educational opportunities have preferred to emigrate to the United States rather than former colonizer Great Britain because of the United States' closer proximity and stronger trade ties with Belize. Belizeans also emigrate to Canada, Mexico, and English-speaking Caribbean countries. The emigration of a large share of Creoles (Afro-Belizeans) and the influx of Central American immigrants, mainly Guatemalans, Salvadorans, and Hondurans, has changed Belize's ethnic composition. Mestizos have become the largest ethnic group, and Belize now has more native Spanish speakers than English or Creole speakers, despite English being the official language. In addition, Central American immigrants are establishing new communities in rural areas, which contrasts with the urbanization trend seen in neighboring countries. Recently, Chinese, European, and North American immigrants have become more frequent.

Immigration accounts for an increasing share of Belize's population growth rate, which is steadily falling due to fertility decline. Belize's declining birth rate and its increased life expectancy are creating an aging population. As the elderly population grows and nuclear families replace extended households, Belize's government will be challenged to balance a rising demand for pensions, social services, and healthcare for its senior citizens with the need to reduce poverty and social inequality and to improve sanitation.

Age structure: (../docs/notesanddefs.html?fieldkey=2010&term=Age structure) (../fields/2010.html#bh)

0-14 years: 33.95% (male 62,454/female 59,896)

15-24 years: 20.55% (male 37,730/female 36,339)

25-54 years: 36.62% (male 66,880/female 65,082)

55-64 years: 4.99% (male 8,834/female 9,130)

65 years and over: 3.89% (male 6,562/female 7,439) (2017 est.)

population pyramid:

Dependency ratios: (../docs/notesanddefs.html?fieldkey=2261&term=Dependency ratios) (../fields/2261.html#bh)
total dependency ratio: 56.8
youth dependency ratio: 50.9
elderly dependency ratio: 5.9
potential support ratio: 17 (2015 est.)
Median age: (../docs/notesanddefs.html?fieldkey=2177&term=Median age) (../fields/2177.html#bh)
total: 22.7 years
male: 22.5 years
female: 22.9 years (2017 est.)
country comparison to the world: 176 (../rankorder/2177rank.html#bh)
Population growth rate: (../docs/notesanddefs.html?fieldkey=2002&term=Population growth rate) (../fields/2002.html#bh)
1.8% (2017 est.)
country comparison to the world: 58 (../rankorder/2002rank.html#bh)
Birth rate: (../docs/notesanddefs.html?fieldkey=2054&term=Birth rate) (../fields/2054.html#bh)
24 births/1,000 population (2017 est.)
country comparison to the world: 53 (../rankorder/2054rank.html#bh)
Death rate: (../docs/notesanddefs.html?fieldkey=2066&term=Death rate) (../fields/2066.html#bh)
6 deaths/1,000 population (2017 est.)
country comparison to the world: 164 (../rankorder/2066rank.html#bh)
Net migration rate: (../docs/notesanddefs.html?fieldkey=2112&term=Net migration rate) (../fields/2112.html#bh)
0 migrant(s)/1,000 population (2017 est.)
country comparison to the world: 73 (../rankorder/2112rank.html#bh)
Population distribution: (../docs/notesanddefs.html?fieldkey=2267&term=Population distribution) (../fields/2267.html#bh)
approximately 25% to 30% of the population lives in the former capital, Belize City; over half of the overall population is rural;
population density is slightly higher in the north and east
Urbanization: (../docs/notesanddefs.html?fieldkey=2212&term=Urbanization) (../fields/2212.html#bh)
urban population: 45.7% of total population (2018)
rate of urbanization: 2.32% annual rate of change (2015-20 est.)
Major urban areas - population: (../docs/notesanddefs.html?fieldkey=2219&term=Major urban areas - population)
(../fields/2219.html#bh)
BELMOPAN (capital) 23,000 (2018)
Sex ratio: (../docs/notesanddefs.html?fieldkey=2018&term=Sex ratio) (../fields/2018.html#bh)
at birth: 1.05 male(s)/female
0-14 years: 1.04 male(s)/female
15-24 years: 1.04 male(s)/female
25-54 years: 1.03 male(s)/female
55-64 years: 0.97 male(s)/female
65 years and over: 0.89 male(s)/female
total population: 1.03 male(s)/female (2017 est.)
Maternal mortality ratio: (../docs/notesanddefs.html?fieldkey=2223&term=Maternal mortality ratio) (../fields/2223.html#bh)
28 deaths/100,000 live births (2015 est.)
country comparison to the world: 116 (../rankorder/2223rank.html#bh)
Infant mortality rate: (../docs/notesanddefs.html?fieldkey=2091&term=Infant mortality rate) (../fields/2091.html#bh)
total: 18.9 deaths/1,000 live births
male: 21.3 deaths/1,000 live births
female: 16.4 deaths/1,000 live births (2017 est.)
country comparison to the world: 85 (../rankorder/2091rank.html#bh)
Life expectancy at birth: (../docs/notesanddefs.html?fieldkey=2102&term=Life expectancy at birth) (../fields/2102.html#bh)
total population: 68.9 years
male: 67.3 years
female: 70.6 years (2017 est.)
country comparison to the world: 163 (../rankorder/2102rank.html#bh)
Total fertility rate: (../docs/notesanddefs.html?fieldkey=2127&term=Total fertility rate) (../fields/2127.html#bh)
2.85 children born/woman (2017 est.)
country comparison to the world: 59 (../rankorder/2127rank.html#bh)
Contraceptive prevalence rate: (../docs/notesanddefs.html?fieldkey=2258&term=Contraceptive prevalence rate)
(../fields/2258.html#bh)
51.4% (2015)
Health expenditures: (../docs/notesanddefs.html?fieldkey=2225&term=Health expenditures) (../fields/2225.html#bh)
5.8% of GDP (2014)
country comparison to the world: 109 (../rankorder/2225rank.html#bh)

Physicians density: (../docs/notesanddefs.html?fieldkey=2226&term=Physicians density) (../fields/2226.html#bh)
0.77 physicians/1,000 population (2009)
Hospital bed density: (../docs/notesanddefs...ml?fieldkey=2227&term=Hospital bed density) (../fields/2227.html#bh)
1.3 beds/1,000 population (2014)
Drinking water source: (../docs/notesanddefs.html?fieldkey=2216&term=Drinking water source) (../fields/2216.html#bh)
improved:
urban: 98.9% of population
rural: 100% of population
total: 99.5% of population
unimproved:
urban: 1.1% of population
rural: 0% of population
total: 0.5% of population (2015 est.)
Sanitation facility access: (../docs/notesanddefs.html?fieldkey=2217&term=Sanitation facility access) (../fields/2217.html#bh)
improved:
urban: 93.5% of population
rural: 88.2% of population
total: 90.5% of population
unimproved:
urban: 6.5% of population
rural: 11.8% of population
total: 9.5% of population (2015 est.)
HIV/AIDS - adult prevalence rate: (../docs/notesanddefs.html?fieldkey=2155&term=HIV/AIDS - adult prevalence rate)
(../fields/2155.html#bh)
1.8% (2016 est.)
country comparison to the world: 27 (../rankorder/2155rank.html#bh)
HIV/AIDS - people living with HIV/AIDS: (../docs/notesanddefs.html?fieldkey=2156&term=HIV/AIDS - people living with HIV/AIDS)
(../fields/2156.html#bh)
4,300 (2016 est.)
country comparison to the world: 107 (../rankorder/2156rank.html#bh)
HIV/AIDS - deaths: (../docs/notesanddefs.html?fieldkey=2157&term=HIV/AIDS - deaths) (../fields/2157.html#bh)
<200 (2016 est.)
Major infectious diseases: (../docs/notesanddefs.html?fieldkey=2193&term=Major infectious diseases) (../fields/2193.html#bh)
degree of risk: high
food or waterborne diseases: bacterial diarrhea, hepatitis A, and typhoid fever
vectorborne diseases: dengue fever and malaria
note: active local transmission of Zika virus by Aedes species mosquitoes has been identified in this country (as of August 2016); it
poses an important risk (a large number of cases possible) among US citizens if bitten by an infective mosquito; other less common
ways to get Zika are through sex, via blood transfusion, or during pregnancy, in which the pregnant woman passes Zika virus to her
fetus (2016)
Obesity - adult prevalence rate: (../docs/notesanddefs.html?fieldkey=2228&term=Obesity - adult prevalence rate)
(../fields/2228.html#bh)
24.1% (2016)
country comparison to the world: 60 (../rankorder/2228rank.html#bh)
Children under the age of 5 years underweight: (../docs/notesanddefs.html?fieldkey=2224&term=Children under the age of 5 years
underweight) (../fields/2224.html#bh)
4.6% (2015)
country comparison to the world: 81 (../rankorder/2224rank.html#bh)
Education expenditures: (../docs/notesanddefs.html?fieldkey=2206&term=Education expenditures) (../fields/2206.html#bh)
7.4% of GDP (2017)
country comparison to the world: 29 (../rankorder/2206rank.html#bh)
School life expectancy (primary to tertiary education): (../docs/notesanddefs.html?fieldkey=2205&term=School life expectancy (primary
to tertiary education)) (../fields/2205.html#bh)
total: 13 years
male: 13 years
female: 13 years (2015)
Unemployment, youth ages 15-24: (../docs/notesanddefs.html?fieldkey=2229&term=Unemployment, youth ages 15-24)
(../fields/2229.html#bh)
total: 18.9%
male: 12.1%
female: 29.6% (2015 est.)

country comparison to the world: 69 (../rankorder/2229rank.html#bh)

Government :: BELIZE

Country name: (../docs/notesanddefs.html?fieldkey=2142&term=Country name) (../fields/2142.html#bh)

conventional long form: none

conventional short form: Belize

former: British Honduras

etymology: may be named for the Belize River, whose name possibly derives from the Maya word "belix," meaning "muddy-watered"

Government type: (../docs/notesanddefs.html?fieldkey=2128&term=Government type) (../fields/2128.html#bh)

parliamentary democracy (National Assembly) under a constitutional monarchy; a Commonwealth realm

Capital: (../docs/notesanddefs.html?fieldkey=2057&term=Capital) (../fields/2057.html#bh)

name: Belmopan

geographic coordinates: 17 15 N, 88 46 W

time difference: UTC-6 (1 hour behind Washington, DC, during Standard Time)

Administrative divisions: (../docs/notesanddefs.html?fieldkey=2051&term=Administrative divisions) (../fields/2051.html#bh)

6 districts; Belize, Cayo, Corozal, Orange Walk, Stann Creek, Toledo

Independence: (../docs/notesanddefs.html?fieldkey=2088&term=Independence) (../fields/2088.html#bh)

21 September 1981 (from the UK)

National holiday: (../docs/notesanddefs.html?fieldkey=2109&term=National holiday) (../fields/2109.html#bh)

Battle of St. George's Caye Day (National Day), 10 September (1798); Independence Day, 21 September (1981)

Constitution: (../docs/notesanddefs.html?fieldkey=2063&term=Constitution) (../fields/2063.html#bh)

previous 1954, 1963 (preindependence); latest signed and entered into force 21 September 1981; amended several times, last in 2012 (2016)

Legal system: (../docs/notesanddefs.html?fieldkey=2100&term=Legal system) (../fields/2100.html#bh)

English common law

international law organization participation: (../docs/notesanddefs.html?fieldkey=2220&term=International law organization participation) (../fields/2220.html#bh)

has not submitted an ICJ jurisdiction declaration; accepts ICCt jurisdiction

Citizenship: (../docs/notesanddefs.html?fieldkey=2263&term=Citizenship) (../fields/2263.html#bh)

citizenship by birth: yes

citizenship by descent: yes

dual citizenship recognized: yes

residency requirement for naturalization: 5 years

Suffrage: (../docs/notesanddefs.html?fieldkey=2123&term=Suffrage) (../fields/2123.html#bh)

18 years of age; universal

Executive branch: (../docs/notesanddefs.html?fieldkey=2077&term=Executive branch) (../fields/2077.html#bh)

chief of state: Queen ELIZABETH II (since 6 February 1952); represented by Governor General Sir Colville Norbert YOUNG, Sr. (since 17 November 1993)

head of government: Prime Minister Dean Oliver BARROW (since 8 February 2008); Deputy Prime Minister Patrick FABER (since 7 June 2016)

cabinet: Cabinet appointed by the governor general on the advice of the prime minister from among members of the National Assembly

elections/appointments: the monarchy is hereditary; governor general appointed by the monarch; following legislative elections, the leader of the majority party or majority coalition usually appointed prime minister by the governor general; prime minister recommends the deputy prime minister

Legislative branch: (../docs/notesanddefs.html?fieldkey=2101&term=Legislative branch) (../fields/2101.html#bh)

description: bicameral National Assembly consists of the Senate (12 seats; members appointed by the governor general - 6 on the advice of the prime minister, 3 on the advice of the leader of the opposition, and 1 each on the advice of the Belize Council of Churches and Evangelical Association of Churches, the Belize Chamber of Commerce and Industry and the Belize Better Business Bureau, and the National Trade Union Congress and the Civil Society Steering Committee; members serve 5-year terms) and the House of Representatives (31 seats; members directly elected in single-seat constituencies by simple majority vote to serve 5-year terms)

elections: House of Representatives - last held on 4 November 2015 (next to be held in November 2020)

election results: percent of vote by party - UDP 50%, PUP 47.3%, other 2.7%; seats by party - UDP 19, PUP 12

Judicial branch: (../docs/notesanddefs.html?fieldkey=2094&term=Judicial branch) (../fields/2094.html#bh)

highest court(s): Supreme Court of Judicature (consists of the Court of Appeal with the court president and 3 justices, and the Supreme Court with the chief justice and 2 judges); note - in 2010, Belize ceased final appeals in civil and criminal cases to the Judicial Committee of the Privy Council (in London) and acceded to the Caribbean Court of Justice

judge selection and term of office: Court of Appeal president and justices appointed by the governor general upon advice of the prime minister after consultation with the National Assembly opposition leader; justices' tenures vary by terms of appointment; Supreme Court chief justice appointed by the governor-general upon the advice of the prime minister and the National Assembly opposition leader; other judges appointed by the governor-general upon the advice of the Judicial and Legal Services Section of the Public Services Commission and with the concurrence of the prime minister after consultation with the National Assembly opposition leader; judges can be appointed beyond age 65 but must retire by age 75; in 2013, the Supreme Court chief justice overturned a constitutional amendment that had restricted Court of Appeal judge appointments to as short as 1 year

subordinate courts: Magistrate Courts; Fam' ourt

Political parties and leaders: (../docs/notesanddefs.html?fieldkey=2118&term=Political parties and leaders) (../fields/2118.html#bh)

Belize Progressive Party or BPP [Patrick ROGERS] (formed in 2015 from a merger of the People's National Party, elements of the Vision Inspired by the People, and other smaller political groups)

People's United Party or PUP [Johnny BRICENO]

United Democratic Party or UDP [Dean Oliver BARROW]

International organization participation: (../docs/notesanddefs.html?fieldkey=2107&term=International organization participation) (../fields/2107.html#bh)

ACP, AOSIS, C, Caricom, CD, CDB, CELAC, FAO, G-77, IADB, IAEA, IBRD, ICAO, ICC (NGOs), ICRM, IDA, IFAD, IFC, IFRCS, ILO, IMF, IMO, Interpol, IOC, IOM, ITU, LAES, MIGA, NAM, OAS, OPANAL, OPCW, PCA, Petrocaribe, SICA, UN, UNCTAD, UNESCO, UNIDO, UPU, WCO, WHO, WIPO, WMO, WTO

Diplomatic representation in the US: (../docs/notesanddefs.html?fieldkey=2149&term=Diplomatic representation in the US) (../fields/2149.html#bh)

chief of mission: Ambassador Francisco Daniel GUTIERREZ (since 21 July 2017)

chancery: 2535 Massachusetts Avenue NW, Washington, DC 20008

telephone: [1] (202) 332-9636

FAX: [1] (202) 332-6888

consulate(s) general: Los Angeles

Diplomatic representation from the US: (../docs/notesanddefs.html?fieldkey=2007&term=Diplomatic representation from the US) (../fields/2007.html#bh)

chief of mission: Ambassador (vacant); Charge d'Affaires Adrienne GALANEK (since 20 January 2017)

embassy: Floral Park Road, Belmopan City, Cayo District

mailing address: P.O. Box 497, Belmopan City, Cayo District, Belize

telephone: [011] (501) 822-4011

FAX: [011] (501) 822-4012

Flag description: (../docs/notesanddefs.html?fieldkey=2081&term=Flag description) (../fields/2081.html#bh)

royal blue with a narrow red stripe along the top and the bottom edges; centered is a large white disk bearing the coat of arms; the coat of arms features a shield flanked by two workers in front of a mahogany tree with the related motto SUB UMBRA FLOREO (I Flourish in the Shade) on a scroll at the bottom, all encircled by a green garland of 50 mahogany leaves; the colors are those of the two main political parties: blue for the PUP and red for the UDP, various elements of the coat of arms - the figures, the tools, the mahogany tree, and the garland of leaves - recall the logging industry that led to British settlement of Belize

note: Belize's flag is the only national flag that depicts human beings; two British overseas territories, Montserrat and the British Virgin Islands, also depict humans

National symbol(s): (../docs/notesanddefs.html?fieldkey=2230&term=National symbol(s)) (../fields/2230.html#bh)

Baird's tapir (a large, browsing, forest-dwelling mammal), keel-billed toucan, Black Orchid; national colors: red, blue

National anthem: (../docs/notesanddefs.html?fieldkey=2218&term=National anthem) (../fields/2218.html#bh)

name: "Land of the Free"

lyrics/music: Samuel Alfred HAYNES/Selwyn Walford YOUNG

note: adopted 1981; as a Commonwealth country, in addition to the national anthem, "God Save the Queen" serves as the royal anthem (see United Kingdom)

Economy :: BELIZE

Economy - overview: (../docs/notesanddefs.html?fieldkey=2116&term=Economy - overview) (../fields/2116.html#bh)

Tourism is the number one foreign exchange earner in this small economy, followed by exports of sugar, bananas, citrus, marine products, and crude oil.

The government's expansionary monetary and fiscal policies, initiated in September 1998, led to GDP growth averaging nearly 4% in 1999-2007, but GPD growth has averaged only 2.1% from 2007-2016, with 2.5% growth estimated for 2017. Belize's dependence on energy imports makes it susceptible to energy price shocks.

Although Belize has the third highest per capita income in Central America, the average income figure masks a huge income disparity between rich and poor, and a key government objective remains reducing poverty and inequality with the help of international donors. High unemployment, a growing trade deficit and heavy foreign debt burden continue to be major concerns. Belize faces continued pressure from rising sovereign debt, and a growing trade imbalance.

GDP (purchasing power parity): (../docs/notesanddefs.html?fieldkey=2001&term=GDP (purchasing power parity)) (../fields/2001.html#bh)

$3.23 billion (2017 est.)

$3.151 billion (2016 est.)

$3.176 billion (2015 est.)

note: data are in 2017 dollars

country comparison to the world: 187 (../ran`   er/2001rank.html#bh)

GDP (official exchange rate): (../docs/notesanddefs.html?fieldkey=2195&term=GDP (official exchange rate)) (../fields/2195.html#bh)

$1.819 billion (2017 est.)

GDP - real growth rate: (../docs/notesanddefs.html?fieldkey=2003&term=GDP - real growth rate) (../fields/2003.html#bh)

2.5% (2017 est.)

-0.8% (2016 est.)

2.9% (2015 est.)

country comparison to the world: 128 (../rankorder/2003rank.html#bh)

GDP - per capita (PPP): (../docs/notesanddefs.html?fieldkey=2004&term=GDP - per capita (PPP)) (../fields/2004.html#bh)

$8,300 (2017 est.)

$8,400 (2016 est.)

$8,700 (2015 est.)

note: data are in 2017 dollars

country comparison to the world: 150 (../rankorder/2004rank.html#bh)

Gross national saving: (../docs/notesanddefs.html?fieldkey=2260&term=Gross national saving) (../fields/2260.html#bh)

11% of GDP (2017 est.)

11.3% of GDP (2016 est.)

12.1% of GDP (2015 est.)

country comparison to the world: 152 (../rankorder/2260rank.html#bh)

GDP - composition, by end use: (../docs/notesanddefs.html?fieldkey=2259&term=GDP - composition, by end use) (../fields/2259.html#bh)

household consumption: 75.6%

government consumption: 14.1%

investment in fixed capital: 23%

investment in inventories: 1%

exports of goods and services: 57.8%

imports of goods and services: -71.5% (2017 est.)

GDP - composition, by sector of origin: (../docs/notesanddefs.html?fieldkey=2012&term=GDP - composition, by sector of origin) (../fields/2012.html#bh)

agriculture: 9.7%

industry: 13.8%

services: 62.2% (2017 est.)

Agriculture - products: (../docs/notesanddefs.html?fieldkey=2052&term=Agriculture - products) (../fields/2052.html#bh)

bananas, cacao, citrus, sugar; fish, cultured shrimp; lumber

Industries: (../docs/notesanddefs.html?fieldkey=2090&term=Industries) (../fields/2090.html#bh)

garment production, food processing, tourism, construction, oil

Industrial production growth rate: (../docs/notesanddefs.html?fieldkey=2089&term=Industrial production growth rate) (../fields/2089.html#bh)

-2% (2017 est.)

country comparison to the world: 194 (../rankorder/2089rank.html#bh)

Labor force: (../docs/notesanddefs.html?fieldkey=2095&term=Labor force) (../fields/2095.html#bh)

120,500

note: shortage of skilled labor and all types of technical personnel (2008 est.)

country comparison to the world: 181 (../rankorder/2095rank.html#bh)

Labor force - by occupation: (../docs/notesanddefs.html?fieldkey=2048&term=Labor force - by occupation) (../fields/2048.html#bh)

agriculture: 10.2%

industry: 18.1%

services: 71.7% (2007 est.)

Unemployment rate: (../docs/notesanddefs.html?fieldkey=2129&term=Unemployment rate) (../fields/2129.html#bh)

10.1% (2017 est.)

11.1% (2016 est.)

country comparison to the world: 141 (../rankorder/2129rank.html#bh)

Population below poverty line: (../docs/notesanddefs.html?fieldkey=2046&term=Population below poverty line) (../fields/2046.html#bh)

41% (2013 est.)

Household income or consumption by percentage share: (../docs/notesanddefs.html?fieldkey=2047&term=Household income or consumption by percentage share) (../fields/2047.html#bh)

lowest 10%: NA%

highest 10%: NA%

Budget: (../docs/notesanddefs.html?fieldkey=2056&term=Budget) (../fields/2056.html#bh)

revenues: $500 million

expenditures: $550 million (2017 est.)

Taxes and other revenues: (../docs/notesanddefs.html?fieldkey=2221&term=Taxes and other revenues) (../fields/2221.html#bh)

27.5% of GDP (2017 est.)

country comparison to the world: 102 (../rankorder/2221rank.html#bh)

Budget surplus (+) or deficit (-): (../docs/notesanddefs.html?fieldkey=2222&term=Budget surplus (+) or deficit (-))
(../fields/2222.html#bh)

-2.7% of GDP (2017 est.)

country comparison to the world: 105 (../rankorder/2222rank.html#bh)

Public debt: (../docs/notesanddefs.html?fieldkey=2186&term=Public debt) (../fields/2186.html#bh)

88.5% of GDP (2017 est.)

91.4% of GDP (2016 est.)

country comparison to the world: 28 (../rankorder/2186rank.html#bh)

Fiscal year: (../docs/notesanddefs.html?fieldkey=2080&term=Fiscal year) (../fields/2080.html#bh)

1 April - 31 March

Inflation rate (consumer prices): (../docs/notesanddefs.html?fieldkey=2092&term=Inflation rate (consumer prices))
(../fields/2092.html#bh)

1.8% (2017 est.)

0.6% (2016 est.)

country comparison to the world: 79 (../rankorder/2092rank.html#bh)

Central bank discount rate: (../docs/notesanddefs.html?fieldkey=2207&term=Central bank discount rate) (../fields/2207.html#bh)

9.86% (1 November 2017 est.)

10.01% (1 November 2016 est.)

country comparison to the world: 24 (../rankorder/2207rank.html#bh)

Commercial bank prime lending rate: (../docs/notesanddefs.html?fieldkey=2208&term=Commercial bank prime lending rate)
(../fields/2208.html#bh)

9.6% (31 December 2017 est.)

9.84% (31 December 2016 est.)

country comparison to the world: 88 (../rankorder/2208rank.html#bh)

Stock of narrow money: (../docs/notesanddefs.html?fieldkey=2214&term=Stock of narrow money) (../fields/2214.html#bh)

$737.5 million (31 December 2017 est.)

$735.9 million (31 December 2016 est.)

country comparison to the world: 162 (../rankorder/2214rank.html#bh)

Stock of broad money: (../docs/notesanddefs.html?fieldkey=2215&term=Stock of broad money) (../fields/2215.html#bh)

$1.311 billion (31 December 2017 est.)

$1.475 billion (31 December 2016 est.)

country comparison to the world: 168 (../rankorder/2215rank.html#bh)

Stock of domestic credit: (../docs/notesanddefs.html?fieldkey=2211&term=Stock of domestic credit) (../fields/2211.html#bh)

$1.1 billion (31 December 2017 est.)

$1.278 billion (31 December 2016 est.)

country comparison to the world: 166 (../rankorder/2211rank.html#bh)

Market value of publicly traded shares: (../docs/notesanddefs.html?fieldkey=2200&term=Market value of publicly traded shares)
(../fields/2200.html#bh)

$NA

Current account balance: (../docs/notesanddefs.html?fieldkey=2187&term=Current account balance) (../fields/2187.html#bh)

$-145 million (2017 est.)

$-163 million (2016 est.)

country comparison to the world: 85 (../rankorder/2187rank.html#bh)

Exports: (../docs/notesanddefs.html?fieldkey=2078&term=Exports) (../fields/2078.html#bh)

$483.4 million (2017 est.)

$442.7 million (2016 est.)

country comparison to the world: 175 (../rankorder/2078rank.html#bh)

Exports - commodities: (../docs/notesanddefs.html?fieldkey=2049&term=Exports - commodities) (../fields/2049.html#bh)

sugar, bananas, citrus, clothing, fish products, molasses, wood, crude oil

Exports - partners: (../docs/notesanddefs.html?fieldkey=2050&term=Exports - partners) (../fields/2050.html#bh)

Burma 30.7%, US 22.6%, UK 19.3% (2016)

Imports: (../docs/notesanddefs.html?fieldkey=2087&term=Imports) (../fields/2087.html#bh)

$944.4 million (2017 est.)

$916.2 million (2016 est.)

country comparison to the world: 182 (../rankorder/2087rank.html#bh)

Imports - commodities: (../docs/notesanddefs.html?fieldkey=2058&term=Imports - commodities) (../fields/2058.html#bh)
machinery and transport equipment, manufa   ed goods; fuels, chemicals, pharmaceutica   ood, beverages, tobacco
Imports - partners: (../docs/notesanddefs.htm /fieldkey=2061&term=Imports - partners) (../fields/2061.html#bh)
US 37.2%, China 11.6%, Mexico 10.8%, Guatemala 7% (2016)

Reserves of foreign exchange and gold: (../docs/notesanddefs.html?fieldkey=2188&term=Reserves of foreign exchange and gold)
(../fields/2188.html#bh)
$368.3 million (31 December 2017 est.)
$376.7 million (31 December 2016 est.)
country comparison to the world: 153 (../rankorder/2188rank.html#bh)

Debt - external: (../docs/notesanddefs.html?fieldkey=2079&term=Debt - external) (../fields/2079.html#bh)
$1.326 billion (31 December 2017 est.)
$1.338 billion (31 December 2016 est.)
country comparison to the world: 162 (../rankorder/2079rank.html#bh)

Exchange rates: (../docs/notesanddefs.html?fieldkey=2076&term=Exchange rates) (../fields/2076.html#bh)
Belizean dollars (BZD) per US dollar -
2 (2017 est.)
2 (2016 est.)
2 (2015 est.)
2 (2014 est.)
2 (2013 est.)

Energy :: BELIZE

Electricity access: (../docs/notesanddefs.html?fieldkey=2268&term=Electricity access) (../fields/2268.html#bh)
electrification - total population: 100% (2016)

Electricity - production: (../docs/notesanddefs.html?fieldkey=2232&term=Electricity - production) (../fields/2232.html#bh)
248 million kWh (2015 est.)
country comparison to the world: 183 (../rankorder/2232rank.html#bh)

Electricity - consumption: (../docs/notesanddefs.html?fieldkey=2233&term=Electricity - consumption) (../fields/2233.html#bh)
413 million kWh (2015 est.)
country comparison to the world: 173 (../rankorder/2233rank.html#bh)

Electricity - exports: (../docs/notesanddefs.html?fieldkey=2234&term=Electricity - exports) (../fields/2234.html#bh)
0 kWh (2016 est.)
country comparison to the world: 108 (../rankorder/2234rank.html#bh)

Electricity - imports: (../docs/notesanddefs.html?fieldkey=2235&term=Electricity - imports) (../fields/2235.html#bh)
230 million kWh (2015 est.)
country comparison to the world: 90 (../rankorder/2235rank.html#bh)

Electricity - installed generating capacity: (../docs/notesanddefs.html?fieldkey=2236&term=Electricity - installed generating capacity)
(../fields/2236.html#bh)
191,000 kW (2015 est.)
country comparison to the world: 164 (../rankorder/2236rank.html#bh)

Electricity - from fossil fuels: (../docs/notesanddefs.html?fieldkey=2237&term=Electricity - from fossil fuels) (../fields/2237.html#bh)
52.4% of total installed capacity (2015 est.)
country comparison to the world: 147 (../rankorder/2237rank.html#bh)

Electricity - from nuclear fuels: (/docs/notesanddefs.html?fieldkey=2239&term=Electricity - from nuclear fuels)
(../fields/2239.html#bh)
0% of total installed capacity (2015 est.)
country comparison to the world: 51 (../rankorder/2239rank.html#bh)

Electricity - from hydroelectric plants: (../docs/notesanddefs.html?fieldkey=2238&term=Electricity - from hydroelectric plants)
(../fields/2238.html#bh)
28.3% of total installed capacity (2015 est.)
country comparison to the world: 74 (../rankorder/2238rank.html#bh)

Electricity - from other renewable sources: (../docs/notesanddefs.html?fieldkey=2240&term=Electricity - from other renewable sources)
(../fields/2240.html#bh)
19.4% of total installed capacity (2015 est.)
country comparison to the world: 32 (../rankorder/2240rank.html#bh)

Crude oil - production: (../docs/notesanddefs.html?fieldkey=2241&term=Crude oil - production) (../fields/2241.html#bh)
2,000 bbl/day (2016 est.)
country comparison to the world: 90 (../rankorder/2241rank.html#bh)

Crude oil - exports: (../docs/notesanddefs.html?fieldkey=2242&term=Crude oil - exports) (../fields/2242.html#bh)
3,000 bbl/day (2014 est.)
country comparison to the world: 66 (../rankorder/2242rank.html#bh)

Crude oil - imports: (../docs/notesanddefs.html?fieldkey=2243&term=Crude oil - imports) (../fields/2243.html#bh)

0 bbl/day (2014 est.)
country comparison to the world: 99 (../rank   r/2243rank.html#bh)
  Crude oil - proved reserves: (../docs/notesanddefs.html?fieldkey=2244&term=Crude oil - proved reserves) (../fields/2244.html#bh)
6.7 million bbl (1 January 2017 est.)
country comparison to the world: 96 (../rankorder/2244rank.html#bh)
  Refined petroleum products - production: (../docs/notesanddefs.html?fieldkey=2245&term=Refined petroleum products - production)
  (../fields/2245.html#bh)
33.05 bbl/day (2014 est.)
country comparison to the world: 110 (../rankorder/2245rank.html#bh)
  Refined petroleum products - consumption: (../docs/notesanddefs.html?fieldkey=2246&term=Refined petroleum products -
  consumption) (../fields/2246.html#bh)
3,700 bbl/day (2015 est.)
country comparison to the world: 181 (../rankorder/2246rank.html#bh)
  Refined petroleum products - exports: (../docs/notesanddefs.html?fieldkey=2247&term=Refined petroleum products - exports)
  (../fields/2247.html#bh)
0 bbl/day (2014 est.)
country comparison to the world: 134 (../rankorder/2247rank.html#bh)
  Refined petroleum products - imports: (../docs/notesanddefs.html?fieldkey=2248&term=Refined petroleum products - imports)
  (../fields/2248.html#bh)
3,638 bbl/day (2014 est.)
country comparison to the world: 172 (../rankorder/2248rank.html#bh)
  Natural gas - production: (../docs/notesanddefs.html?fieldkey=2249&term=Natural gas - production) (../fields/2249.html#bh)
0 cu m (2013 est.)
country comparison to the world: 110 (../rankorder/2249rank.html#bh)
  Natural gas - consumption: (../docs/notesanddefs.html?fieldkey=2250&term=Natural gas - consumption) (../fields/2250.html#bh)
0 cu m (2013 est.)
country comparison to the world: 159 (../rankorder/2250rank.html#bh)
  Natural gas - exports: (../docs/notesanddefs.html?fieldkey=2251&term=Natural gas - exports) (../fields/2251.html#bh)
0 cu m (2013 est.)
country comparison to the world: 70 (../rankorder/2251rank.html#bh)
  Natural gas - imports: (../docs/notesanddefs.html?fieldkey=2252&term=Natural gas - imports) (../fields/2252.html#bh)
0 cu m (2013 est.)
country comparison to the world: 93 (../rankorder/2252rank.html#bh)
  Natural gas - proved reserves: (../docs/notesanddefs.html?fieldkey=2253&term=Natural gas - proved reserves)
  (../fields/2253.html#bh)
0 cu m (1 January 2014 est.)
country comparison to the world: 117 (../rankorder/2253rank.html#bh)
  Carbon dioxide emissions from consumption of energy: (../docs/notesanddefs.html?fieldkey=2254&term=Carbon dioxide emissions
  from consumption of energy) (../fields/2254.html#bh)
700,000 Mt (2013 est.)
country comparison to the world: 173 (../rankorder/2254rank.html#bh)

Communications :: BELIZE

  Telephones - fixed lines: (../docs/notesanddefs.html?fieldkey=2150&term=Telephones - fixed lines) (../fields/2150.html#bh)
total subscriptions: 23,000
subscriptions per 100 inhabitants: 6 (July 2016 est.)
country comparison to the world: 172 (../rankorder/2150rank.html#bh)
  Telephones - mobile cellular: (../docs/notesanddefs.html?fieldkey=2151&term=Telephones - mobile cellular)
  (../fields/2151.html#bh)
total: 227,000
subscriptions per 100 inhabitants: 63 (July 2016 est.)
country comparison to the world: 181 (../rankorder/2151rank.html#bh)
  Telephone system: (../docs/notesanddefs.html?fieldkey=2124&term=Telephone system) (../fields/2124.html#bh)
general assessment: above-average system; trunk network depends primarily on microwave radio relay
domestic: fixed-line teledensity of only about 6 per 100 persons; mobile-cellular teledensity approaching 65 per 100 persons
international: country code - 501; landing point for the Americas Region Caribbean Ring System (ARCOS-1) fiber-optic
telecommunications submarine cable that provides links to South and Central America, parts of the Caribbean, and the US; satellite
earth station - 8 (Intelsat - 2, unknown - 6) (2016)
  Broadcast media: (../docs/notesanddefs.html?fieldkey=2213&term=Broadcast media) (../fields/2213.html#bh)
8 privately owned TV stations; multi-channel cable TV provides access to foreign stations; about 25 radio stations broadcasting on
roughly 50 different frequencies; state-run radio was privatized in 1998 (2009)
  Internet country code: (../docs/notesanddefs.html?fieldkey=2154&term=Internet country code) (../fields/2154.html#bh)

.bz

Internet users: (../docs/notesanddefs.html? key=2153&term=Internet users) (../fields/2 html#bh)

total: 157,735

percent of population: 44.6% (July 2016 est.)

country comparison to the world: 174 (../rankorder/2153rank.html#bh)

Transportation :: BELIZE

National air transport system: (../docs/notesanddefs.html?fieldkey=2269&term=National air transport system) (../fields/2269.html#bh)

number of registered air carriers: 2

inventory of registered aircraft operated by air carriers: 28

annual passenger traffic on registered air carriers: 935,603

annual freight traffic on registered air carriers: 2,463,420 mt-km (2015)

Civil aircraft registration country code prefix: (../docs/notesanddefs.html?fieldkey=2270&term=Civil aircraft registration country code prefix) (../fields/2270.html#bh)

V3 (2016)

Airports: (../docs/notesanddefs.html?fieldkey=2053&term=Airports) (../fields/2053.html#bh)

47 (2013)

country comparison to the world: 92 (../rankorder/2053rank.html#bh)

Airports - with paved runways: (../docs/notesanddefs.html?fieldkey=2030&term=Airports - with paved runways) (../fields/2030.html#bh)

total: 6

2,438 to 3,047 m: 1

914 to 1,523 m: 2

under 914 m: 3 (2017)

Airports - with unpaved runways: (../docs/notesanddefs.html?fieldkey=2031&term=Airports - with unpaved runways) (../fields/2031.html#bh)

total: 41

2,438 to 3,047 m: 1

914 to 1,523 m: 11

under 914 m: 29 (2013)

Roadways: (../docs/notesanddefs.html?fieldkey=2085&term=Roadways) (../fields/2085.html#bh)

total: 2,870 km

paved: 488 km

unpaved: 2,382 km (2011)

country comparison to the world: 169 (../rankorder/2085rank.html#bh)

Waterways: (../docs/notesanddefs.html?fieldkey=2093&term=Waterways) (../fields/2093.html#bh)

825 km (navigable only by small craft) (2011)

country comparison to the world: 70 (../rankorder/2093rank.html#bh)

Merchant marine: (../docs/notesanddefs.html?fieldkey=2108&term=Merchant marine) (../fields/2108.html#bh)

total: 756

by type: bulk carrier 53, container ship 3, general cargo 373, oil tanker 55, other 272 (2017)

country comparison to the world: 29 (../rankorder/2108rank.html#bh)

Ports and terminals: (../docs/notesanddefs.html?fieldkey=2120&term=Ports and terminals) (../fields/2120.html#bh)

major seaport(s): Belize City, Big Creek

Military and Security :: BELIZE

Military expenditures: (../docs/notesanddefs.html?fieldkey=2034&term=Military expenditures) (../fields/2034.html#bh)

1.17% of GDP (2016)

1.09% of GDP (2015)

1.06% of GDP (2014)

1.1% of GDP (2013)

0.97% of GDP (2012)

country comparison to the world: 100 (../rankorder/2034rank.html#bh)

Military branches: (../docs/notesanddefs.html?fieldkey=2055&term=Military branches) (../fields/2055.html#bh)

Belize Defense Force (BDF): Army, BDF Air Wing; Belize Coast Guard; Belize Police Department (2017)

Military service age and obligation: (../docs/notesanddefs.html?fieldkey=2024&term=Military service age and obligation) (../fields/2024.html#bh)

18 years of age for voluntary military service; laws allow for conscription only if volunteers are insufficient; conscription has never been implemented; volunteers typically outnumber available positions by 3:1; initial service obligation 12 years (2012)

Transnational Issues :: BELIZE

Disputes - international: (../docs/notesanddefs.html?fieldkey=2070&term=Disputes - international) (../fields/2070.html#bh)

Guatemala persists in its territorial claim to approximately half of Belize, but agrees to the Line of Adjacency to keep Guatemalan squatters out of Belize's forested interior; both countries agreed in April 2012 to hold simultaneous referenda, scheduled for 6 October 2013, to decide whether to refer the dispute to the ICJ for binding resolution, but this vote was suspended indefinitely; Belize and Mexico are working to solve minor border demarcation discrepancies arising from inaccuracies in the 1898 border treaty

Trafficking in persons: (../docs/notesanddefs.html?fieldkey=2196&term=Trafficking in persons) (../fields/2196.html#bh)

current situation: Belize is a source, destination, and transit country for men, women, and children subjected to forced labor and sex trafficking; the coerced prostitution of women and children by family members has not led to arrests; child sex tourism, involving primarily US citizens, is on the rise; sex trafficking and forced labor of Belizean and foreign women and LGBT individuals occurs in bars, nightclubs, brothels, and domestic service; workers from Central America, Mexico, and Asia may fall victim to forced labor in restaurants, shops, agriculture, and fishing

tier rating: Tier 3 – Belize does not comply fully with the minimum standards for the elimination of human trafficking and is not making significant efforts to do so; authorities did not initiate any new trafficking investigations of prosecutions, and cases from previous years remain pending; law enforcement efforts to use informal means to identify and refer victims were ineffective and draft procedures for referring victims to services are still not finalized; trafficking victims were more commonly arrested, detained, or deported based on immigration violations than provided with assistance; the government did not make progress in implementing the 2012-14 anti-trafficking national strategic plan (2015)

Illicit drugs: (../docs/notesanddefs.html?fieldkey=2086&term=Illicit drugs) (../fields/2086.html#bh)

major transshipment point for cocaine; small-scale illicit producer of cannabis, primarily for local consumption; offshore sector money-laundering activity related to narcotics trafficking and other crimes

TAB 'BB'

Belize 2018 Crime & Safety — OSAC (01/31/2018)

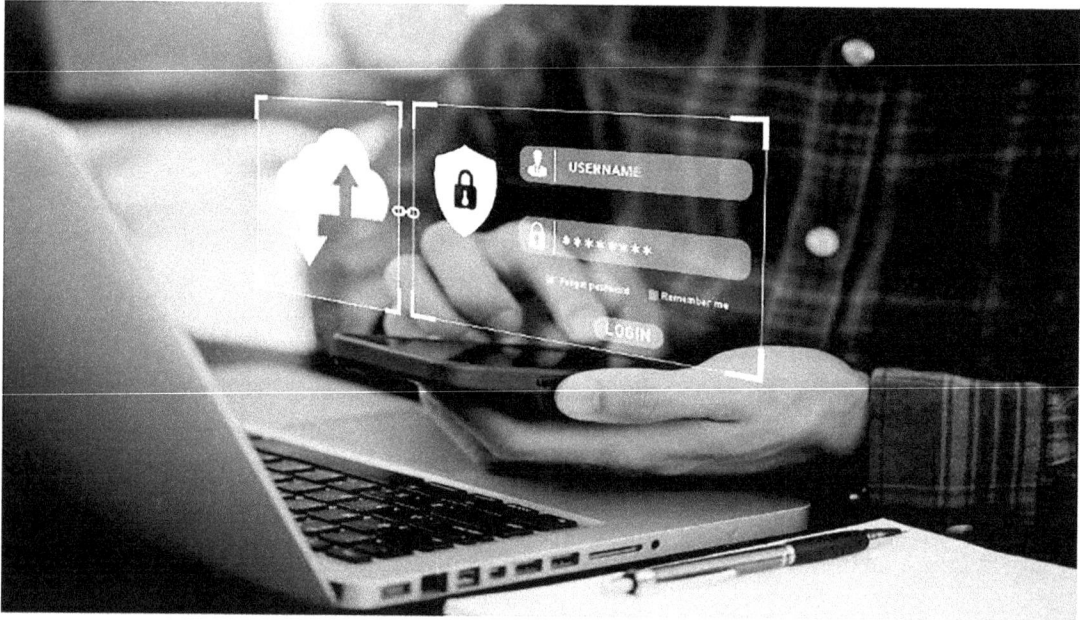

UNITED STATES DEPARTMENT OF STATE

OSAC

BUREAU OF DIPLOMATIC SECURITY

Belize 2018 Crime & Safety Report

Travel Health and Safety; Transportation Security; Stolen items; Political Violence; Natural Disasters; Maritime; Other; Disease Outbreak; Financial Security; Crime

Western Hemisphere > Belize; Western Hemisphere > Belize > Belmopan

1/31/2018

According to the current U.S. Department of State Travel Advisory at the date of this report's publication, Belize has been assessed as Level 2: exercise increased caution.

Overall Crime and Safety Situation

U.S. Embassy Belmopan does not assume responsibility for the professional ability or integrity of the persons or firms appearing in this report. The American Citizen Services (ACS) Unit cannot recommend a particular individual or location and assumes no responsibility for the quality of service provided.

The U.S. Department of State has assessed Belmopan as being a HIGH-threat location for crime directed at or affecting official U.S. government interests.

Please review OSAC's Belize-specific webpage for proprietary analytic reports, consular messages, and contact information.

OSAC

Belize, formerly known as British Honduras, is the only English-speaking country in Central America and lies along the Caribbean Sea. Belize is located south of Mexico and borders Guatemala in the west and south. Approximately 25-30% of the population lives in Belize City, and nearly 50% are located in rural communities. Tourism is a major part of the economy, with high season running November-April. Approximately 1.5 million tourists visited Belize in 2017, including daily visitors from cruise ships. Most popular destinations include the cayes (islands) off the eastern coast, including Ambergris Caye and Caye Caulker, and the southern coastal areas of Hopkins and Placencia.

Crime Threats

There is no indication that foreigners are being actively targeted in Belize, although tourists are more susceptible to incidents of crime when not displaying situational awareness. Major crimes continue to shift from being concentrated in the population area of Belize City to districts in the north, west, and south of Belize, as reported in 2016.
Confrontational crimes, such as armed robbery and theft, have increased in tourist areas. Violent crimes remain uncommon in tourist areas; however, they do happen. Murder, sexual assault, and armed robberies occurred in areas frequented by tourists and expats in 2017. Those who practice good personal security are less likely to be impacted. Criminal acts, including extremely violent acts, occur in all areas of Belize.
Notable murders of U.S. citizens have occurred in 2016-2017, including the widely-publicized murders of U.S. citizens in the Cayo District in January 2016, in the Corozal District in April 2017, in the Belize District in July 2017, and in the Stann Creek District in December 2017. The police are actively investigating; however, all four murders remain unsolved.
Domestic violence is prevalent, and crimes due to domestic violence are high.
Incidents of pickpocketing, burglary, and hotel room theft are the most common types of non-violent crimes committed against U.S. citizens; and they occur throughout Belize. Non-confrontational petty thieves are particularly active in tourist areas and on public transportation. Reports of theft from lodging are common, and visitors are encouraged to keep doors locked, even when at home, and secure valuables in locked containers or provided safes. If confronted by an intruder, cooperation is generally advised.
Break-ins and vandalism of automobiles do occur. Use of a car alarm is a necessary precaution in deterring vehicle thefts and break ins. Theft of easily pilfered items and sound systems is a common crime.

UNITED STATES DEPARTMENT OF STATE

OSAC

BUREAU OF DIPLOMATIC SECURITY

Corruption, human smuggling/trafficking, the drug trade, money laundering (institutional and trade-based), and local criminal gang activity remain significant criminal problems exacerbated by the low conviction rate. Criminal organizations and individuals often operate beyond the ability of the police to disrupt them.

There is some evidence to suggest that Salvadoran and Guatemalan-based transnational criminal organizations provide logistical support to international drug and human trafficking organizations and utilize Belize as a transit country along smuggling routes. Gang tags from 18th Street (*Barrio 18*) and MS-13 (*Mara Salvatrucha*) have been reported in multiple districts. In 2017, Police reported arrests of individuals with possible gang ties, although there is no indication that formal gang cliques have been established in Belize.

Belize is a source, transit, and destination country for those subjected to forced labor and sex trafficking. No human trafficking cases were prosecuted in 2017. Cases from previous years remain pending, and limited resources are available to victims.

Due to the small population and high per capita murder rate, Belize consistently ranks among the top 10 countries in the world for homicides, according to the United Nations Office on Drugs and Crime. Belize averages approximately 40 homicides per 100,000 residents. The murder rate in 2017 countrywide totaled 142, with a number of cases that could later be classified as murders pending the conclusion of investigations. The highest murder rate on record in Belize is 145, which occurred in 2012. In previous years, the increase was likely attributed to the displacement of crime from the central hub of criminal gang activity in south Belize City. The murder rate in the Belize District increased by 13 in 2017, and brought the per capita murder rate of Belize City to just over 90 homicides per 100,000 residents. Three out of six districts experienced an increase in murders in 2017.

Murder

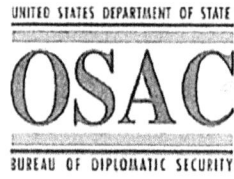

UNITED STATES DEPARTMENT OF STATE

OSAC

BUREAU OF DIPLOMATIC SECURITY

2015

2016

2017

Belize

66

70

82

Cayo

27

34

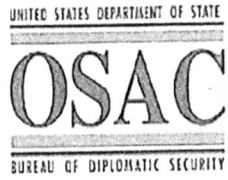

UNITED STATES DEPARTMENT OF STATE

OSAC

BUREAU OF DIPLOMATIC SECURITY

28

Orange Walk

7

11

9

Stann Creek

8

11

12

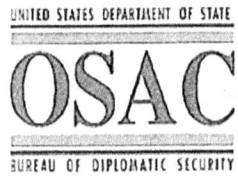

Corozal

6

7

8

Toledo

5

5

3

Total

119

138

142

The Belize District, which includes Belize City, continues to have the highest number of murders due in large part to dozens of street gangs that operate in the city. Belmopan, the tiny capital with a population of approximately 16,000 residents and home to several diplomatic missions, including the U.S. Embassy, recorded 11 murders in 2017. In 2017, 58% of the murders in Belize were carried out by a gun, 19% by knife, and 8% by machete.

Cases of fraud related to credit/debit cards have been reported in areas frequented by tourists, particularly in Belize City and San Pedro. Skimming, the theft of credit card information during an otherwise legitimate transaction, is most likely to occur in restaurants, bars, and hotels when the victim's card is out of view. For more information, please review OSAC's Report, "The Overseas Traveler's Guide to ATM Skimmers & Fraud.

There have been numerous reports of fraud committed against expatriates and Belizeans who have attempted to purchase land in Belize. Corrupt officials have reportedly been involved in fraudulently facilitating land title transfers. Consult with a reputable Belizean attorney when purchasing property. Many expatriates have reported being the victim of scams in which land is purchased that was not available, was legally owned by other parties, or was subsequently sold without their knowledge. Due to media coverage implicating high level complicity in land fraud, the government has renewed efforts to address property disputes by converting physical records to electronic records.

Several high-profile investigations have been reported linking Belizean Ministerial-level and immigration department officials in the alleged sale of illegal Belizean identity documents including passports.

Other Areas of Concern

UNITED STATES DEPARTMENT OF STATE

OSAC

BUREAU OF DIPLOMATIC SECURITY

It is recommended that travel to the south side of Belize City be minimized to official business only and that personal trips be avoided due to gang activity there. The Belizean government has designated certain areas as crime-ridden, thereby enabling law enforcement and security authorities to conduct random searches without a warrant.

Several tourist areas along the western border with Guatemala have active military patrols due to border incidents that are reported each year. Some excursions require a military patrol to view ruins on the western border with Guatemala.

Transportation-Safety Situation
For more information, please review OSAC's Report, "Security in Transit: Airplanes, Public Transport, and Overnights."

Road Safety and Road Conditions
Road conditions are improving but are still characterized as very poor. The road systems range from short stretches of newly paved roads in Belize City, to decades-old pavement on the major highways that run north-south and east-west. Roads in rural areas/villages are typically dirt or loose gravel, and road conditions worsen during the rainy season. The primary highways – Philip SW Goldson Highway (northern), George Price Highway (western), Hummingbird, and Southern highways – are in generally better condition (paved) than most roads. The combination of inconsistent paving, bridges with low guard rails, and slick roadways due to rain have been contributing factors in several fatal accidents. Traffic fatalities remain an urgent, very real danger.

The major highways are the only reliable avenues to transit the country, aside from airplanes operated by two Belizean commercial carriers. Pedestrians, bicyclists, cars, and buses utilize the same roads. Stray dogs and wildlife also wander freely in close proximity to the many small villages that line the major highways.

Driving can be extremely hazardous after dusk and during rainstorms.

Defensive driving is critical to navigate the road systems. Local drivers may use turn signals to signify different vehicle movements. For example, a left turn signal may be a signal for your car to pass on the left or it could indicate a left turn by the vehicle. Drivers should always use maximum follow distances to ensure an appropriate reactionary gap.

Due to the absence of stoplights and vehicular police patrols, speed bumps control speeds, especially in/around small villages, schools, and population centers. Speed bumps can be a significant hazard, as they tend to be very large and are often unmarked. Drivers should

always be aware of them, especially during dusk, dawn, and night driving, as vehicles may slam on their brakes to avoid hitting an unmarked bump.

Most parking is on the street. If left overnight, ensure you park in an area that is well illuminated, with security guards (most larger hotels have security guards), and within view of your destination. For more information on self-driving, please review OSAC's Report "Driving Overseas: Best Practices."

The police regularly operate checkpoints, especially in/around Belize City, Belmopan, and occasionally along the major highways leading west and south. The police may ask for a form of identification, and vehicles are expected to stop at these checkpoints and fully cooperate. Reports of false checkpoints or extortion have been reported but are uncommon.

Public Transportation Conditions

Taxi stands and plazas are located throughout major cities and villages. Taxis can be identified by green license plates. Taxis should generally only be hailed from reputable establishments. Make it clear to the driver that you do not wish to pick up additional passengers. Many vehicles imported into Belize are salvage vehicles from neighboring countries that may not have operational security features such as airbags.

Buses often operate under poor conditions and lack adequate maintenance. Bus drivers often exceed the speed limits, pull over without warning for passengers, and pass where it is unsafe.

Buses and cars often do not yield to pedestrians. Walking or exercising after dark is not recommended, especially for women. Make a note of emergency telephone numbers and locations you may need: police, fire, your hotel, and the U.S. Embassy.

Other Travel Conditions

Water taxis are an inexpensive and reliable method to travel from Belize City to the cayes (Caye Caulker, San Pedro). Water taxis are generally safe, but caution should be exercised while using them. Travelers should ensure that there are adequate life vests on board.

Individuals wishing to travel via personally-owned vehicles through the interior of Mexico and other Central American countries should exercise caution and seek country specific information.

Terrorism Threat

The U.S. Department of State has assessed Belmopan as being a LOW-threat location for terrorist activity directed at or affecting official U.S. government interests.

Local, Regional, and International Terrorism Threats/Concerns

UNITED STATES DEPARTMENT OF STATE

OSAC

BUREAU OF DIPLOMATIC SECURITY

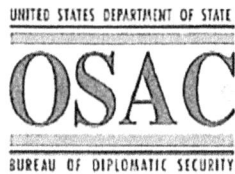

The Worldwide Caution highlights information on the continuing threat of terrorist actions and violence against U.S. citizens and interests. Recent terrorist attacks serve as a reminder that U.S. citizens need to maintain a high level of vigilance and take steps to increase their security awareness.

In 2017, an individual identified by police as a Belizean citizen with suspected ties to the Ansar Al-Khilafah Philippines (AKP) terrorist group was killed by police in the Philippines.

Political, Economic, Religious, and Ethnic Violence

The U.S. Department of State has assessed Belmopan as being a LOW-threat location for political violence directed at or affecting official U.S. government interests.

Civil Unrest

Political violence is rare. Lawful protests/demonstrations do occur but are generally peaceful and orderly. The Belizean government requires a permit that must be requested at least 24 hours prior to a planned protest. Even demonstrations intended to be peaceful can escalate into violence. Avoid areas of demonstrations and exercise caution if in the vicinity of any large gatherings, protests, or demonstrations.

Post-specific Concerns

Environmental Hazards

The most frequent natural disasters to affect Belize are hurricanes and tropical storms. Hurricane season in the western Caribbean is June 1-November 30; however, September-October is when tropical storms have generally affected Belize.

In 2016, Belize suffered a direct hit by Category 1 Hurricane Earl, resulting in power outages throughout 65% of the country, extensive flooding, and the blockage of major highways. The eye of the hurricane crossed Belmopan, causing serious damage across the Cayo district.

The National Emergency Management Office (NEMO) analyzed Belize's vulnerability to hurricanes and established an evacuation plan, although response capabilities would be limited even for a Category 1 storm. Hurricane shelters exist along the coast, but emergency

UNITED STATES DEPARTMENT OF STATE

OSAC

BUREAU OF DIPLOMATIC SECURITY

food/water stockpiles would be exhausted quickly by the high number of potential victims. Waterways require frequent dredging, so flooding would be exacerbated.

Because Belize is tropical and has regular rainfall, clogged drainage and waterways often lead to flooding of roadways, even during the dry season. Severe storms cut off vehicular movement in many coastal and inland areas as the low bridges flood.

There is a significant risk of forest fires during the dry season (December-May).

Earthquakes and tsunami warnings have occurred in Belize. Few earthquakes have their epicenter in Belize, but major earthquakes on fault lines outside of Belize can be felt in the country, typically in the south.

Much of Belize is protected rainforest, and there is the threat of attack by indigenous animals. Rivers contain crocodiles, and isolated attacks have been reported. For more information, please review OSAC's Report "When Wildlife Attacks."

There are significant safety concerns for tourists who engage in diving and snorkeling activities. While engaging in diving, snorkeling, cave tubing etc., it is prudent to assume that safety procedures and standards are not up to U.S. standards, and careful consideration should be given prior to engaging in "at your own risk" activities that can involve long hikes, climbs, and dive sites that are not within cell phone range. It is recommended to have portable first aid kits and satellite phones available. Several U.S. citizens died while diving or snorkeling in 2017. Inconsistent and overall lax safety standards may have been a factor in some of these deaths, along with age, pre-existing health conditions, swimming capability, inexperience of the divers, and/or poor weather conditions.

Personal Identity Concerns

While Belize is generally a friendly, accommodating society, females should be particularly attentive to risks associated with being in public alone or in the company of only one other female.

There is significant hostile sentiment toward individuals who identify themselves as LGBT. LGBT issues are frequently highlighted in the press and can spur passionate discussions at community forums and on social media. There have been instances of violence reported against LGBT individuals.

Drug-related Crimes

Due to Belize's location, the transit of drugs (including cocaine and precursor chemicals for methamphetamine) has risen.

UNITED STATES DEPARTMENT OF STATE

OSAC

BUREAU OF DIPLOMATIC SECURITY

In 2015, U.S. Embassy Belmopan issued a Security Message to U.S. Citizens to avoid the Roaring Creek, Camalote, and Teakettle Corridor due to an uptick in violent crime believed to stem from a dispute over local narcotic distribution networks in the area.

The Misuse of Drugs Act (MODA) was introduced in 2017 and possession of marijuana/cannabis in quantities of 10g or less was decriminalized as it is done in a private domicile with the owner's permission. Smoking in public locations, including parks, is still illegal and importation of marijuana/cannabis is a violation of Belizean law. All U.S. citizens are advised that the purchase of drugs is still against the law, and violators are subject to substantial penalties, including jail time.

Kidnapping Threat

While kidnapping is rare in Belize, in 2016, one U.S. citizen and a number of Canadian nationals were reportedly kidnapped and extorted by threat of kidnapping in the western portion of Belize. The American was released unharmed within a few hours.

Police Response

The police have limited funding and limited resources, and as a result of perceived response and corruption, they do not enjoy the full confidence and cooperation of the general population. Crime is likely under-reported and often resolved by confrontation due to absence of an immediate police response. Investigative units generally have the will to respond; however, availability of transportation and lack of professional training in investigative techniques remain obstacles. Equipment shortages (radios, vehicles) limit their ability to deter or respond to crimes expeditiously. Other impediments to effective law enforcement are unsupportive laws, general distrust, and the limited cooperation between the police, prosecutors, and corrections. The conviction rate remains low. Response times from police are generally slow. When criminal acts happen in some of the more remote areas, there is little protection or assistance available for the victims. Senior police leadership have taken measures to address some of these issues.

All people traveling in Belize are subject to Belizean laws. Drug and firearm offenses come with strict penalties and can result in lengthy jail sentences.

How to Handle Incidents of Police Detention or Harassment

Reports of police harassment and extortion attempts of American tourists are rare but do occur and should be reported.

UNITED STATES DEPARTMENT OF STATE

OSAC

BUREAU OF DIPLOMATIC SECURITY

In 2016, Western tourists reported being offered drugs and were "set-up" for arrest and payment of a cash fine.

In 2017, a U.S. citizen tourist was detained and robbed by three police officers in San Pedro. Two of the officers were suspended, and the investigation is ongoing.

Crime Victim Assistance

If you are the victim of a crime, you should contact the local police first to obtain a Belize police report (tel: 911 or +501-822-2222) and the U.S. Embassy in Belmopan at +501-822-4011. The police and emergency telephone lines may be busy, and contacting police can be difficult. In 2017, U.S. citizens reported difficulties in receiving police reports due to a lengthy and time consuming reporting structure, which may contribute to under reporting of thefts in tourist areas.

Emergency assistance for U.S. citizens is available from the U.S. Embassy. The U.S. Embassy Consular Section should be contacted in the event of an arrest, medical emergency, death, violent crime, or other emergency. During regular business hours (Mon-Fri 800-1200 and 1300 to 1700), U.S. citizens with emergencies may visit the Embassy Consular Section or may call 822-4011. If you are a U.S. citizen with an after-hours emergency, please call the duty officer at (501) 610-5030. If you are calling from the U.S., you must first dial 011-501 and then the seven-digit number. Contact the U.S. Embassy to report a passport lost or stolen. The Embassy's consular staff can assist in finding appropriate medical care, contacting family members or friends, and explaining how U.S. funds may be transferred to Belize.

Police/Security Agencies

Belize Police Headquarters: Belize Police are headquartered in Belmopan and can be contacted at +501-802-2221. Most police contact information can be found on the Belize Police Department webpage.

National Crimes Investigations Branch (NCIB): This unit, under the Commissioner of Police, is the lead investigative agency for serious crimes. NCIB can be reached at +501-802-3818.

Belize City Police Station: Responsible for the Eastern District of Belize, including Belize City, and can be reached at +501-227-2222.

San Pedro Substation: Responsible for San Pedro and can be reached at 702-0137.

Other police:
Belize City: +501-207-2222
Belmopan: +501-802-2221
Benque Viejo: +501-803-2038
Caye Caulker: +501-226-0179
Corozal: +501-402-2022
Dangriga: +501-522-2022
Independence: +501-523-2022
Orange Walk: +501-322-2022
Punta Gorda: +501-722-2022
San Ignacio: +501-804-2022
San Pedro: +501-206-2022

Medical Emergencies

Medical care in Belize can be costly and inadequate by U.S. standards. There are nine hospitals and numerous medical clinics throughout Belize. While certain hospitals are equipped to treat certain medical emergencies, clinics treat only outpatient cases and are not staffed to handle emergencies. Belize City is the center for medical care in Belize with three major hospitals considered best equipped to handle serious medical problems: Belize Medical Associates, Belize Health Care Partners, and Karl Heusner Memorial Hospital (KHMH). Medical facilities outside Belize City are not adequate to handle serious medical conditions and often fail to meet basic U.S. standards. Emergency medical care and search and rescue capabilities are extremely limited, particularly on the Cayes and in remote areas in Belize. Travelers should be prepared with their legally-prescribed drugs that they may need during their visit and take caution to ensure that those medications are legally permitted to enter Belize before travel. There are reasonably well-stocked pharmacies in most major towns and tourist destinations, and prescriptions are usually not required. Travelers should use caution as counterfeit medication is found throughout Belize. For more information, please refer to OSAC's Report, "Traveling with Medications."

Contact Information for Available Medical Services

The U.S. Embassy has compiled an Emergency and Medical Listing of licensed medical providers in Belize.

Available Air Ambulance Services

UNITED STATES DEPARTMENT OF STATE

OSAC

BUREAU OF DIPLOMATIC SECURITY

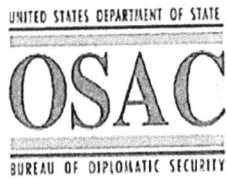

If an air ambulance is required, the Embassy provides a Listing of Air Ambulance Companies servicing Belize.

For those traveling the more remote areas of Belize or to the off-shore cayes, emergency transportation to adequate medical facilities may be unavailable. Astrum Helicopters provides MEDEVAC flights in coordination with the Belize Emergency Response Team (BERT). For emergency response and transportation, BERT and BES are Belize's only qualified providers.

Astrum Helicopters
Mile 3.5 George Price Highway
Belize City, Belize
Office: +501-222-5100
Fax: +501-222-5105

www.astrumhelicopters.com

Belmopan Emergency Services (BES)
19 Cardinal Avenue
Belmopan, Belize
Tel: +501-223-3292
Email: besservice@yahoo.com

Belize Emergency Response Team (BERT)
P.O. Box 1370

UNITED STATES DEPARTMENT OF STATE

OSAC

BUREAU OF DIPLOMATIC SECURITY

1675 Sunrise Avenue
Coral Grove Area
Belize City, Belize
Tel: +501-223-3292
Cell: +501-610-3890
Fax: +501-223-0549
Email: info@bertbelize.org

Insurance Guidance
Those who experience serious or life-threatening medical problems and require evacuation to
the U.S. may require an air ambulance service. It is recommended to check with your
insurance company to verify you have sufficient coverage before traveling, or purchase
supplemental medevac insurance.
Country-specific Vaccination and Health Guidance
The Zika virus was identified in Belize in August 2016.
The CDC offers additional information on vaccines and health guidance for Belize.

OSAC Country Council Information
There is no Country Council in Belmopan. Interested private-sector security managers should
contact OSAC's Western Hemisphere team with any questions.

U.S. Embassy Location and Contact Information
Embassy Address and Hours of Operation
U.S. Embassy Belmopan
4 Floral Park Road
Belmopan, Belize
Hours of Operation: Mon-Fri, 0800-1200 and 1300-1700; closed on American and Belizean
holidays. https://bz.usembassy.gov/holiday-calendar/
Embassy Contact Numbers
If you are calling from the U.S., you must first dial 011-501 and then the seven-digit number.
Main Embassy Number: +501-822-4011
After-hours emergency: +501-610-5030

UNITED STATES DEPARTMENT OF STATE

OSAC

BUREAU OF DIPLOMATIC SECURITY

Website: https://bz.usembassy.gov/
Embassy Guidance
Americans are encouraged to register with the Smart Traveler Enrollment Program (STEP) or contact the American Citizens Service Office located in the Consular Section.
Additional Resources
Belize Country Information Sheet

TAB 'CC'

Belize Travel Advisory – U.S. Department of State (01/10/2018)

Travel.State.Gov
U.S. DEPARTMENT OF STATE — BUREAU OF CONSULAR AFFAIRS

Search [Q]

U.S. Passports | **International Travel** | **U.S. Visas** | **Intercountry Adoption** | **International Parental Child Abduction**

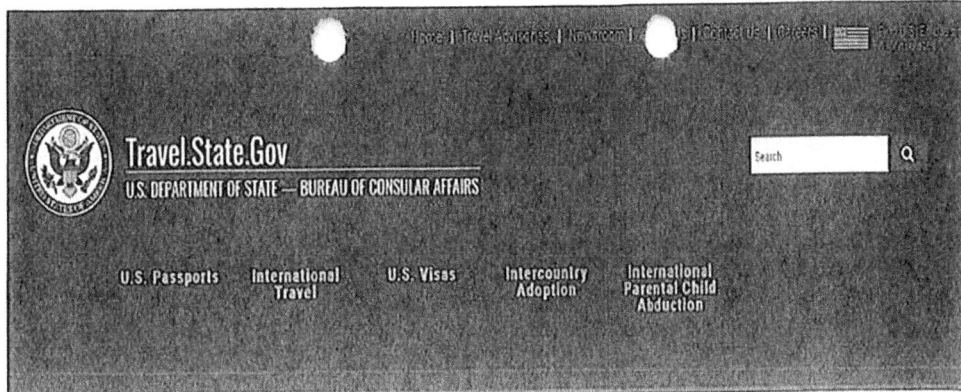

Travel.State.Gov > Travel Advisories > Belize Travel Advisory

Belize Travel Advisory

Travel Advisory
January 10, 2018

Belize - Level 2: Exercise Increased Caution

(C)

Exercise increased caution in Belize due to **crime**.

Violent crime, such as sexual assault, armed robbery, and murder, is common. Local police lack the resources to respond effectively to serious criminal incidents.

Read the Safety and Security section on the country information page.

If you decide to travel to Belize:

- Be aware of your surroundings.
- Avoid walking or driving at night.
- Do not physically resist any robbery attempt.
- Be extra vigilant when visiting banks or ATMs.
- Do not display signs of wealth, such as wearing expensive watches or jewelry.
- Enroll in the Smart Traveler Enrollment Program (STEP) to receive Alerts and make it easier to locate you in an emergency.
- Follow the Department of State on Facebook and Twitter.
- Review the Crime and Safety Report for Belize.
- U.S. citizens who travel abroad should always have a contingency plan for emergency situations. Review the Traveler's Checklist.

Travel Advisory Levels

1. Exercise normal precautions
2. Exercise increased caution
3. Reconsider travel
4. Do not travel

Assistance for U.S. Citizens

U.S. Embassy Belmopan
4 Floral Park Road
Belmopan, Belize

Telephone
+(501) 822-4011

Emergency
+(501) 610-5030

Fax
+(501) 822-4012

Email
ACSBelize@state.gov

Website
U.S. Embassy
Belmopan

TAB 'DD'

Belize 2017 Human Rights Report – U.S. Department of State

BELIZE 2017 HUMAN RIGHTS REPORT

EXECUTIVE SUMMARY

Belize is a constitutional parliamentary democracy. In November 2015 the United Democratic Party (UDP) won 19 of 31 seats in the House of Representatives following generally free and fair multiparty elections.

Civilian authorities maintained effective control over the security forces.

The most significant human rights issues included allegations of unlawful killings by security officers, which the authorities investigated and prosecuted; allegations of corruption by government agents; allegations that several killings were motivated by sexual orientation or gender identity; trafficking in persons; and child labor.

In some cases the government took steps to prosecute public officials who committed abuses, both administratively and through the courts, but there were few successful prosecutions. While some lower-ranking officials faced disciplinary action and/or criminal charges, higher-ranking officials were less likely to face punishment, resulting in a perception of impunity.

Section 1. Respect for the Integrity of the Person, Including Freedom from:

a. Arbitrary Deprivation of Life and Other Unlawful or Politically Motivated Killings

There were allegations that government agents committed an arbitrary or unlawful killing. In June police officers shot and killed a man in the Corozal District after he allegedly approached the officers with a machete during a routine eviction. The officers involved were not placed on interdiction (a modified suspension with lesser penalties if the case is still under investigation) despite the continuing investigation.

Three police officers in San Pedro Town were initially charged with murder after they allegedly beat a 30-year-old man to death in March while he was detained in police custody on disorderly conduct charges. In October the director of public prosecution downgraded the charges against the three officers from murder to manslaughter, and they were released on bail while awaiting trial.

In August a customs officer shot a man when he refused to hand over contraband. The suspected smuggler died days later. The customs officer was arrested, charged with manslaughter, and transferred to another police branch.

b. Disappearance

There were no reports of disappearances by or on behalf of government authorities.

c. Torture and Other Cruel, Inhuman, or Degrading Treatment or Punishment

The constitution prohibits torture or other inhuman punishment, and there were no reports that government officials employed these practices. There were, however, reports that police, especially the Gang Suppression Unit, used excessive force, and there were other allegations of abuse by security force personnel.

The Ombudsman's Office received 32 new complaints of police overreach in the first six months of the year. The most common complaint was police abuse. The Office of the Ombudsman also noted an increase in complaints against the Immigration and Nationality Department.

In April, two women and two men claimed police brutality while being detained in San Pedro Town. According to reports, police detained two women on the street using excessive force. Civilians gathered and demanded the police minimize the use of force; police physically attacked a bystander recording the event as well as his brother. One of the men was shot in the legs when police fired warning shots into the air and the ground. The Belize Police Department (BPD) investigated the matter, and the two officers were criminally charged for "wounding."

In November, two women, a Belizean and a Salvadoran, accused three police officers of raping them in a Belize City police station after they were removed from a transit bus to be searched for drugs. The police officers remained on active duty as the investigation proceeded.

Prison and Detention Center Conditions

Physical Conditions: There were no reports of prison or detention center conditions that raised major human rights concerns, although prisoners in pretrial detention are not separated from convicted prisoners. Officials used isolation in a small, unlit, unventilated punishment cell, called a "reflection room," to discipline

Country Reports on Human Rights Practices for 2017
United States Department of State • Bureau of Democracy, Human Rights and Labor

206 | Page

inmates. Conditions in the women's area were significantly better than in the men's compound.

There were no reported cases of prison officers abusing their power. Between January and September, prison authorities investigated four cases of inmate-on-inmate assault involving "gross violence." Because inmates were generally not willing to press criminal charges against their attackers, the prison's internal tribunal system handled all cases. Penalties included temporary segregation or temporary suspension of privileges, depending on the severity of the assault.

Administration: The Kolbe Foundation, a local Christian nonprofit organization, administered the country's only central prison, which houses men, women, and juveniles. The government retained oversight and monitoring responsibility.

The law authorizes inmates to complain to the Ombudsman's Office through prison authorities, but inmates (and sometimes their family members) continued to make complaints directly to the ombudsman, who could not fully investigate complaints because of lack of resources and access to the prisoners. The prison administrator's chief of security initially investigates allegations of mistreatment. If the investigation discovers incriminating evidence, the accused officer is disciplined. If there is evidence of officer corruption, the investigation is passed to the administrator's intelligence officer, who further investigates the matter.

Independent Monitoring: The prison administrator permitted visits from independent human rights observers. While the prison generally operated free from government interference, the Ministry of Home Affairs monitored it on site through the Office of Controller of Prisons.

d. Arbitrary Arrest or Detention

While the constitution and law prohibit arbitrary arrest and detention and provide for the right of any person to challenge the lawfulness of his/her arrest or detention in court, there were several allegations made through the media and to the police Professional Standards Branch (PSB) that the government failed to observe these requirements. In addition, due to substantial delays and a backlog of cases in the justice system, the courts did not bring some minors to trial until they reached 18 years. In such cases the defendants were tried as minors.

Role of the Police and Security Apparatus

Country Reports on Human Rights Practices for 2017
United States Department of State • Bureau of Democracy, Human Rights and Labor

207 | P a g e

The police are responsible for internal security. The Ministry of Home Affairs is responsible for oversight of police and prisons, and the Ministry of Defense is responsible for the military. Although primarily charged with external security, the Ministry of Defense also provides limited domestic security support to civilian authorities and has limited powers of arrest that are executed by its Belize Defense Force (BDF) for land and littoral areas and the Belize Coast Guard for coastal and maritime areas.

There were reports of impunity involving the security forces, including reports of police brutality and corruption (primarily extortion cases). The government often ignored reports of police abuse, delayed action, failed to take disciplinary action, or transferred accused officers to other areas within their department.

The PSB investigates complaints against police. The law authorizes the police commissioner to place police personnel on suspension or interdiction. As of October the PSB received 59 formal complaints of police brutality. The PSB reported 44 officers were on interdiction or on suspension. Additionally, authorities use police investigations, coroner inquests, and the Public Prosecutions Office to evaluate allegations against police. While police officers are under investigation, they remain on active duty.

Arrest Procedures and Treatment of Detainees

Police must obtain search or arrest warrants issued by a magistrate, except in cases of hot pursuit, when there is probable cause, or when the presence of a firearm is suspected. Police must inform detainees of their rights at the time of arrest and of the cause of their detention within 48 hours of arrest. Police must also bring a detainee before a magistrate to be charged officially within 48 hours. The BPD faced allegations that its members arbitrarily detained persons beyond 48 hours without charge, did not take detainees directly to a police station, and used detention as a means of intimidation.

The law requires police to follow the Judges' Rules, a code of conduct governing police interaction with arrested persons. Although judges sometimes dismissed cases that involved violations of these rules, they more commonly deemed confessions obtained through violation of the rules to be invalid. Police usually granted detainees timely access to family members and lawyers, although there were reports of persons held in police detention without the right to contact family or seek legal advice.

Country Reports on Human Rights Practices for 2017
United States Department of State • Bureau of Democracy, Human Rights and Labor

208 | Page

By law a police officer in charge of a station or a magistrate's court may grant bail to persons charged with minor offenses. The Supreme Court can grant bail to those charged with more serious crimes, including murder, gang activity, possession of an unlicensed firearm, and specific drug trafficking or sexual offenses. The Supreme Court reviews the bail application within 10 working days.

Pretrial Detention: Lengthy trial backlogs remained, particularly for serious crimes such as murder. As of September 27, there were 491 prisoners on remand at the Belize Central Prison. Problems included police delays in completing investigations, lack of evidence collection, court delays in preparing depositions, and adjournments in the courts.

Judges occasionally were slow to issue rulings, in some cases taking a year or longer. The time lag between arrest, trial, and conviction generally ranged from six months to four years and in some cases up to seven years. Pretrial detention for persons accused of murder averaged three to four years.

The Bar Association of Belize publicly insisted that the chief justice deliver judgments on 30 outstanding civil cases from 2012 to 2015 by the end of the year or tender his resignation. In response, the chief justice began delivering judgments on the pending cases on a strict timeline (at least two each for 15 weeks). In addition the Supreme Court temporarily hired an additional judge for five years to assist with the backlog of cases. In September the Supreme Court swore-in 39 new court arbitrators to assist in judgment for the backlog of cases.

e. Denial of Fair Public Trial

The constitution provides for an independent judiciary, and the government generally respected judicial independence.

Trial Procedures

The law provides for the right to a fair and public trial, and an independent judiciary generally enforced this right, although delays in holding trials occurred.

The law stipulates that nonjury trials are mandatory in cases involving charges of murder, attempted murder, abetment of murder, and conspiracy to commit murder. Government officials stated that this law protects jurors from retribution. A single Supreme Court judge hears these cases. A magistrate generally issues decisions

Country Reports on Human Rights Practices for 2017
United States Department of State • Bureau of Democracy, Human Rights and Labor

209 | P a g e

and judgments for lesser crimes after deliberating on the arguments presented by the prosecution and defense.

Defendants enjoy a presumption of innocence, and standard procedure is for the defendant to be informed promptly of the charges and to be present at the trial. If the defendant is under the influence of drugs or alcohol, or there are language barriers, he/she is informed of the reason of arrest at the earliest possible opportunity. Defendants have the right to defense by counsel and appeal, but the prosecution can apply for the trial to proceed if a defendant skips bail or does not appear in court.

There is no requirement for defendants to have legal representation except in cases involving murder. The Supreme Court's registrar is responsible for appointing an attorney to act on behalf of indigent defendants charged with murder. In lesser cases the court does not provide defendants an attorney, and defendants sometimes represented themselves. The Legal Advice and Services Center, staffed by three attorneys, can provide legal services and representation for a range of civil and criminal cases, including domestic violence and other criminal cases up to attempted murder. These legal aid services are overstretched and cannot reach rural areas or districts. Defendants are entitled to adequate time and facilities to prepare a defense or request an adjournment, a common delay tactic. The court provides Spanish interpreters for defendants upon request. Defendants may not be compelled to testify against themselves or confess guilt.

The law allows defendants to confront and question witnesses against them and present witnesses on their behalf. Witnesses may submit written statements into evidence in place of court appearances. Defendants have the right to produce evidence in their defense and examine evidence held by the opposing party or the court.

The rate of acquittals and cases withdrawn by the prosecution due to insufficient evidence continued to be high, particularly for sexual offenses, murder, and gang-related cases. These actions were often due to the failure of witnesses to testify because of fear for life and personal safety, as well as a lack of basic forensic capability in the country.

Political Prisoners and Detainees

There were no reports of political prisoners or detainees.

Civil Judicial Procedures and Remedies

Individuals and organizations may seek civil remedies for human rights violations through domestic courts, including the Supreme Court. Litigants may appeal cases to the Caribbean Court of Justice, the country's highest appellate court. Individuals can also present petitions to the Inter-American Commission on Human Rights.

Property Restitution

In 2015 and 2016, the government agreed to compensation packages with Belize Telemedia Limited (BTL) and Belize Electricity Limited related to the nationalization of both companies in 2009 and 2011, respectively. The government continued to make payments to the former owner of BTL. In November the Caribbean Court of Justice ruled that the final payment of US $78 million should be made to the previous owners of the company by November 10. The government paid by the deadline.

f. Arbitrary Interference with Privacy, Family, Home, or Correspondence

The constitution prohibits such actions, and there were no reports that the government failed to respect these prohibitions.

Section 2. Respect for Civil Liberties, Including:

a. Freedom of Expression, Including for the Press

The law provides for freedom of expression, including for the press, and the government generally respected these rights. An independent press, an effective judicial system, and a functioning democratic political system combined to promote freedom of expression, including for the press.

Violence and Harassment: In May the sergeant of arms for the National Assembly physically assaulted two members of the press and threatened another, who was covering a protest in the Senate. The government did not immediately censure him, but he was eventually suspended from attending subsequent sessions.

In September a female journalist was physically assaulted by an officer attached to the Special Patrol Unit of the Police while she was covering a political event in Orange Walk. She subsequently made a formal complaint to the PSB. The

Country Reports on Human Rights Practices for 2017
United States Department of State • Bureau of Democracy, Human Rights and Labor

211 | P a g e

minister of state of home affairs responded to the incident by stating, "The police department has a job to do and in that situation we have always asked the media to stay a distance away from the situation."

Internet Freedom

The government did not restrict or disrupt access to the internet or censor online content, and there were no credible reports that the government monitored private online communications without appropriate legal authority. According to local marketing firm, Idea Labs Ltd., 45 percent of the population had internet access as of June 2016.

Academic Freedom and Cultural Events

There were no government restrictions on academic freedom or cultural events.

b. Freedoms of Peaceful Assembly and Association

The law provides for the freedoms of peaceful assembly and association, and the government generally respected these rights

c. Freedom of Religion

See the Department of State's *International Religious Freedom Report* at www.state.gov/religiousfreedomreport/.

d. Freedom of Movement

The law provides for freedom of internal movement, foreign travel, emigration, and repatriation, and the government generally respected these rights.

The government generally cooperated with the Office of the UN High Commissioner for Refugees (UNHCR) and other humanitarian organizations in providing protection and assistance to internally displaced persons, refugees, returning refugees, asylum seekers, stateless persons, or other persons of concern. Although the government committed to provide protection and assistance to refugees, asylum seekers, persons at risk of becoming stateless, or other persons of concern under the UN Convention on the Status of Refugees, the Belize Refugees Act, and the UN Convention for Statelessness, the government has yet to approve any refugee or asylum applications.

Country Reports on Human Rights Practices for 2017
United States Department of State • Bureau of Democracy, Human Rights and Labor

212 | P a g e

Protection of Refugees

Access to Asylum: The law provides for the granting of asylum or refugee status, and the government has established a system for providing protection to refugees. The government does not distinguish between refugees and asylum seekers, as the law itself does not reference asylum seekers--only refuges and recognized refugees. As of September, 3,019 persons (1,754 men and 1,265 women) had requested refugee status. The government has not granted refugee status to any applicant since the early 1990s. The nongovernmental organization (NGO) Help for Progress, UNHCR's implementing partner in the country, continued to assist by providing limited basic services, including shelter, clothing, and food to refugees and asylum seekers.

Employment: Persons awaiting adjudication of their refugee applications were unable to work legally in the country.

Access to Basic Services: Refugees were able to use the education system and the socialized medical system, but the government offered no assistance with housing or food except in extreme cases that involved children and pregnant women.

Temporary Protection: The Immigration Department issued renewable special residency permits for periods of 60 to 90 days to those who applied for refugee status within the 14-day deadline.

Section 3. Freedom to Participate in the Political Process

The law provides citizens the ability to choose their government in free and fair periodic elections held by secret ballot and based on universal and equal suffrage.

Elections and Political Participation

Recent Elections: In 2015 the UDP won 19 seats in the 31-seat National Assembly, equaling the majority with which it entered the election. The Organization of American States observation team reported generally free and fair elections.

Participation of Women and Minorities: No laws limit participation of women and/or members of minorities in the political process, and they did participate. Observers suggested cultural and societal constraints limited the number of women

Country Reports on Human Rights Practices for 2017
United States Department of State • Bureau of Democracy, Human Rights and Labor

213 | P a g e

participating in government. Women remained a clear minority in government. Two of 31 members of the House of Representatives and three of 13 senators were women. Although both major parties declared they took steps to increase female participation, neither adopted party policies that would ensure a percentage of their candidates are women. One of the parties put forward a female candidate for the 2018 mayoral elections.

Section 4. Corruption and Lack of Transparency in Government

The law provides criminal penalties for corruption by officials, but the government did not implement the law effectively, and officials often engaged in corrupt practices with impunity. There were numerous reports of government corruption during the year.

Corruption: Allegations of corruption in government among public officials, including ministers, chief executive officers, and deputy ministers, were numerous, although no substantial proof was presented in most cases. Investigations into corruption within the Immigration and Nationality Department in the 2011-13 period continued and uncovered several instances of questionable activities involving high-ranking government officials, including ministers of government.

Although the Ombudsman's Office reported fewer official complaints than in previous years, citizens continued to allege corruption against the Lands and Surveys Department in the Ministry of Natural Resources for illegally distributing lands to party associates. Despite accusations of political cronyism, the government insisted that it maintained transparency in the distribution of land.

During the year media reported that several land documents indicated questionable transactions in the Lands and Surveys Department. In August the press revealed a transaction believed to be a land hustle involving members of the former deputy prime minister's family. According to documents, during his tenure the department issued land titles to individuals for well below market value, although the parcels were already privately owned. The individuals then sold the parcels of land to close relatives of the former deputy prime minister at still-reduced prices. As of October the BPD had not started a criminal investigation because the complainant had yet to make a formal report to the authorities. This was not the first allegation of its kind.

Financial Disclosure: The law requires public officials to submit annual financial disclosure statements, which the Integrity Commission reviews. At the same time,

Country Reports on Human Rights Practices for 2017
United States Department of State • Bureau of Democracy, Human Rights and Labor

214 | P a g e

the constitution allows authorities to prohibit citizens from questioning the validity of such statements. Anyone who does so outside a rigidly prescribed procedure is subject to a fine of up to 5,000 Belize dollars ($2,500), three years imprisonment, or both. Many public officials did not submit annual financial disclosure statements and suffered no repercussions. In September the Integrity Commission informed 10 members of the National Assembly and 60 members of local governments of their failure to declare their financial affairs in 2016. The commission informed the press that it had submitted the list of names to the Office of the Director of Public Prosecution.

Section 5. Governmental Attitude Regarding International and Nongovernmental Investigation of Alleged Abuses of Human Rights

A variety of domestic and international human rights groups generally operated without government restriction, investigating and publishing their findings on human rights cases. Government officials often were cooperative and responsive to their views.

Government Human Rights Bodies: The ombudsman, although appointed by the government, acts as an independent check on governmental abuses. The Office of the Ombudsman holds a range of procedural and investigative powers, including the right to enter any premise to gather documentation and the right to summon persons. The office operated under significant staffing and financial constraints, although an investigator was added in July to assist with cases. The law requires the ombudsman to submit annual reports, and the office wrote a mid-year report to address problem trends. The office does not have the power to investigate allegations against the judiciary. While the Ombudsman's Office technically has wide investigative powers, noncompliance from the offices it investigates severely limited its effectiveness.

The Human Rights Commission, an independent, volunteer-based government agency, continued to operate, but only on an ad-hoc basis due to funding and staffing limitations. The commission provided human rights training for police recruits, prison officers, and the BDF.

Section 6. Discrimination, Societal Abuses, and Trafficking in Persons

Women

Country Reports on Human Rights Practices for 2017
United States Department of State • Bureau of Democracy, Human Rights and Labor

215 | P a g e

Rape and Domestic Violence: The criminal code criminalizes rape of men or women, including spousal rape. The code states that a person convicted of rape shall be sentenced to imprisonment for eight years to life, although sentences were sometimes much lighter. Challenges to the wider justice system generally resulted in poor conviction rates for rape.

Domestic violence was often prosecuted with charges such as harm, wounding, grievous harm, rape, and marital rape, but charges were treated as civil matters. Police, prosecutors, and judges recognized both physical violence and mental injury. Penalties include fines or imprisonment for violations. The law empowers the Family Court to issue protection orders against accused offenders.

According to data provided by a government ministry in 2016, there were 731 cases of domestic violence filed by women and 123 by men; 460 followed through with court action. The government ran awareness campaigns against gender-based and domestic violence, a domestic violence hotline, and shelters, and major police stations had designated domestic abuse officers, although these measures were not always effective.

Sexual Harassment: The law provides protection from sexual harassment in the workplace, including provisions against unfair dismissal of a victim of sexual harassment in the workplace. The Women's Department recognizes sexual harassment as a subset of sexual violence, but no cases have ever been brought under the sexual harassment protections.

Coercion in Population Control: There were no reports of coerced abortion, involuntary sterilization, or other coercive population control methods. Estimates on maternal mortality and contraceptive prevalence are available at: www.who.int/reproductivehealth/publications/monitoring/maternal-mortality-2015/en/.

There were reports of Mayan women receiving involuntary caesarian sections to discourage large families. There were uncorroborated anecdotes of Mayan women being sterilized unnecessarily because of irregularities found during annual checkups.

For additional information on maternal mortality and other health issues, see the see the World Health Organization website at www.who.int/reproductivehealth/publications/monitoring/maternal-mortality-2015/en/.

Country Reports on Human Rights Practices for 2017
United States Department of State • Bureau of Democracy, Human Rights and Labor

216 | P a g e

Discrimination: The law provides for the same legal status and rights for women as for men. The law also mandates equal pay for equal work, but the labor commissioner verified that men earned on average $90 Belize dollars ($45) more per month than women did because they held higher managerial positions. The law provides generally for the continuity of employment and protection against unfair dismissal, including for sexual harassment in the workplace, pregnancy, or HIV status.

The BDF and Belize Coast Guard maintain a 5 percent and 10 percent limit, respectively, on the number of female service members allowed to serve. Despite legal provisions for gender equality and government programs aimed at empowering women, NGOs and other observers reported that women faced social and economic discrimination. Although participating in all spheres of national life and outnumbering men in university classrooms and high school graduation rates, women held relatively few top managerial or government positions.

Children

Birth Registration: Citizenship is derived by birth within the country's territory, regardless of the parents' nationality. Citizenship may also be acquired by descent if at least one parent is a citizen of the country. The standard provision is for births to be registered no later than a week after birth; registration after a month is considered late and includes a minimal fine. Failure to register does not result in any denial of public service, but it slows the process for receiving a social security card and therefore accessing health care.

Education: Primary education is free, and education is compulsory between the ages of six and 14; however, primary schools may incorporate other fees, and parents may be required to pay for textbooks, uniforms, and meals.

Child Abuse: Abuse of children occurred, and as of December 2016 (the most recent date for which statistics were available), 1,407 cases were reported to authorities of which 78 cases were considered either trafficking or cases of unaccompanied minors.

In June, two 13-year-old primary school girls reported to police (in the company of their parents) that the principal of their school had sexually assaulted them. Police arrested and charged the principal. The investigation continued at year's end.

Country Reports on Human Rights Practices for 2017
United States Department of State • Bureau of Democracy, Human Rights and Labor

217 | Page

The law allows authorities to remove a child from an abusive home environment and requires parents to maintain and support children until the age of 18. There were publicized cases of underage girls being victims of sexual abuse and mistreatment, in most cases in their own home or in a relative's home.

The Family Services Division in the Ministry of Human Development is the government office with the lead responsibility for children's problems. The division coordinated programs for children who were victims of domestic violence, advocated remedies in specific cases before the Family Court, conducted public education campaigns, investigated cases of trafficking in children, and worked with local and international NGOs and UNICEF to promote children's welfare.

Early and Forced Marriage: The legal minimum age to marry is 18, but persons between ages 16 and 18 may marry with the consent of parents, legal guardians, or judicial authority. According to UNICEF, 26 percent of women ages 20 to 24 were married or cohabiting before age 18. The government did not undertake any prevention or mitigation efforts to reduce the rate of early marriage.

Sexual Exploitation of Children: The law establishes penalties for child prostitution, child pornography, child sexual exploitation, and indecent exhibition of a child. It defines a "child" as anyone under age 18. The law stipulates that the offense of child prostitution does not apply to persons exploiting 16- and 17-year-old children in sexual activity in exchange for remuneration, gifts, goods, food, or other benefits.

The legal age for consensual sex is 16, but prostitution is not legal under 18. Sexual intercourse with a girl under age 14 is an offense punishable by 12 years' to life imprisonment. Unlawful sexual intercourse with a girl ages 14-16 is an offense punishable by five to 10 years' imprisonment.

There were anecdotal reports that boys and girls were exploited in child prostitution, including the "sugar daddy" syndrome whereby older men provided money to young women and/or their families for sexual relations. Similarly, there were reports of increasing exploitation of minors, often to meet the demand of foreign sex tourists in tourist-populated areas or where there were transient and seasonal workers. The law criminalizes the procurement or attempted procurement of "a person" under age 18 to engage in prostitution; an offender is liable to eight years' imprisonment. The government did not effectively enforce laws prohibiting child sex trafficking.

Country Reports on Human Rights Practices for 2017
United States Department of State • Bureau of Democracy, Human Rights and Labor

218 | Page

The law establishes a penalty of two years' imprisonment for persons convicted of publishing or offering for sale any obscene book, writing, or representation.

International Child Abductions: The country is a party to the 1980 Hague Convention on the Civil Aspects of International Child Abduction. See the Department of State's *Annual Report on International Parental Child Abduction* at travel.state.gov/content/childabduction/en/legal/compliance.html.

Anti-Semitism

The Jewish population was small, and there were no reports of anti-Semitic acts.

Trafficking in Persons

See the Department of State's *Trafficking in Persons Report* at www.state.gov/j/tip/rls/tiprpt/.

Persons with Disabilities

The law does not expressly prohibit discrimination against persons with physical, sensory, intellectual, and mental disabilities, but the constitution provides for the protection of all citizens from any type of discrimination. The law does not provide for accessibility accommodations for persons with disabilities, and most public and private buildings and transportation were not accessible to them. Certain businesses and government departments had designated clerks to attend to the elderly and persons with disabilities. There were no policies to encourage hiring of persons with disabilities in the public or private sectors.

Mental health provisions and protections generally were poor. Informal government-organized committees for persons with disabilities were tasked with public education and advocating for protections against discrimination. The Ministry of Education, Culture, Youth, and Sports maintained an educational unit offering limited special education programs within the regular school system. There were two schools and four special education centers for children with disabilities.

The special envoy for women and children continued advocacy campaigns on behalf of persons with disabilities, especially children, and supported efforts to promote schools that took steps to create inclusive environments for persons with disabilities.

Country Reports on Human Rights Practices for 2017
United States Department of State • Bureau of Democracy, Human Rights and Labor

219 | P a g e

Indigenous People

No separate legal system or laws cover indigenous persons, since the government maintains that it treats all citizens the same. Employers, public and private, generally treated indigenous persons equally with other ethnic groups for employment and other purposes.

The Maya Leaders' Alliance, composed of the Toledo Maya Council, Q'eche Council of Belize, Toledo Alcaldes Association, Julian Cho Society, and Tumul K'in Center of Learning, monitored development in the Toledo District with the goal of protecting Mayan land and culture. While the government noted the need to respect and consult the Mayan communities when issuing oil exploration licenses in the south, the alliance believed it was not properly consulted before decisions were made.

Acts of Violence, Discrimination, and Other Abuses Based on Sexual Orientation and Gender Identity

In 2016 the Supreme Court struck down the interpretation of Section 53 of the criminal code, which criminalized sexual acts "against the order of nature." The government partially appealed the ruling in September, conceding the decriminalization of homosexuality but questioning a section of the decision that made "sexual orientation" a protected class. The Roman Catholic Church appealed the entire ruling in September. The Court of Appeals had not heard the case as of November.

The Immigration Act prohibits homosexual persons from entering the country, but immigration authorities did not enforce the law. A Venezuelan man intending to visit a Belizean man was harassed by immigration officers, and eventually denied entry and returned to Venezuela, allegedly due to a lack of travel funds.

The extent of discrimination based on sexual orientation or gender identity was difficult to ascertain due to a lack of official reporting. The NGO United Belize Advocacy Movement (UniBAM) registered four killings or attempted killings based on sexual orientation and gender identity from January to September.

According to UniBAM, lesbian, gay bisexual, transgender, and intersex (LGBTI) persons were denied medical services and education and encountered family-based violence.

Country Reports on Human Rights Practices for 2017
United States Department of State • Bureau of Democracy, Human Rights and Labor

220 | Page

HIV and AIDS Social Stigma

There was some societal discrimination against persons with HIV/AIDS, and the government worked to combat it through public education efforts of the National AIDS Commission under the Ministry of Human Development.

The law provides for protection of workers against unfair dismissal, including for HIV status. The government provided free antiretroviral medication and other medical services to persons with HIV registered in the public health system; however, the government sometimes had insufficient supplies of medication.

Section 7. Worker Rights

a. Freedom of Association and the Right to Collective Bargaining

The law, including related regulations and statutes, generally provides for the right to establish and join independent trade unions, bargain collectively, and conduct legal strikes. The law also prohibits antiunion discrimination, dissolution, or suspension of unions by administrative authority. It requires reinstatement of workers fired for union activity. The Ministry of Labor, Local Government, and Rural Development (Ministry of Labor) recognizes unions and employers associations after they are registered, and the law establishes procedures for the registration and status of trade unions and employers organizations and for collective bargaining.

The law allows authorities to refer disputes involving public and private sector employees who provide "essential services" to compulsory arbitration, prohibit strikes, and terminate actions. The national fire service, postal service, monetary and financial services, civil aviation and airport security services, port authority personnel (stevedores and pilots), and security services are deemed essential services beyond the International Labor Organization definition of essential services. There were no reports of antiunion discrimination, but there were some reports that workers were intimidated into either not joining a union, or dropping union membership if they had joined.

Workers can file complaints with the Ministry of Labor or seek redress from the courts, although it remained difficult to prove that terminations were due to union activity. The department generally handled labor cases without lengthy delays and dealt with appeals via arbitration outside of the court system. The court did not

Country Reports on Human Rights Practices for 2017
United States Department of State • Bureau of Democracy, Human Rights and Labor

221 | P a g e

apply the law requiring reinstatement of workers fired for union activity and provided monetary compensation instead.

There was a lack of resources to carry out the mandate of the ministry's Labor Department, including a shortage of vehicles and fuel to ensure compliance, particularly in rural areas. There were complaints of administrative or judicial delays relating to labor complaints and disputes. Information on penalties for violations of freedom of association or collective bargaining was unavailable.

The government and employers did not always effectively enforce the law. Antiunion discrimination and other forms of employer interference in union functions sometimes occurred, and on several occasions, unions threatened or carried out strikes. Authorities threatened not to pay teachers on the days they strike and to pass a law allowing the government to hire temporary teachers to replace those on strike. At least one NGO continued to petition the Inter-American Commission on Human Rights to highlight, among other things, concerns with employers' measures that do not allow migrant workers to unionize and that require migrants to submit to HIV tests in certain industries. The NGO asserted that in certain industries, particularly banana, citrus, and construction, employers often did not respect due process, did not pay minimum wages, and classified workers as contract and nonpermanent employees to avoid providing certain benefits. An NGO noted that both national and migrant workers were denied rights and that the Labor Department was inadequately staffed and under resourced.

b. Prohibition of Forced or Compulsory Labor

The constitution prohibits all forms of forced or compulsory labor. Penalties for forced or compulsory labor are covered under the antitrafficking law and carry prison sentences of one to eight years for adult victims and one to 12 years for child victims, which were comparable to penalties for other major offenses and sufficient to deter violations, although the government did not enforce this law. Resources and inspections to deter violations were limited. The government did not identify any forced labor victims during the year.

Forced labor of both Belizean and foreign women occurred in bars, nightclubs, and domestic service. Migrant men, women, and children were at risk for forced labor in agriculture, fishing, and in the service sector, including restaurants and shops, particularly among the South Asian and Chinese communities.

Country Reports on Human Rights Practices for 2017
United States Department of State • Bureau of Democracy, Human Rights and Labor

BELIZE 19

Also see the Department of State's *Trafficking in Persons Report* at
www.state.gov/j/tip/rls/tiprpt/.

c. Prohibition of Child Labor and Minimum Age for Employment

The law sets the minimum age for employment at 12 years old generally, with the
exception of work in wholesale or retail trade or business, for which the minimum
age is 14. "Light work," which is not defined in the law, is allowed for children
ages 12 to 13. Children ages 14 to 18 may be employed only in an occupation that
a labor officer has determined is "not injurious to the moral or physical
development of nonadults." Children over age 14 are explicitly permitted to work
in "industrial undertakings"--activities that include mining, manufacturing, and
construction. Children under age 16 are excluded from work in factories, and
those under age 18 are excluded from working at night or in certain kinds of
employment deemed dangerous. The Labor Department used a list of dangerous
occupations for young workers as guidance, but the list has not been adopted as
law.

The law permits children to work on family farms and in family-run businesses.
National legislation does not address a situation in which child labor is contracted
between a parent and the employer. The National Child Labor Policy distinguishes
between children engaged in work that is beneficial to their development and those
engaged in the worst forms of child labor. The policy identifies children involved
in the worst forms of child labor as those engaged in hazardous work, trafficking
and child slavery, commercial sexual activities, and illicit activities.

The Labor Department has primary responsibility for implementing labor policies
and enforcing labor laws, but it had limited dedicated resources to investigate
complaints. Inspectors from the Labor and Education Departments are responsible
for enforcing these regulations, with the bulk of the enforcement falling to truancy
officers. The penalty for employing a child below minimum age is a fine not
exceeding $20 Belize dollars ($10) or imprisonment not exceeding two months.
On a second offense, the law stipulates a fine not exceeding $50 Belize dollars
($25) or imprisonment not exceeding four months. There was not enough
information provided to determine if the penalties, remediation, and inspections
were sufficient to deter violations. There was no information on whether child
labor laws were well enforced. There is also a National Child Labor Committee
under the National Committee for Families and Children, a statutory interagency
group that advocates for policies and legislation to protect children and eliminate
child labor.

Country Reports on Human Rights Practices for 2017
United States Department of State • Bureau of Democracy, Human Rights and Labor

223 | P a g e

Some children were vulnerable to forced labor, particularly in the agricultural and service sectors. Commercial sexual exploitation of children occurred (see section 6, Children). According to the most recent data available from the Statistical Institute of Belize, the country's child labor rate was 3.7 percent, with the problem most prevalent in rural areas. Boys accounted for 74 percent of children illegally employed.

Also see the Department of Labor's *Findings on the Worst Forms of Child Labor* at www.dol.gov/ilab/reports/child-labor/findings/.

d. Discrimination with Respect to Employment and Occupation

The law and regulations prohibit discrimination on the basis of race, sex, gender, language, HIV-positive status or other communicable diseases, or social status. The government did not effectively enforce those laws and regulations. The law does not explicitly prohibit discrimination in employment with respect to disability, sexual orientation, and/or gender identity. There were reports that discrimination in employment and occupation occurred with respect to sexual orientation. One NGO reported that members of the LGBTI community often had problems gaining and retaining employment due to discrimination in the workplace. There were no officially reported cases of discrimination at work based on ethnicity, culture, or skin color; although anecdotal evidence suggested that such cases occurred.

e. Acceptable Conditions of Work

The national minimum wage was $3.30 Belize dollars ($1.65) per hour. A full-time worker receiving the minimum wage earned between 1.5 to two times the poverty limit income, depending on the district. The law sets the workweek at no more than six days or 45 hours and requires premium payment for overtime work. Workers are entitled to two workweeks' paid annual holiday. Additionally there are 13 days designated as public and bank holidays. Employees who work on public and bank holidays are entitled to pay at time-and-a-half, except for Good Friday and Christmas, which are paid at twice the normal rate.

Several different health and safety regulations cover numerous industries. The law, which applies to all sectors, prescribes that the employer must take "reasonable care" for the safety of employees in the course of their employment. The law further states that every employer who provides or arranges

Country Reports on Human Rights Practices for 2017
United States Department of State • Bureau of Democracy, Human Rights and Labor

224 | Page

accommodation for workers to reside at or in the vicinity of a place of employment shall provide and maintain sufficient and hygienic housing accommodations, a sufficient supply of wholesome water, and sufficient and proper sanitary arrangements.

The Ministry of Labor did not always effectively enforce minimum wage and health and safety regulations. The ministry's Labor Department had 25 labor officers in 10 offices throughout the country. Inspections were not sufficient to secure compliance, especially in the more remote areas. Fines varied according to the infraction but generally were not very high and thus not sufficient to deter violations. Several cases were pending. In January a labor tribunal was established.

The minimum wage was generally respected. Nevertheless, anecdotal evidence from NGOs and employers suggested that undocumented Central American workers, particularly young service workers and agricultural laborers, were regularly paid below the minimum wage.

While no known reports were made to the Labor Department, several individuals alleged in the media that employers in certain industries often did not respect due process, did not pay minimum wages, and classified workers as contract and nonpermanent employees to avoid certain benefits.

There were no officially reported complaints of major industrial factory fires or mine disasters. It was unclear whether workers could remove themselves from situations that endangered health or safety without jeopardy to their employment or whether authorities effectively protected employees in this situation.

Country Reports on Human Rights Practices for 2017
United States Department of State • Bureau of Democracy, Human Rights and Labor

225 | P a g e

CERTIFICATE OF SERVICE

Jeremy Edward BURROWES
A078-112-433

I, Christopher A. Reed, hereby certify that I am a resident of or employed in the County of Los Angeles, over 18 years of age, not a party to the within action and that I am employed at and my business address is:

Law Offices of Brian D. Lerner, APC
3233 E. Broadway
Long Beach, CA 90803
Telephone: (562) 495-0554
Facsimile: (562) 608-8672

On July 9, 2018, I served a copy of the attached **SUPPLEMENTAL DOCUMENTS FOR APPLICATION FOR CANCELLATION OF REMOVAL AND ADJUSTMENT OF STATUS FOR CERTAIN NONPERMANENT RESIDENTS #2** on the following person(s) by the method(s) indicated:

Office of the Chief Counsel
Department of Homeland Security
606 S. Olive Street, 8ᵗʰ Floor
Los Angeles, CA 90014
(USPS First-Class Mail)

I declare under penalty of perjury that the foregoing is true and correct. Executed in Long Beach, California.

DATED: July 9, 2018

By: _____
Christopher A. Reed
Attorney at Law

ABOUT THE AUTHOR

Brian D. Lerner is an Immigration Lawyer and runs a National Immigration Law Firm for nearly 30 years. He is an attorney who is a certified specialist that might help in Immigration & Nationality Law as issued by the California State Bar, Board of Legal Specialization. Attorney Lerner is an expert in Immigration Law, Removal and Deportation, Citizenship, Waiver and Appeals.

He has been a licensed attorney since 1992 and started the Law Offices of Brian D. Lerner, APC. The immigration practice consists of Immigration and Nationality Law, and everything involved with and regarding immigration which includes citizenship, investment visas, family and employment visas, removal and deportation hearings, appeals, waivers, adjustment, consulate processing and all types of immigration and citizenship matters.

He has represented clients from all over the U.S. and in many countries around the world. One side of his practice is dedicated to keeping people in the U.S. and fighting for their immigration rights, while another side is to get people back who have been deported and removed from the U.S.

Also, there is the affirmative part of Immigration Law which Brian Lerner has helped numerous people come into the U.S. on business visas, investment visas, student visas, fiancée and marriage visas, religious visas and many more. Attorney Lerner has helped immigrants who are victims of crime and domestic violence or ones that are married to abusers.

In other words, Attorney Lerner has a firm that helps people all over the U.S. He has dedicated significant time to preparing numerous petitions and applications for you to get at a fraction of the price of hiring an attorney. He says it is the next best thing to a real attorney because they are real petitions prepared by an expert.

www.ingramcontent.com/pod-product-compliance
Lightning Source LLC
Chambersburg PA
CBHW051753200326
41597CB00025B/4536